A. S. Byatt

Twayne's English Authors Series

Kinley E. Roby, Editor

Northeastern University

TEAS 529

A.S. BYATT
Photograph by Jane Brown. Courtesy of A. S. Byatt.

A. S. Byatt

Kathleen Coyne Kelly

Northeastern University

Twayne Publishers
An Imprint of Simon & Schuster Macmillan
New York

Prentice Hall International
London • Mexico City • New Delhi • Singapore • Sydney • Toronto

Twayne's English Authors Series No. 529

A. S. Byatt
Kathleen Coyne Kelly

Twayne Publishers
An Imprint of Simon & Schuster Macmillan
1633 Broadway
New York, New York 10019

Library of Congress Cataloging-in-Data

Kelly, Kathleen Coyne.
    A. S. Byatt / Kathleen Coyne Kelly.
        p.   cm. — (Twayne's English authors series ; TEAS 529)
    Includes bibliographical references and index.
    ISBN 0-8057-7043-7
    1. Byatt, A. S. (Antonia Susan), 1936–   —Criticism and interpretation.
I. Title. II. Series.
PR6052.Y2Z73   1996
823'.914—dc20
                                                                        96-23773
                                                                        CIP

The paper used in this publication meets the minimum requirements of American
National Standard for Information Sciences—Permanence of Paper for Printed Library
Materials, ANSI Z39.48–1984. ∞

10 9 8 7 6 5 4 3 2 1

Printed in the United States of America

Contents

Preface

Perhaps the most important thing to say about my books is that they try to be about the life of the mind as well as of society and the relations between people. I admire—am excited by— intellectual curiosity of any kind (scientific, linguistic, psychological) and also by literature as a complicated, huge, interrelating pattern. I also like recording small observed facts and feelings. I see writing and thinking as a passionate activity, like any other.

A. S. Byatt, in Contemporary Authors (1991)

As the above passage demonstrates, Antonia Susan Byatt is her own best reader: this comment serves as a gloss on almost all of her work, both fiction and nonfiction.

A painterly, writerly writer, A. S. Byatt has been publishing fiction and criticism since the early 1960s. Interest in her work has slowly increased over the years, especially since the publication of *Possession: A Romance* (1990), which has found the largest audience of any of her works. It is part academic novel, part suspense story, part romance, and part study of "the life of the mind." The novel showcases Byatt's sheer range of knowledge—literary, literary-critical, philosophical, scientific, psychological—which is evident in everything else she writes as well. This range is not always seen as a virtue; it has been described as "a density . . . problematic to some who complain of overloading and extravagance." But there is another viewpoint: the result of such a reach is, rather, "spellbinding, intriguing . . . brocaded, allegorical, and tapestried."[1] Either way, the sheer power, poetry, and depth of Byatt's fiction cannot be denied.

Byatt has always been clear about those writers who have most influenced her, not only in her fiction writing but in her scholarly work about other people's fiction writing. Her scholarly work is never far from her fiction; in a way, her books and articles on romantic literary criticism and the novels of Iris Murdoch provide a guide to her own developing history as a writer. At this point, instead of tracing out these influences in detail, I would like to locate such influences within two larger contexts: realism and postmodernism. An understanding of these concepts is an essential preliminary to understanding Byatt's work.

Realism and the Novel

One can find examples of realism in every literary period. However, while most critics can agree on what the general outlines of realism are, not all agree on particular applications of the term.

Realism as most critics have described it captures something about the reality or truth of human existence: "Realism is, in the broadest sense, simply fidelity to actuality."[2] The realistic novel, for example, is so plotted that one accepts the outcome as somehow natural: that is, not contrived or influenced by events beyond human control. The scale of the realistic novel is therefore human-sized. Realistic fiction is like a window through which one observes average people going about their everyday lives. At the same time, realistic fiction is *not* a window; it is the sum of a particular set of conventions that, like any other set of conventions, can be subject to analysis. It is often pointed out, for example, how "realistic" effects have their source in a scrupulous attention to detail. The realistic novel, then, is an *illusion* of reality, a text manipulated by an author in a particular way. It is not a document that can be read like a transcript of actual events (though it has been so read), no matter how often a reader may be struck by the "truth" of the text in its apparent faithfulness to human experience.

In her use of realism, Byatt is influenced by a number of writers, who, taken together, may be seen as constituting a veritable movement. George Eliot and Honoré de Balzac in the 19th century and Iris Murdoch in the 20th are writers of realistic fiction whom Byatt often invokes as models for her fiction. Byatt happily acknowledges her debts, saying that Balzac "knew how complicated the world is. And he knew language is provisional. He also knew that it always had been intensely emotive *and* had described the world."[3] (Actually, by commenting on Balzac's attitude toward language, Byatt questions Balzac's status as a realist writer par excellence.) She also says that she is "moved by Iris Murdoch's critical stand, her call for a large cast, her respect for the opaque individual," and develops her own variations on these matters in her fiction (Kenyon, 51).

Another way to approach realism is as a *mode of representation*, a way of seeing that has no more claim to truth than any other mode. Examples from the visual arts may help us understand realism as a mode, especially since Byatt herself has such a strong visual sense in her writing and clearly acknowledges the influence of, and connections to, certain artists—Vincent Van Gogh and Henri Matisse among them.[4]

To generalize rather crudely, a painter, like a novelist, must make a choice about her or his representation of nature and the real world. To what degree does she intend a painting to be an imitation of nature, an improvement upon it, or a departure from it? Think about a painting by Andrew Wyeth, in which every blade of grass or strand of hair is meticulously rendered; or a painting of fruit in a bowl that looks as if one might pluck an apple right out of the canvas; or a Dürer flower; or an Audubon painting of a robin. Think about experiments with perspective and depth that seem to render a scene so real that one imagines one is looking at a real landscape or at a color photograph. While all such paintings have an element of the "real" in them, they may also be highly idealized or romanticized, or even too real—*hyper*real.

No artist can really paint something "as is," even if she is trying to: the very medium—oils or watercolors or ink—changes that which is to be painted. (And language itself changes what is to be said.) More important, the artist's own cultural and social context influences how she "sees" in the first place. Byatt's awareness of this fact is articulated in her short story "Art Work." Robin is a *neo*realist painter who paints accurate and empty spaces with just one flash of color. His wife Deborah, also an artist, understands his work as "a serious attempt at a serious and terrible problem, an attempt to answer the question every artist must ask him- or herself, at some time: Why bother, why make representations of anything at all?"[5]

When a painter or novelist attempts to incorporate this awareness of the difficulties of representation into her or his work—the thing to be represented and the process of representation itself—we might understand this attempt as a move from an "innocent" realism to a more knowing postmodern vision. In all of her work, Byatt attempts to negotiate the space that exists between realism and other modes of representation. Her vision is at once focused on the flawed lives of everyday individuals—albeit very smart and introspective individuals—and on the language that she uses to construct such characters. *Still Life*, for example, "faces the difficulties of realism today by sharing them with the reader" (Kenyon, 54). Byatt specializes in this paradox that underpins realism—the "implausibility of the realist commenting on the creation of realism," as Kenyon puts it (55).

In other words, Byatt complicates the realist project by reflecting on the process of writing realistic fiction itself. She writes realist fiction and, while doing so, questions its ability to imitate life; she is too steeped in Renaissance and Romantic notions of art and representation to do otherwise. "My characters are real and also metaphors," she says (quoted in Kenyon, 62). As the next section will show, Byatt's characters are also very conscious of their function as icons of the real and the metaphorical.

A. S. Byatt and Postmodernism

Byatt is often labeled a postmodern writer, and while she herself may take exception to any sort of categorization, the term is useful in a number of ways with respect to her fiction. But "postmodern" and "postmodernism" are also vexed terms; it is worth spending some time on them here, for they will surface again and again throughout this study of Byatt's fiction. As one critic defines it, postmodern writing is "open, playful, optative, provisional, (open in time as well as in structure or space), disjunctive, or indeterminate . . . a discourse of ironies and fragments"; it is an amalgam of "ubiquitous interactions, immanent codes."[6] Let us explore this definition further.

First, the "post" in "postmodern" indicates that there is something chronological about the phenomenon. However, while a number of scholars may attempt to locate the end of modernism and the beginning of postmodernism sometime in the 1950s, it makes more sense to think about postmodernism as an aesthetic choice or strategy. Granted, it is not always clear whether one can really step out of one's cultural condition in order to exercise such a choice, but we can note, with respect to the controversy over the opposition of modernism and postmodernism, that currently one might write or paint or compose music or build in a modern style or in a postmodern style—or in a classical, Gothic, or baroque style, for that matter. This eclecticism is precisely what some would recognize as postmodern: the ability to range over a number of periods and places and to create an amalgam of styles and moods.

Modernism is usually described as an early 20th-century reaction against what were seen as the stifling 19th-century bourgeois aesthetic values of continuity and coherence—F. R. Leavis and his group are critics and promoters of the modern in this respect. The novels of James Joyce and Gertrude Stein were often described as experimental and avant-garde because they reject realist or naturalist ideas about plot and structure and dialogue. Pablo Picasso, with his fragmented "portraits" and geometric canvases, is another example of what we have come to call modernism. Collage, multiple points of view, and juxtaposition of forms bespeak a disenchantment with the idea that life is unified and coherent and benevolent. World War I had certainly disabused many of the idea that this was indeed the best of all possible worlds.

Postmodernism is not so much a reaction to modernism as it is, according to some, a continuation of the sense of disorientation, alienation, and fragmentation characteristic of a society that is undergoing deep and profound cultural change. (It is in this sense that Joyce's work, usually understood as epitomizing the "modern," has also been described recently as "postmodern.") On the other hand, it has been argued that postmodernism resides not so much in a particular work of art as in the reader: modernism and postmodernism are ways of reading. Richard Pearce goes so far as to say that "there is no difference between modernism and postmodernism. It is only that revolutionary writers had to be read in a conservative way. . . . At best . . . modernism is the way people learned to read writers like Joyce."[7] In other words, partially because of modernism, we have become more able to deal with texts that are full of gaps and contradictions. A visual example is the MTV video, with its many cuts from scene to scene and its employment of tantalizing images that are never fully explained. At first, many viewers are frustrated and puzzled, but most come to accept the once-radical techniques of the music video and to understand that the lack of closure, the inability to interpret, is part of the pleasure.

The cultural angst that created modernism—an angst that was in turn fueled by the art certain writers and painters produced—had a purpose, many argue, and that purpose was to explore meaning through symbol and other forms of representation in order to reaffirm coherence in the face of evidence to the contrary. Postmodern angst, on the other hand, seems to be tinged with despair and hopelessness and can lead to an ironic celebration of the superficial and a cynical promotion of the fragmentary, with no expectation of achieving any final, absolute truth. However, it can be argued that the postmodern critic/writer invites us to an act of courage leading to increased freedom: by abandoning the comforts and restrictions of certainty, by understanding that truth is always contingent, one can engage in a free play of the mind. Examples of contemporary novels that are often labeled—not without debate—postmodern include Thomas Pynchon's *The Crying of Lot 49*, *Gravity's Rainbow*, and *V*, and Vladimir Nabokov's *Pale Fire*.

Postmodernism has threatened some very strongly held notions about the nature of the author and the relationship of author to text. Can we ever really recover the intention of an author once a text leaves her or his hands? If meaning cannot be recovered in the intention of the writer, where does it reside—if it even exists? Is it the reader who really creates meaning through the act of reading? What happens when the distinctions between author, narrator, and character are disabled? A number of novelists have taken up these questions in their work and sometimes do so by inviting the reader to interpret not only the product—the text in hand—but also the process by which the text is made. In these novels, we may get glimpses of the actual author—or at least, a persona that the author creates for us to imagine as author. We see this in Julian Barnes's *Flaubert's Parrot*. Trey Ellis writes two versions of a character's life in *Platitudes*, in which two fictional authors vie for control of the novel.

We may see an author manipulating the stuff of plot and narrative so that we imagine the novel itself as a metaphor for the act of creating fiction, as in John Fowles's *The French Lieutenant's Woman*. The line between fiction and reality may be deliberately blurred, as in Umberto Eco's *The Name of the Rose*, which is offered as a true historical document, and in Michael Crichton's *Eaters of the Dead*, which also purports to be a historical document that tells the "true" story of the myth of Beowulf.

When Tim O'Brien has his characters chase an AWOL soldier all the way from Vietnam to Paris in *Going after Cacciato*, we realize that he is deliberately violating our sense of what a novel is supposed to do. In this novel, as in most of the other novels mentioned so far, the author—or the text, if you prefer—challenges us to rethink our expectations about texts and textuality and to contemplate the very nature of making fiction. In a way, a postmodern novel asks us to stop believing in a distinction between fiction and reality. Postmodern fiction is ambiguous, open-ended, big enough for multiple and conflicting interpretations. If this leaves us puzzled and frustrated, all the better; the world itself is puzzling and frustrating, subject to multiple and conflicting interpretations.

Byatt entered the university in the 1950s—the very decade when modernism allegedly began to give way to postmodernism. Her teacher F. R. Leavis might be described as one of the last great exponents of modernism. Under his influence, Byatt has retained a modernist sense of the moral power of literature, of the supremacy of language and its ability to capture something authentic about human experience, and of the intrinsic coherence of the world. Byatt believes, along with Leavis, that "words are somehow healthiest when they approach the condition of things," as Terry Eagleton puts it, and that language is somehow "alienated" "unless it is crammed with the physical textures of actual experience."[8] At the same time, Byatt regrets the postmodern tendency to "see language as a system signing to itself."[9] Under the influence of reading Proust, she wants it both ways, so that it may be "possible for a text to be supremely mimetic . . . and at the same time to think about form, its own form, its own formation."[10] Byatt's novels are often sites of controversy: she passionately uses description and allusion and metaphor as if they could capture some truth, while her plots are often open-ended and celebratory of the inability to do so.

Acknowledgments

Thanks to Mary Annas, Barry Hoberman, Nuria Ortega-Lopez, and Lolly Ockerstrom, who either read chapters in progress or helped with the bibliography. A. S. Byatt's secretary, Liz Allen, was always helpful, and Yves Yancithe and Salvatore Genovese, of the interlibrary loan staff at Northeastern University, have been invaluable. Kinley Roby, the Twayne English Authors editor who first encouraged me to take up this project, deserves special mention. I am also grateful to editor Anne Davidson for her patience and gentle promptings. Copy editor Cindy Buck did a superb job of saving me from myself; all errors that remain, of course, are my own. Production editor Andrew Libby was consistently gracious and reassuring. La Vinia Jennings, a fellow Twayne author, was always there to sympathize with, and Barry Hoberman displayed marvelous forebearance throughout the project.

Chronology

1936   Antonia Susan Drabble born 24 August in Sheffield, England.

1957   Receives B.A., with first-class honors, from Newnham College, Cambridge University.

1957–58   English Speaking Union Fellowship.

1958   Attends Bryn Mawr College.

1958–59   Attends Somerville College, Oxford University.

1959   Marries Ian Byatt.

1960   Daughter Antonia is born.

1961   Son Charles is born.

1962–71   University of London, staff member in extra-mural department.

1964   *The Shadow of the Sun* (begun 1954)

1965–69   Central School of Art and Design, part-time lecturer in department of liberal studies.

1965   *Degrees of Freedom: The Novels of Iris Murdoch*.

1967   *The Game* (begun 1957).

1969   Divorces Ian Byatt. Marries Peter Duffy.

1970   Daughter Isabel is born. *Wordsworth and Coleridge in Their Time* (published 1973 in the United States).

1972   Son Charles dies.

1972–80   University College, lecturer.

1973   Daughter Miranda is born.

1974–77   Member of the BBC Social Effects of Television Advisory Group

1976   *Iris Murdoch*.

1978   British Council lecturer in Spain. *The Virgin in the Garden* (begun around 1972).

1979   George Eliot, *The Mill on the Floss*, edited by Byatt.

Chapter One
"Points on a Circle"

Antonia Susan Drabble Byatt is one of those writers who has been writing all her life. "From being very little, reading and living were . . . only finished off if you could write them down" (Musil, 100). This sense that writing made real, or more real, one's intellectual growth and pleasure and one's experiences certainly pervades Byatt's mature work, in both her fiction and nonfiction. In many ways, Byatt is a metawriter: a writer whose writing is both self-reflexive and consciously crafted. She continually provides a commentary on her own reading and writing and asks us to pay attention to her doing so. Her writing is like a Möbius strip on which life experience, reading experience, and writing combine to make a perpetual loop.

Byatt has commented on the fact that while many writers want to separate their fiction from their nonfiction, she has never desired such a separation: "From my early childhood, reading and writing seemed to me to be points on a circle. Greedy reading made me want to write, as if this were the only adequate response to the pleasure and power of books" (*PM*, xiii). This greediness reveals itself in a number of ways in her work, but especially through literary allusion and thick description.

Byatt named her 1991 collection of literary essays *Passions of the Mind*, and this title captures one of many paradoxes about her: life experience does not turn to dry dust in her novels, no matter how much it may be filtered through art. As the reviewer Caryn McTighe puts it, Byatt's "works [are] dominated by an absorbing, discriminating mind which finds intellectual passions as vibrant and consuming as emotional ones."[1]

Early Life and Education

A. S. Byatt was born in Sheffield, Lincolnshire, on 24 August 1936. Her father was a judge and writer; her mother was a secondary-school teacher who gave up her job to raise her four children but who never gave up teaching. Both parents valued intellectual achievement and provided a home rich in books, conversation, music, and art. They converted to Quakerism late in life.

However, home life was not always harmonious. Byatt's mother never got over her anger at having to give up her career to become a housewife and mother. Byatt was to say later that, in searching for a subject upon which to write, she wanted to avoid "approaching her [mother's] perpetual rage, depression, and frustration, which were, in fact, the driving force that made sure none of her daughters became housebound."[2]

At age ten, after suffering a near-fatal ovarian infection, Byatt spent weeks in bed convalescing, and during this time she developed her life-long reading habits, devouring Charles Dickens, Alfred Lord Tennyson, and Jane Austen, among others. Her mother gave her plenty of Browning to read—an experience that would later allow Byatt to write wonderful pastiches of Browning's poetry in *Possession: A Romance*. Byatt says now that "the novelist I most love is Marcel Proust. After him Balzac, Dickens, Eliot, Thomas Mann and James, Iris Murdoch, Ford Maddox Ford, and Willa Cather. And Leo Tolstoy and Fyodor Dostoevsky" (McTighe, 71).

Perhaps the first formative experience of Byatt's young life was World War II, during which she was evacuated from Sheffield to Pontrefract, Yorkshire. (She went to school with the actress Judi Dench). When she was 13, in 1949, she and her sister were sent to Mount School, a Quaker boarding school in York. Byatt was not a forthcoming child. She was ter-rified of the outside world and often experienced, she says, "panic," because "I had a strong sense of not knowing how to behave socially, handed down from my mother's anxiety about having got herself right out of her class." Byatt adds, "I always knew I had on the wrong clothes."[3] Some of Byatt's feelings about school seem to have made their way into her fiction; in *The Game*, Cassandra has very bad memories of

> when she was sent away to school, a colourless eleven years old in liberty bodice, wrinkled lisle stockings, and a tunic bought prudently one size too large. The other girls were enemies, the building menacing, objects threatening: the notice-board with dangerous pins, the gallows-like wooden swing, the horn spoon with which they ate their Sunday eggs. She wept all night, and then the weeping had spilled over into the day; she sat on benches, immobile, with a wet face, and grew thinner. The terror wore off gradually.[4]

The sense of place is strong in Byatt's fiction, and Yorkshire looms large in the lives of many of her characters. They are either from there (like William Adamson in *Morpho Eugenia*) or visit there (like Anna Severell [*The Shadow of the Sun*] and Randolph Ash and Christabel La-

Motte [*Possession: A Romance*]). The narrator of *Morpho Eugenia* tells us that the part of Yorkshire from which Adamson comes "consisted of foul black places amongst fields and rough land of great beauty."[5] When we consider that Byatt describes her childhood as unhappy, and most of her time at Mount School as difficult, we might imagine these words as representing her memories of her early life, in which "foul black places" were mixed with "great beauty."

The reviewer Myra Stout writes that Byatt considered her collection of short stories *Sugar* to be so autobiographical that Byatt gave her a copy "to help with the factual background of her Yorkshire childhood and family relationships" (24). The cathedral city in "Racine and the Tablecloth," with its medieval walls that Emily Bray traverses on her lonely walks to church, may well be based on York. In fact, the character Emily Bray may be a cover for Byatt herself: both seem to have been shy, undersized (and therefore not very athletic—a major drawback at boarding schools, which give over a good deal of time to sports), and unable to make many friends easily because they are so much brighter than the rest.

Byatt says that she first began writing seriously at Mount School, escaping to the basement boiler room to do so. This detail makes its way into another story, the Jamesian "The Changeling," in which a woman writer creates a child who retreats behind the furnace when he is feeling threatened.

Both parents, all of her siblings, and Byatt attended Cambridge University. "It was paradisal," says Byatt of her university years. "We were the pre-political generation. We believed in unfashionable concepts such as objectivity, impartiality, listening to people, pragmatics, suspension of judgement."[6] At the same time, Byatt says of herself and other women that "we had fought, much harder than the men, who outnumbered us eleven to one, to be allowed to study at Cambridge, and we were fatally torn, when thinking of our futures, by hopes of marriage . . . [and] some work" (*SS*, ix). She graduated from Cambridge with a B.A. degree, with honors, in 1957.

The next year, Byatt spent some time in the United States studying at Byrn Mawr College in Pennsylvania (1957–58), then returned to England to continue her studies at Somerville College, Oxford (1958–59). It was at Oxford that Byatt started but then abandoned a dissertation on religious allegory in the 17th century. She says about her projected dissertation that "it is not too much to say that this unwritten work, with its neoplatonic myths, its interest in the incarnation, in fallen and unfallen (adequate and inadequate) language to describe reality, has haunted both my novels and my reading patterns ever since" (*PM*, xv).

Her adviser was Dame Helen Gardner, one of the few women dons (the British equivalent of an American university professor) at Oxford, and an extremely accomplished one at that. In the late 1950s, Gardner and other scholars were reading John Donne, Andrew Marvell, and George Herbert with renewed interest and excitement, all under the influence of the poet T. S. Eliot, who wrote the bulk of his literary criticism in the 1920s and 1930s. Byatt calls Eliot "seductive," especially with respect to his interest in and reading of the metaphysical poets (*PM*, xiv). Eliot single-handedly revived academic interest in these Renaissance poets, who were remarkable for their paradoxical imagery and for blending the intellectual and theological with the erotic. Byatt's interest in the sensual and symbolic potentialities of language as exemplified by Donne and others has continued to inform her work.

Cambridge and F. R. Leavis

There are many threads to Byatt's intellectual life, threads she gathers up and weaves into her fiction and nonfiction alike. However, what constitutes an important part of the warp and woof of Byatt's fiction is the influence of one particular Cambridge teacher and literary critic: Franklin Raymond Leavis (1895–1978). It is important that we spend a bit of time on F. R. Leavis, not only because of his direct influence on Byatt but also because he shaped the entire trajectory of Anglo-American 20th-century literary criticism, an understanding of which is essential to reading Byatt's fiction.

By the time Byatt went to all-female Newnham College, Cambridge, in 1957 to earn her B.A., Leavis, then 62, was the reigning intellectual, a position he had occupied for 30 years. Leavis, his wife Q. D. (known as "Queenie"), and their circle, which included such critics as I. A. Richards and William Empson, exerted tremendous influence on the literary taste of the day. (In fact, Leavis and Richards taught Byatt's mother when she was at Cambridge.) It is hard now to imagine Leavis as a radical, since he is so often critiqued for his elitist, exclusive judgments.

However, consider the shape of university life as it was found—and then rejected—by Leavis when he entered Cambridge immediately after World War I. Until the very end of the 19th century, taking up the study of "literature" in the university meant studying the classics—that is, texts in Greek and Latin. For the most part, the university was closed to women, the study of literature was almost exclusively a male pursuit, and it was a pursuit limited to the leisured and moneyed class. The study of literature, with its emphasis on language learning, was subsumed under the heading of "philology." It was expected that gentlemen would read Shakespeare, Milton, Pope, Dryden, Wordsworth, and other now-canonical figures on their own, and that they would be ready to quote at length from these authors' works while tramping over the English countryside or engaged in polite drawing-room conversation. If young men read novels—from Fielding to Dickens and beyond—that was certainly acceptable, but not quite the sign of an educated taste. (Nineteenth-century women, many of whom were forbidden by their fathers and husbands to read parts of the daily newspapers, let alone novels, kept their reading habits strictly to themselves.)

Leavis and his circle rejected the notion that reading English literature was simply a diversion for dilettantes and strove to make it central to university study, and central to the understanding of culture. Suspicious of the values of the upper class, rejecting of post-Victorian social and political mores, Leavis and his circle represented a new kind of student in England and America. The dictum (ironically meant or not) of T. S. Eliot took on the significance of a mantra: "Our literature is a substitute for religion, and so is our religion."[7] As has been noted by a number of literary historians, for Leavis and his group, "literature becomes more than just a handmaiden for moral ideology: it *is* moral ideology for the modern age." (Eagleton, 27)

In 1932, the Leavises founded the journal *Scrutiny*, which served, until it folded in 1953, as the primary organ for their ideas on culture and literature, ideas informed by an "intense moral seriousness," as Byatt puts it, and an antipathy to the Marxism of the 1930s and 1940s. The name of the journal gives us a clue to the method of the Leavisites (a term that came to be used for his followers and that was not always meant to be complimentary). Following a Romantic strain that can be partially traced back through T. S. Eliot to Samuel Coleridge, Leavisites rejected the dominant paradigm of biographical and historical criticism in order to focus on the text itself. A poem was to be subjected to rigorous, attentive reading; Leavisites scrutinized the "words on the page," as they were fond of saying, in order to yield up the ambiguities, ironies, and paradoxes to be found there. An appreciation of imagery, metaphor, and symbol, scarcely recognized in the older, historically bound method, was deeply emphasized.

In other words, in order to read à la Leavis, one does not need to understand, say, Shakespeare's life or the fortunes of the Tudor dynasty to appreciate his works: theoretically and quite simply, one should be able to pick up a poem and make a "close reading"—the term used to describe this text-bound, language-steeped method. And herein lies a paradox: by freeing texts from their authors' biographical and historical circumstances, Leavis seemed to espouse a new egalitarian kind of reading, one that did not depend upon an exclusive—and expensive—training in philology and history. In this respect, American interpreters of the Leavisite method enthusiastically embraced the possibilities of what came to be known in the United States as the New Criticism (as opposed to the old historical, textual, and biographical criticism).

In reality, however, an older kind of elitist attitude was replaced by a new. Not everyone, alas, was capable of recognizing the subtle complexities that make a poem a poem. And not every poem was worth a close reading. Few critics, and fewer readers, Leavis believed, possessed the intellectual and moral wherewithal to make a sound judgment on what was worth reading. His pronouncements in such works as *New Bearings in English Poetry* (1932), *Revaluation* (1936), and *The Great Tradition* (1948) of what was "good" and what was "bad" were to influence *what* was read and *how* it was read for decades. Chaucer, Shakespeare, the metaphysical poets, Wordsworth, George Eliot, T. S. Eliot, and D. H. Lawrence were in; Spencer, Fielding, Shelley, most of the Victorian novelists, and Joyce were not.

While extremely controversial in its beginnings, the New Criticism became the dominant paradigm for English studies in both Great Britain and America until the 1960s. In many respects, it remains so, though post–New Critical paradigms, including structuralism, Marxism, feminism, and deconstructionism, have certainly made a number of inroads.

Byatt is certainly familiar with and deft at handling these newer critical approaches, as the more academic stretches of *Possession* demonstrate. However, she remains committed to the idea that literature contains a moral dimension, and that language can indeed capture both abstract truths and felt experience. As she says of her days at Cambridge, she learned that writing "was to be taught, in order to make the world better, more just, more discriminating" (*SS*, x). Reflecting back on her experience at "Leavis's Cambridge" (viii), as Byatt refers to it, she is able to respect and admire the moral seriousness with which Leavis attempted to place "English Literature at the centre of university studies and also of social morality" (Eagleton, 27).

However, Byatt says now that "I felt then that these claims were extravagant and absurdly exclusive" (*PM*, xiv). She continues to believe in the power and beauty of language, and in literature as having a moral depth and compass. She speaks of Leavis's great "moral ferocity which dismissed all literature but the greatest, which was great for *moral* reasons. He could show you the toughness of a sentence, the strength and the grace of it, the way another one failed and betrayed itself, but you paid a terrible price for this useful technical knowledge" (*SS*, x).

Her 1991 introduction to the reissue of *The Shadow of the Sun*, so often quoted in this chapter, is an exercise in retrospective in which she brings her mature and informed sensibilities to bear not only on her first novel but on the intellectual climate in which it was written. For just as Anna Severell must move out of the "shadow" of her novelist-father in *The Shadow of the Sun*, so has Byatt been impelled to move out of the shadow that Leavis and her Cambridge education represent. She says that "the only way to deal with it was to read so much and so variously that no particular writer or system could overpower me" (*PM*, xiii). Indeed, her "early novels are in one aspect a sort of questioning quarrel with Leavis's vision and values, which nevertheless I inherit and share" (xiv).

Other Literary Influences

After F. R. Leavis, the names that crop up most often when Byatt speaks or writes about herself as a writer are Iris Murdoch, Marcel Proust, and George Eliot. Murdoch is a contemporary British novelist who has written over 20 novels and a number of critical and philosophical studies. Both Byatt and Murdoch write packed, textured novels that take for granted an audience with the time and the desire to linger over words and philosophical knots. Other contemporary English novelists with whom Byatt is often associated include Margaret Drabble—her younger sister[8]—Faye Weldon, A. N. Wilson, and David Lodge.

Murdoch's essay "Against Dryness: A Polemical Sketch" is one that Byatt often quotes as a way to understand her own aims as a novelist.[9] Murdoch argues that "through literature we can re-discover a sense of the density of our lives" (20); that at the end of the 20th century, "we have been left with far too shallow and flimsy an idea of human personality" (16). In this essay, Murdoch also identifies and argues for what she calls the "crystalline" novel: "a small quasi-allegorical object portraying the human condition." It is, she says, "what the more serious writers want to create" (18).

When Byatt writes in one of her critical studies of Murdoch that "there is a large number of suspicious reviewers and readers who find the elaborate, in some ways intensely artificial, world of her novels difficult to take," she is partly responding to her own critics.[10] While there are many differences between Byatt and Murdoch, they are alike in that they see themselves writing realistic fiction and are committed to a search for truth, to seeing things as they really are—and part of this seeing is to capture the complexity of human relations.

Byatt tells the story of her first reading of Proust in graduate school at Cambridge. While working on her thesis and on *The Shadow of the Sun* at the same time, she went to see Dame Helen Gardner, who told Byatt that she was reading Proust, in English. Gardner dismissed Byatt's fiction writing, telling her "to get on with her thesis." Byatt says that, in a rage, "she fled out of the room and went to Blackwells where I purchased Proust in French, read all of his work, and stopped writing my thesis. I needed to read Proust to learn how to write from him at that time, and Proust is all over *Shadow* in big chunks" (Musil, 196).[11] Byatt says that in her own writing, she would like "to include everything, like Proust" (Kenyon, 55). She "shares [Proust's] use of the novel to speculate on consciousness, on death; and on the impossibility of fully knowing another person. . . . They both use language to attempt to make permanent moments in time" (Kenyon, 68).

Marriage, Family, and Writing

While the particulars of Anna Severell's Cambridge experience in *The Shadow of the Sun* might not be the same as Byatt's, what both character and author have in common is the same sense of a "battle," as Byatt puts it, between "sexuality, literary criticism, and writing" (*SS*, viii). When Byatt says that her first four books were "too densely written," she attributes this fault to her attempt to balance writing, teaching, and motherhood (Foote, 61).

In 1959, Antonia Drabble married Ian Byatt, a British economist, and subsequently had two children, Antonia (born in 1960 and described by her mother as a "born writer" [Kellaway, 45]) and Charles (1961). In 1962, she began teaching part-time at the University of London, and in 1965, at the Central School of Art and Design. Her first novel, *The Shadow of a Sun*, which she had begun at Cambridge when she was seventeen, was published in 1964. These years were incredibly busy for Byatt as she attended to her family, kept up her teaching, wrote fiction, and began to branch out into literary criticism with *Degrees of Freedom: The Novels of Iris Murdoch* (1965). She was also beginning to write reviews, do talks and interviews for the BBC, and write scholarly essays.

In 1957, when Byatt was 21, she had begun her second novel, *The Game*, which would not be published until 1967. Her next project, the scholarly study *Wordsworth and Coleridge in Their Time*, was published in 1970, then renamed and reissued as *Unruly Times* in 1973.

At this point, events in Byatt's personal life had a number of profound effects on her progress as a writer. In 1969, she and Ian Byatt divorced; later that same year, she married Peter Duffy, to whom she is still married. They have had two children, Isabel (1970) and Miranda (1973). In 1972, her 11-year-old son Charles was killed by a drunk driver while he was walking home from school. "It took me eleven years to recover *at all*," says Byatt (Kellaway, 45). It is not surprising to find that Byatt has since woven in themes of mourning and loss into her writing. Stout characterizes Byatt as full of a "permanent sadness" (15). It is difficult not to draw parallels between her personal grief and the subject matter of "The Changeling," "The July Ghost," "The Next Room," "The Dried Witch," and *The Conjugial Angel*. "The July Ghost," another Jamesian story, is about a woman who is too "sensible" to see her own son's ghost and can only be comforted secondhand, through her lodger, who, to his consternation, is able to see the ghost.[12]

After Charles's death, Byatt began to teach full-time at University College, until 1983. His death understandably interrupted the completion of her next book, *The Virgin in the Garden*, which was finally published in 1978. It is the first of a series of four novels that follow the lives of the Potter family. A minor character is Mrs. Thone, who is inconsolable after the death of her son. Guilt and grief are explored in brief here and would continue to be touched upon in Byatt's later work. However, it must be said that in these works Byatt is doing more than simply reworking the stuff of autobiography into fiction, as later chapters in this study will show.

Meanwhile, Byatt completed another, shorter critical study of Iris Murdoch's novels (*Iris Murdoch*, 1976) and edited George Eliot's *The Mill on the Floss* for Penguin (1979). In 1985, she published *Still Life*, for which she won the British Silver Pen Award.

Sugar and Other Stories (1987), Byatt's first collection of short stories, represents, she says, her first sustained work as a full-time writer. "I wrote them in a kind of *joie de vivre* about being a full-time writer."[13] She describes the collection as "about losses: of possibilities, of parents, of children, of love, of ideas, of . . . hope."[14]

Possession: A Romance

Possession: A Romance was published in 1990 and became a best-seller in England and in America. By March 1991, *Possession* had sold more than 100,000 copies in the United States alone. Byatt won the prestigious British Booker Prize for the novel in 1990. Warner Brothers bought the film rights in 1991, and the playwright Henry David Hwang (*M. Butterfly*) has written the screenplay.

When Byatt's American publisher, Random House, asked her to omit some of the poetry and place description—the novel is 555 pages in hardcover—she refused. However, she did agree to make a slight but telling change in her description of Roland, who in the American edition acquires a "smile of amused friendliness" and is able to arouse "feelings of warmth, and sometimes more, in many women."[15] Byatt tells this story with some amusement.

Possession, Byatt says, is the first book she wrote without interruption. "That's why it reads easier. I was actually able to make my own rhythm, hold everything balanced in my head" (Foote, 61). She adds, "I knew people would like [*Possession*]. It is the only one I've written to be liked, and I did it partly to show off." But she also says that "there is very little *life* in *Possession*. It's all art" (Stout, 14).

However, these and other comments Byatt makes about her work must be taken with the proverbial grain of salt—there is indeed a good deal of art in *Possession*, and sometimes the life becomes imprisoned within the art, but in its exploration of love and loss, the novel often rings true and deep. Authors are not always the best commentators on their own work, though Byatt as a literary critic is better than most in this regard. Still, Byatt is as susceptible as the next author to the "interview effect": an author, forced to make pronouncements on the ineluctable creative process, loses or obscures a bit of the truth of it.

Byatt identifies an inspiratory moment for *Possession* as the time she saw a well-known Coleridge scholar working in the British Library and "mused that much of what she [Byatt] knew of Coleridge had been filtered through that individual. . . . 'I thought, it's almost like a case of demonic possession, and I wondered, has she eaten up his life or has he eaten up hers?'" Byatt thought of writing a novel based on the Brownings but concluded that she couldn't do it "because, (A) the Browning scholars might sue for libel, and (B) that left me no room for invention." She adds that she wanted to portray Browning "with the kind of warmth of a Shakespearean comedy."[16] She also says *Possession: A Romance* was "partly provoked" by John Fowles's *The French Lieutenant's Woman* (Kellaway, 45).

Eleven years before writing *Possession: A Romance*, Byatt quoted B. S. Johnson, who rails against writers who attempt to recreate the 19th-century novel: "No matter who the writers are who now attempt it," he says, "it cannot be made to work for our time, and the writing of it is anachronistic, invalid, irrelevant and perverse."[17] *Possession: A Romance*, insofar as it includes elements of the 19th-century novel, has proven Johnson wrong.

Personal Details

Byatt currently lives in Putney, in southwestern London (her house has a Latin inscription above the doorway: *semper eadem*, "always the same," which was Queen Elizabeth I's motto), and has a cottage in the south of France, in the Cévennes Mountains. She lives with a border collie named William (as in Wordsworth). As a SAD (seasonal affective disorder) sufferer, she finds that her French cottage is more than just a vacation home to her. (Certainly the sun, sunlight, and heat figure prominently in a number of her fictions, such as "On the Day That E. M. Forster Died," in which the woman works best in summertime.) Byatt says, "What I write is heliotropic," and this is apparently true metaphorically and literally (*SS*, xiv). Byatt also says she likes TV nature programs ("snails and slugs and intestinal tapeworms"), an interest that one can trace from *The Game* and *Possession* through *Morpho Eugenia*. Byatt likes to watch snooker (a kind of pool): "I like the *narrative* of it, the drama. I love it the way you love a Matisse!" (Stout, 14).

Byatt, according to Stout, "looks a picture of assured authority, a cross between a school headmistress and the Foreign Secretary. Yet close up, she is soft, dimpled and plump, with a strikingly feminine cupid's bow mouth and disheveled gray-brown curls. Beneath her animated, bulldog-firm manner, she often displays surprising vulnerability." She says of herself that "I am a novelist who happens to be quite good academically. And I am *not* motherly, or donnish. That is a stereotype because of my being . . . circular" (Stout, 11, 14).

Byatt describes herself as a member of the Radical Party and says, "Of course I am a feminist. But I don't want to be required to write to a feminist programme, and I feel uneasy when this seems to be asked of me" (McTighe, 71). In another interview, she said, "Now is the only time to be a woman" (Kellaway, 45).

Current Work and Interests

Passions of the Mind, a collection of Byatt's previously published critical essays, quickly followed publication of *Possession: A Romance*, and her earlier novels were reissued. In 1992, Byatt published two novellas under the umbrella title of *Angels and Insects*. (The first novella, *Morpho Eugenia*, was made into a film in 1995, directed by Peter Haas.) In 1994, *The Matisse Stories*, a collection of three short stories, was published in England (and in the United States in 1995). A collection of fairy stories, *The Djinn in the Nightingale's Eye*, was published in 1994 in Great Britain, and will be published in the United States by Random House in 1997. *Babel Tower*, the next book in her tetralogy (*A Virgin in the Garden* is the first, *Still Life* the second), was published in the spring of 1996, too late to be considered for this study. Byatt has already planned one last novel in the series, titled *A Whistling Woman*. She says, "I hope to write it in an unbroken run, as I've got two more books in my head I want to write." Of her writing habits, she has said: "I plan all my books in notebooks of Coleridgean complexity, thinking out the ideas and the narrative and the images, and then I write them, like knitting, in one thread. I used to write twenty drafts, partly for the rhythm, but now I make do with two, or even one."[18]

Byatt has very decided opinions about readers, writers, and the novel. For example, she calls Elizabeth Bowen's definition of the ultimate goal of a novel "as good a statement of the complex relations of truth and fiction as I know." Bowen says: "Plot must further the novel towards its object. What object? The non-poetic statement of a poetic truth. . . . Have not all poetic truths already been stated? The essence of a poetic truth is that no statement of it can be final."[19] In Byatt's view, poetic truth is not necessarily opposed to realism, however. She is also interested in "the problem of the 'real' in fiction," which, along with "the adequacy of words to describe it, has occupied me for the last twenty years" (*PM*, xv). Writing in 1991, Byatt said that she is "exercised by the problem of communicable detail . . . How many readers will have read Milton's *Paradise Lost* or . . . *The Aeneid*? How many who have not will be annoyed to find them in my books? (This is a reaction I still find puzzling)" (McTighe, 71).

More recently, Byatt says that "I am passionately in favour of keeping alive the teaching of as much of the past as can be managed. I don't subscribe to the view that the contemporary, the living writer is necessarily any more accessible or 'relevant' to the experience of the student . . . than the dead."[20] Taken together, these two statements illustrate Byatt's abiding belief in the accessibility of fiction.[21]

Though Byatt does not currently teach, she has many years of classroom experience and is quick to acknowledge that her writing and reading experience has been shaped by the special demands of teaching (*PM*, xiii, xvi). In "Reading, Writing, Studying: Some Questions about Changing Conditions for Writers and Readers," she asks, what is "the effect on the whole culture of readers and writers, inside and outside teaching structures, of the almost immediate teaching of books, as they are written?" ("Reading," 4). Byatt goes on to note that she belongs to a generation of writers who have an already constituted group of "professional readers"—the members of the university.

At the time of her first novel, Byatt recalls,

I found the idea of being eventually studied both exciting and consoling—however daunting it might also have been. It meant that if one constructed complicated shifts in tone in sentences, felt out ambiguities, referred to texts about which one cared passionately—*Paradise Lost, The Faerie Queene*—somewhere, somehow, there might be someone on the lookout for the subtleties which you couldn't expect everyone to understand. ("Reading," 5).

Five novels, one Booker Prize, and dozens of short stories and critical essays later, Byatt has established a place for herself in the literary canon. One cannot imagine a course on the contemporary British novel without her.

Chapter Two
Early Fiction: *The Shadow of the Sun* and *The Game*

The Shadow of the Sun

After *Possession* had considerably enlarged Byatt's audience, a number of her earlier novels were reissued, including her first, *The Shadow of the Sun*, which Byatt began when she was at Cambridge in 1954 and published in 1964. While Byatt's art has certainly matured over the past 30 years, her preoccupation with the artist, the imagination, and the impossibility of love and the inevitability of loss has remained constant. *The Shadow of the Sun* is the most Coleridgean of her novels in its opposition of the demands of the world and the demands of the creative imagination.

At the same time, *The Shadow of the Sun* is a coming-of-age story, a portrait not of the artist but of the artist's daughter as a young woman. As such, the novel explores what Harold Bloom calls the "anxiety of influence": the difficulty of the poet in coming to terms with the works of writers who have preceded him in order to make space for his own imagination. (The masculine pronoun is deliberate, for Bloom writes only about male poets and their precursors. However, the notion of anxiety of influence has a much wider application.) Anna Severell must fight against the influence of her father, his overpowering genius and personality, in order to find something that she can claim for her own. At the end of the novel, it is not clear that she has succeeded (or will succeed); what is clear is just what she is up against in the person of Henry Severell.

In 1991, Byatt wrote an introduction to the reissue of *The Shadow of the Sun* in which she reflects on its original making and her attitudes toward it some 30 years later:

> Reading it now, or skimming and remembering it, I reexperience a kind of fear. I didn't want to write a "me-novel" as we scornfully labelled them then, literary sophisticates, inexperienced human beings. But I had the eternal first novelist's problem. I didn't *know* anything—about life, at least. I remember thinking out the primitive first idea of it, which was

that of someone who had the weight of a future life, amorphously drag-
ging in front of her, someone whose major decisions were all to come,
and who found that they had got made whilst she wasn't looking, by
casual acts she thought didn't impair her freedom. (viii)

In this introduction, Byatt charts a minihistory of herself as a novelist
and, in doing so, asks us to focus not on the young Byatt who wrote
then but on the mature Byatt who writes now. The postmodern Byatt is
at work here: she recognizes that she has indeed written a "me-novel,"
however transformed it may be by art. She says that *The Shadow of the
Sun* is not an allegory of her own life ("it isn't, of course, it has its own"
[xi]). Nonetheless, as is often the case with Byatt's novels, *The Shadow of
the Sun* is both autobiographical and not at the same time. In discussing
the significance of the title, Byatt says that "Coleridge saw the human
intellect as a light like the moon, reflecting the light of the primary consciousness, the Sun. My Anna was not even a reflected light, she was a
shadow of a light only." "I feared that fate," adds Byatt (*SS*, xiii).[1]

Byatt took the title of the novel from Sir Walter Raleigh's "A Farewell to False Love," which is a spurned lover's meditation on love. In
the poem, love is fragile and fraught with danger: "A substance like the
shadow of the sun, / A goal of grief for which the wisest run."[2] Note
the ironic *for*: we would expect that the wise would run *from* false love,
but Raleigh twists the meaning so that we understand how willing even
the wisest are to embrace love's folly. Byatt also uses a stanza from
"False Love" as an epigraph for the novel and says that she initially read
the poem as "a wry comment on the female belief in, or illusion of, the
need to be 'in love'" (*SS*, xii). She adds that the "desiderata of the feminine mystique, the lover, the house, the nursery, the kitchen, were
indeed a 'goal of grief for which the wisest run' and my mother was
there to prove it" (xiii). In *The Shadow of the Sun*, Byatt attempts to capture the trajectory of so many educated young women of her generation
who were unable to escape domesticity and the oppressive influence of
parents and propriety.

Byatt furnishes a revealing anecdote (as it is intended to be) about
the title. Her original editor at Chatto and Windus, the poet and critic
Cecil Day Lewis, suggested, she tells us, that she change the title from
"The Shadow of *the* Sun" to "The Shadow of *a* Sun." This story captures
how Byatt uses the symbol of the shadow, for the young Byatt could not
say no to the older and established Lewis, just as her character Anna
cannot say no to her father. Only in the 1991 edition has her original
title been restored (*SS*, xiii).

Influences on *The Shadow of the Sun*, Byatt says, include Françoise Sagan's *Bonjour Tristesse*, the novels of Marcel Proust, Iris Murdoch, and—as a reaction against the "sensibility" of Woolf—novelists such as Forster, Elizabeth Bowen, and Rosamond Lehmann (*SS*, xii). D. H. Lawrence—"whom," says Byatt, "I cannot escape and cannot love" (xii)—haunts the novel as well. Anna is "a descendant of Birkin, a portrait of the artist with the artist left out" (xii). She adds, "What I said at the time was that the novel was about the paradox of Leavis preaching Lawrence when if the two had ever met they would have hated each other" (xi).

The Story

Seventeen years old, stubborn and shy, troubled Anna must learn to make her own way in the world. Her journey into adulthood is particularly complicated by the fact that her father is a famous novelist, but "distant and largely unknown" to her (*SS*, 12). Not only will Anna never achieve the intellectual power that he so lightly wields, she will never win the affection and the recognition that she so desperately wants from him. To make matters worse, her no-nonsense mother Caroline neglects Anna and her 12-year-old brother in order to create a safe and nurturing environment for her husband. For Caroline, Anna is a bother who constantly disrupts the seeming tranquillity of her home.

The events of the first half of the novel take place over a single summer, during which Oliver and Margaret Canning come to visit the Severells at their home in the country at Darton. Oliver is a literary critic and university teacher who often writes about the novels of Anna's father. He spends his visit tutoring Anna, finally convincing her to go on to Cambridge. While at Darton, Oliver is keenly aware of how Anna is neglected by her parents in their different ways, and an odd intimacy develops between the two.

An important theme that begins to emerge at this point is the fragility of human relationships and how inadequate most people are in dealing with each other—and how good they are at deceiving others as well as themselves.

At the same time, the first half of the novel is a description of genius at work and of the price one must pay in order to do any creative work. Genius, it seems, cannot coexist with human emotions; Henry chooses to avoid contending with those around him, the novel suggests, as much as he is chosen by his gifts to do so.

The second half of the novel covers Anna's time at Cambridge, where she has an affair with Oliver, leading to her pregnancy and the breakup of his marriage. As she looks back at her life, Anna begins to feel that she has never really taken control of it, and that she has allowed others to make all of her decisions. We are left wondering if Anna will ever move out from the "shadow" of her father—and Oliver—and determine her own destiny.

Suns and Other Influences

At the center of the novel is Henry Severell, who, according to the reviewer R. D. Spector, "has a Dickensian exaggeration that startles and arouses the imagination. . . . Henry dominates the reader's mind just as surely as he does the fictional characters who live in his shadow."[3] Henry is selfish and self-absorbed, accustomed to having a wife who takes care of mundane domestic duties—including the raising of his children—so that he has space and time to write. Byatt's narrator tells us that "visitors . . . were almost always in awe of Henry Severell, and assumed that his needs must be different and more pressing than those of others, a feeling which Caroline did her best to encourage" (*SS*, 5). At the same time, Henry can be kind in a remote, Olympian way. He is capable of some tenderness but reserves to himself his emotional energy, which he then pours into his work. Henry looks like "a cross between God, Alfred Lord Tennyson, and Blake's Job, respectable, odd, and powerful all at once" (9). At one point, we are told that the weather at Darton had been unusually hot for England, the air full of a brilliant heat. Henry "liked sun, responded to heat like a salamander . . . moving and walking more violently as the temperature increased" (44). This preoccupation with light and heat parallels Marcus's visionary experiences in *The Virgin in the Garden*, in turn inspired by Van Gogh's visions (see chapter 4).

Though he is a successful and well-respected novelist, Henry becomes periodically obsessed with a scholarly project titled *Analysis of the English Romantic Movement*. Henry cannot move past the note-taking stage in his study of Wordsworth and Coleridge. Caroline sees his attempts to work on the *Analysis* as "almost always a prelude to fits of strange behaviour" (*SS*, 8). "Strange behaviour" consists of an English version of a walkabout (cf. Leonard Bast's night walk in E. M. Forster's *Howards End*). In the early part of the novel, for example, Henry, feeling restless, goes on a visionary walk, a journey, a quest, lumbering over everything that comes in his way, wading rivers and climbing over fences. By the time he has circled back toward home, muddy and grass-stained, he has transformed himself into a Green Man—a "Wild Man of the Wood" figure (56ff, 84ff).

The walkabouts are agonizing for the Severells, who are left behind to wait for Henry's return. They choose not to talk about these episodes, and Caroline simply ministers to Henry when he comes home. Anna is embarrassed and angered by Henry's journeys, but she also wants to understand and emulate her father. She reads his quests as a commentary on the lack of her own: "One knew so little, could follow him in imagination only far enough to stick fast at a consciousness of one's own inability to follow further." (*SS*, 52). This is the "shadow" that Anna lives under and that hovers over her at Cambridge, where she cannot find her own way.

In her introduction to *The Shadow of the Sun*, Byatt invokes her own "sun" when she says of her teacher F. R. Leavis that, "in his shadow his pupils, would-be critics and would-be poets and novelists alike shrivelled into writing-blocks" (*SS*, x). While Henry Severell is not F. R. Leavis, both men seem to share a certain power over those with whom they come in contact. At the same time, Byatt identifies with Henry, saying that he is "partly simply my secret self. . . . Someone who saw everything too bright, too fierce, too much" (x). In reflecting on the relationship between Anna and her father, Byatt thinks of Henry as "an ideal and unapproachable father, who, being male, could have what she and I felt we perhaps ought not to want, singlemindedness, art, vision" (ix). The figure of Henry is refashioned elsewhere in Byatt's works: he shares this terrible clarity of vision with Marcus in *The Virgin in the Garden*, as I have mentioned, and with Cassandra in *The Game*. Roland, at the very end of *Possession*, begins to write with the same "singlemindedness." The Tennyson in *The Conjugial Angel* is Henry in advanced old age, left to contemplate his diminishing powers. Finally, the ideal male reader in "Racine and the Tablecloth" is a much more sympathetic version of Henry Severell.

Oliver, not without problems of his own, understands the Severell family very well. "'I can see it can't be very pleasant for you, living under his shadow. Great men are always hard on the next generation,'" he says to Anna (*SS*, 53; cf. 83). Byatt says that Oliver "represents a kind of public vision . . . a scholar, a critic, a *user* of literature, not a maker, a natural judge" (xi). Oliver and Henry have an uneasy relationship: they are not quite friends, and not quite colleagues, but spend a good deal of time together, primarily because of Oliver's efforts. Oliver is Henry's best reader and, at the same time, his most annoying reader.

Henry complains that "he pries, he nibbles, he draws conclusions, he defines, on scraps of information that no one with any real tact would try to make anything out of. He will ask questions all the time" (6–7).

But it is Anna the novel focuses on. Byatt has given her all the awkwardness of adolescence. She is

> small for her age . . . and thin, with pronounced hollows above the bones at the base of her neck; she suffered, nevertheless, from that late adolescent padding of flesh [that] contributes a certain squareness to the whole appearance. . . . She was dressed, as usual, in a shapeless Aertex shirt, which had been her school hockey shirt, and boy's heavy jeans, held somewhere between the waist and hips by an old Girl Guide belt. (*SS*, 10)

Anna is a difficult girl, not at all outgoing, as her mother and Jeremy would prefer her to be. She uses an old hut at the bottom of the garden as a refuge, as a place to hide from social obligations and her family ("it was horrible to dislike one's family so much" [13]).

Anna is physically clumsy and admires the beautiful and "golden" Margaret. She is also very bright. However, she is unwilling to commit to the intellectual life, because of the formidable reputation of her father. Living with genius can be intimidating: "Watching Henry drained her dreams of their force," she thinks (*SS*, 16).

At the same time, Anna does share in Henry's overabundance of feeling and sensation. The narrator tells us of a moment for Anna when

> things became suddenly beautiful, intolerably beautiful, and she intolerably aware of them: she found herself, despite herself, driven to tears by the intense green she saw, looking up through the apple trees at the summer sky, unable to reduce the profusion of the gold-edged crossing twigs and the overlapping, deepening, glittering rounds of the leaves against that uncompromising midsummer blue to any order that she could comprehend. (*SS*, 19)

This moment of heightened perception is very much like what Henry experiences, though Anna could not know this, since she rarely talks to her father.

Henry's walkabouts are also echoed in small by Anna when she runs away from boarding school to York, where she spends her days in movie theaters and her nights in a bleak bed-and-breakfast. She is expelled from school, and Caroline worries that Anna will be a burden to her parents. For Caroline, Anna has become "some evil spirit who had taken possession of the life she had arranged round her husband and her house, and was brooding over it, weighing on it, would never leave it" (SS, 28).

Oliver makes up the third crucial element in the triangulated relationship that includes Anna and Henry. He teaches at a training college for women—somewhat like an American community college—and is at once bitter about, ashamed, and proud of his working-class roots. Oliver says to Anna about Henry that "one doesn't know where he starts from. . . . It's nowhere I've ever been. I'm not sure it's a legitimate place for most people to go, or to be preoccupied with. . . . I accept his view *because he knows*, not because I know" (SS, 52). Oliver is admiring, but also envious and critical.

While Oliver and Margaret have an active sexual life—and, we learn, one that is often abusive to Margaret—they do not share in a life of the mind. She is beautiful, fashionable, feminine—and empty, trained solely for marriage and children. Margaret's shortcomings may not necessarily be her fault, however; the narrative seems to suggest that she is simply a woman of her time.[4]

The climax of part 1 comes on the day before the Cannings are to return to London. Caroline arranges a picnic by the sea, which is a part of her idea, or fantasy, that the Severells are a normal family. However, the day degenerates into a number of quarrels. There is a confrontation between Oliver and Henry over the relationship between novelist and reviewer. Henry and Margaret have an emotional conversation in which Margaret, as if seeing into her desperate future, extracts a promise of help from Henry about Oliver.

That night, Anna waits up for the storm that has been building for weeks. By accident, she encounters Oliver in the bathroom, and as the weather finally breaks, so do their inhibitions: "And then, as the thunder bore down upon them again, Oliver reached out for her and held her back by the hair . . . and she, after her first involuntary stiffening, clutched at his shoulders with sharp fingers and held out her mouth to him. . . . Oliver's love-making was painful" (SS, 136).

We move from this beginning in the midst of endings—of the summer, of the Cannings' visit, of Anna's childhood—to part 2, in which Anna goes to Cambridge. She does well, writing, the narrator tells us, essays that are "precise, correct, unadventurous." It is as if Anna deliberately holds back and will not allow herself the intellectual free rein that just might make her more like her father, a condition she both longs for and fears. Her cautiousness—or better, her detachment—carries over into her personal relationships: "Her view of love was still through the small end of the telescope; if it looked . . . as though it might have been anything else, she took care to complicate it until it was safely impossible and remote again" (*SS*, 145). Again, Anna cannot see how she may share these feelings with her father.

Her feelings about love color her attitude toward Peter Hughes-Winterton, an earnest, proper, almost stereotypical, Cambridge aristocrat. We first meet him in his smoky rooms at a party expressly organized "for Anna, whom he loved. He had hoped she might blossom in candlelight and good manners" (*SS*, 147). For Anna, however, Peter "remain[s] a protector, an opener of doors, a bringer of flowers, a provider of coats against the rain and cushions in punts, and Anna laughed at his punctiliousness, admired him for it and came to rely on it, all at once" (148).

At the party, Anna drinks too much. As she sits on the cold college lawn, on the verge of being sick, Oliver appears, and she goes home with him. This is not a romantic or even auspicious beginning to their affair, but it is a beginning nonetheless.

Anna can be more honest with Oliver than she can with Peter or with any of her tutors. She tells him that "I always do what comes easiest" (*SS*, 153), and, "Shall I tell you, I don't like literature? I—it seems to me—it's like a religion to them. They go to D. H. Lawrence like the Ten Commandments, to show them how to live" (157). (It may be that she likes literature very much, but that the way it is taught is the source of the problem.) She also tells Oliver, "But I don't want nothing. I want something. I want it badly. But I don't know what it is" (158). Oliver blames her father for her confusion: "Who did the seeing at home? Whose literature and the law and the Ten Commandments, whose authority and vision won't you take at second hand?" he demands (158).

While Anna and Oliver settle into a routine of seeing each other and sleeping together, Henry gets a letter from Margaret, who is feeling neglected and expects Henry to determine what Oliver has been up to. Caroline is the one who tells Henry not to help.

> People . . . won't grow up and accept life as it is. They can't cope with the fact that marriage can be boring, that it isn't all love and companionship, it can't be, not if a man is worth anything. They get bored, they say they aren't fulfilled and shout for help. They should learn to sacrifice themselves. Where would you be, for instance, if I was always trying to talk to you, or "fulfilling myself" instead of coping with the bank and the grocer and the telephone? (*SS*, 173)

Caroline's own unhappiness dominates this criticism of Margaret—or perhaps this betrayal of Margaret. Henry at least is made uncomfortable—"irritated"—by what lies beneath his wife's words. He decides to see Margaret, who has become a kind of mad housewife, subsisting on Bloody Marys and cigarettes. Henry agrees to see Oliver, to "do" something. The narrator tells us that "the idea that [Margaret's] life must be a string of . . . lies exasperated him. It was a waste of consciousness, a waste of the possibilities of movement, to spend a whole human energy on such a fabrication" (*SS*, 189). Apparently, Henry is able to see this insight as a truth about Margaret yet unable to apply it to his own wife.

Henry goes to Cambridge. Father and daughter have what seems to be their first real conversation—Henry begins to win Anna over and offers to give her money to go away, to find out what she really wants, for he sees that Cambridge is not for her (*SS*, 195ff). She says:

> "A lot of the time I feel as though I could live life tremendously—as though if I could find just the one *thing*, the event that would happen, all these little annoying bits of life would fall into place, and become important. . . . I've watched you working, I've watched you just going about, I know *you* know."
>
> "It's a question simply of the best way of finding it," said Henry with a roar of triumph that lifted Anna's head so that for a moment they smiled steadily at each other. He said, "You're all right, that's all right. . . . You're like me, you know. Whether you like it or not. You're my daughter." (*SS*, 200)

The narrator tells us that "he had found an answer for Anna, he had helped, he had made contact. And before he had had time to possess any of his achievements, he made his mistake. He thought he could say anything to Anna, now; he wanted, having begun to talk, to talk on, to tell her how he saw things, to confirm in her the power to see things his way that he had decided she possessed" (*SS*, 203). When Henry begins to discuss the Cannings, she reacts so violently that he finally realizes the truth. Anna feels betrayed and convinces herself that her father had come to separate her from Oliver, and that the offer of money was a bribe. And because the two had never really talked before, they are unable to solve this crisis.

Henry seeks Oliver out in the library and has as little success with him as he had with Anna. What has simmered beneath the surface is finally spoken: Henry says, "I've always felt—right from the beginning—something in your attitude to me—or my books, I think both—a kind of grabbing, a pulling down—a hatred" (*SS*, 217). Henry asks

Oliver to not get Anna mixed up in these feelings; Oliver says she's better off without Henry, and with him. When Anna and Oliver next meet,
Anna is feeling sick—the first intimations for the reader that she is
pregnant.

On her way home, Anna comes close to a Henry-like epiphany:

> And then the cutting edge of the vision melted . . . she had not been
> stirred out of herself, she had been moved only as far as a secondhand
> reflection, in a literary manner, in Oliver's manner, on a piece of prose . . .
> about an experience that in its real, far, unimaginable depth belonged
> properly to her father. She was still small, and self-contained and watch-
> ing, and the possible glory was gone. (*SS*, 238)

These visionary moments are important to Anna's maturing, to her
struggle with her identity. We might imagine that, if she had enough of
such moments, she would indeed break free from the influence of her
father and Oliver.

Caroline's reaction to the news of Anna's pregnancy is to blame her.
She continues to see Anna only as a trouble (*SS*, 246–48). Caroline's
tears have a strange effect on Henry, who up to this point could not
write because he was so agitated. It is "as though Caroline's family
anguish, Caroline's outrage, Caroline's sense of failure in her part,
relieved him of his own burden" (249). The narrator tells us how Henry
"felt sick for a moment, and for a moment as he said Anna's name his
imagination touched at her, and love tore him. But under that, he was
still and cold, waiting quiescent. And under that again, the old life
stirred, a tiny flame, which warmed him, in spite of himself, which he
knew he must protect before anything" (267).

Caroline, Henry, Oliver, and Margaret have a confrontation. Afterward, Henry retreats to his study, where he begins to work on his manu-
script. Oliver follows him and rails: "But you got away, didn't you? You
don't care now, do you? Not really *care*? You must write your quota of
pages tonight and the rest of us must shift as we can" (*SS*, 273). Margaret, says Oliver, is able to see the world for what it is: "Here, she says,
is a tree." But Henry sees "a transfigured tree, an ideal and shining
tree." What Oliver and Anna see is a hole. "It's positively a lack of trees,
a space for a tree, *no* tree. *No* tree" (276). Oliver thus sums up the different ways of seeing that cause so much trouble for the principals in *The
Shadow of the Sun.*

Anna, in the meantime, has run away to the Hughes-Wintertons,
having said she would marry Peter, who knows about her pregnancy.

Once she meets his mother, and after staying at her house and imagining her future as Peter's wife, Anna runs away once more. As she begins to make plans, her mood lightens, and we begin to think that Anna is finally doing something for herself ("She stood up, in a blaze of decision. . . . The thing to do is go, now. Alone" (*SS*, 297). However, Oliver follows her and takes over. We are left watching Anna "wake up out of a dream, seeing that what one did was indeed done, one was what one did, this as well, this above all, watching her last chance, or illusion, which? slip away" (297). Byatt thus eschews the conventionality—and comfort—of a happy ending in order to make a point about the unfinished quality of real life: straightening out the tangled threads of our existence is a complicated business indeed.

The Game

Starting it in 1957, Byatt had written a partial draft of *The Game* before finishing *The Shadow of the Sun*. In *The Game* (1967), Byatt continues to explore a number of themes begun in *The Shadow of the Sun*, but from different angles. As in her first novel, Byatt writes about the entanglements of love relationships and about writers and the creative imagination. She continues in a realist vein, studying, as Iris Murdoch would say in "Against Dryness," "the difficulty and complexity of the moral life and the opacity of persons" and affirming "a respect for the contingent" (20).

Both of these novels, along with the first two of Byatt's novel sequence (*The Virgin in the Garden* and *Still Life*), focus on family relationships. In the later sequence, Byatt explores the "powerhouse" effect: parents are so liberal that children have little to rebel against as they break away from their parents and struggle to develop an identity of their own (see chapter 4). We see the beginnings of Byatt's interest in the powerhouse family in *The Game*, in which siblings have trouble, not with separating themselves from their parents, but with developing identities apart from one another. One of the epigraphs with which Byatt opens *The Game* is taken from Charlotte Brontë's 1835 poem "Retrospection":

> We wove a web in childhood
> A web of sunny air;
> We dug a spring in infancy
> Of water pure and fair.[5]

However, the nostalgia invoked by these lines hardly applies to the childhood of the main characters in the novel, the sisters Julia and Cassandra Corbett. At the end of the novel, the epigraph takes on a darker cast. At this point, Julia reads Cassandra's journal and comes across the following passage: "When we were children, we were not quite separate. We shared a common vision, we created a common myth. And this, maybe, contained and resolved our difficulties. We wove a web in childhood, a web of sunny air. . . . We are food for thought. The web is sticky. I trail dirty shreds of it" (*G*, 230). What may be normal sibling rivalry in most families (as among, for example, the Brontë sisters) proves to be dangerous for the Corbett sisters.[6] This rivalry, this love/hate relationship, drives the plot of the novel.

I should add at this point that it is difficult to approach *The Game*, a tale of two sisters, without being conscious of the rivalry—real, imagined, or exaggerated by the literary press—between Byatt and her novelist sister Margaret Drabble. Our reading of the novel may well oscillate between an interest in the autobiographical and an appreciation of the text in itself.[7]

The Story

The Game is set in the early sixties, when Cassandra and Julia are in their late thirties; however, we get flashbacks to various points in their childhood from both their points of view. As children, we learn, Cassandra and Julia played a Brontëan "game" of medieval battles and courtly romance, using a set of figures not unlike chess pieces. The narrator tells us how the sisters "had worked out . . . attitudes to all sorts of adult problems which [Julia] for one had found alternatively percipient and fantastically thwarting—how did one ever rid oneself of a longing for a devouring love which one saw, wisely, to be impossible, but had enjoyed in such verisimilitude and detail when nothing else was happening to one at all?" (*G*, 46–47). The game takes on a more sinister aspect as they get older; in many ways, people around the sisters become figures to be manipulated, to be captured, then lost, and won back again (103). This game is the originary game that gives the novel its title and central metaphor.

Cassandra and Julia are not close in the way that encourages sisterly confidences. They find their shared history stifling; their problem is that they are *too* close, that they know each other too well. They continue to have an antagonistic relationship well into adulthood, a relationship based on a series of betrayals. For example, when they are teenagers,

Julia publishes as her own a story that she and Cassandra had written together; she later takes over Cassandra's only friend, Simon Moffitt. In turn, Cassandra is withholding and cold, qualities that seem to compel Julia into even more betrayals, small and large. Cassandra, as the eldest, feels that she can have no peace from the insecure and inquisitive Julia; Julia feels that she cannot develop a sense of self in the shadow of her sister. Julia, reflecting on her version of their childhood, says, "I've always been scared stiff of waking up and finding out I was nothing but a thought in Cassandra's mind" (*G*, 86). At another point, Julia tells Simon that Cassandra "made perfectly normal behaviour into crimes— like borrowing books, like telling people things. She locked me out until I was crazy to get in. And then she saw to it I was guilty of real crimes, that what I'd done I couldn't change or undo. She made me—take things—and then left me in possession" (232–33).

What is so striking about their childhood difficulties is that Cassandra and Julia are raised in a liberal Quaker home in which generosity toward others is the rule. In this case, however, charity does not begin at home; misunderstandings, jealousies, and pettinesses too often drive a wedge between the two sisters.

What happens in the Cassandra-Simon-Julia triangle is not a simple case of sisters quarreling over a man, of love betrayed. Simon colludes as well; he genuinely likes them both, Cassandra for her cleverness and seriousness, and Julia for her more "feminine" lightheartedness. But Simon has his own unwholesome reasons for wanting to come between the sisters, reasons that have less to do with them and more to do with his own need to manipulate others.

Julia's reasons for her interest in Simon are complicated. As the younger sister, she looked up to Cassandra, and when they were children, this adoration often took the form of imitation, which Cassandra felt as stifling and intrusive. Julia wanted Cassandra's toys when they were children, her diary when they were adolescents, and her friend Simon in young womanhood. Though Julia likes Simon and imagines that she is in love with him, his chief attraction is that he is forbidden, off-limits. Julia fancies herself as one who likes danger; she thinks in terms of winning and losing, of being in competition with Cassandra, who simply wants to be left alone.

Cassandra finds Julia's obsessive interest in her life a burden because she feels so fragmented herself; she has problems enough with the boundaries of her personality without Julia's testing the limits. She feels alienated and is deeply unhappy. Her psychic survival, she is sure, involves erecting a wall around herself, an act that, of course, isolates her even further. These feelings shape her early and tenuous relationship with Simon, for the two are not lovers, not girlfriend and boyfriend in the conventional sense; both seem incapable of taking the friendship beyond a purely intellectual plane. In fact, the Corbetts seem to have had no idea that Cassandra was seeing Simon and regard him as Julia's boyfriend.[8]

When Julia and Cassandra begin a tentative conversation about Simon (who has abandoned them both and gone to Malaya), Julia describes Simon as "an awful emotional dabbler" (*G*, 95). Julia wants to share her Simon experience with Cassandra, but Cassandra withdraws and will not listen. As usual, Julia's motives are not completely innocent: while she may want to make up with her sister, she still wants to hurt her, and by beginning to talk about the sexual aspect of her relationship with Simon, she wounds Cassandra.

Julia eventually marries a Quaker social worker named Thor (thus recapitulating her own unhappy childhood) and becomes a successful popular novelist of domestic life. Yet she covets even more recognition; she longs to be a part of the larger London literary scene. The narrator says of Julia:

> She didn't want simplicity. She wanted the complicated, irreducible social world outside, where it was possible to believe in people who really cared more for their motor-cars than for anything else, people who spent *most of their time* thinking about who had snubbed whom at whose party in what dress. . . . She needed them, she wanted them, she wrote about them, she fed off them. She expected nothing, and this seemed to her the only possible form of moral activity. (*G*, 40)

Cassandra, by contrast, grows into a bookish and introverted Oxford professor of medieval literature. She had converted to Anglo-Catholicism when she was 18 and suffers from an obsessive religiosity. While Julia is the picture of contemporary fashion—Byatt's descriptions of her clothing are eerily reminiscent of descriptions of 1950s Barbie doll fashions—Cassandra deliberately dresses the part of the religious eccentric: "She affected cuffed and pointed black velvet slippers. [Her] clothes gave her a certain monastic, anachronistic grace; she was thin, and carried herself well although a little rigidly." In addition, Cassandra is loaded down with rings, crosses, medallions, and chains (*G*, 19).

When Simon returns to London from fieldwork in the Amazon, his presence rekindles old hostilities between the sisters. Julia writes a novel about Cassandra's affair with Simon, and while she sees it as the best work she's ever done, it is quite a blow to Cassandra once it is published.

Possessed of an indomitable will and pride that tip her over into madness, Cassandra kills herself. At the end of the novel, Julia begins to
resemble one of her own heroines in her popular fiction as she attempts
to deal with her sister's death, Thor's desertion, and the anger of her
daughter Deborah. Byatt's description of *The Game* is helpful here. She
says that it is "about the fear of the 'woman's novel' as an immoral
devouring force" (*SS*, xii). Cassandra, along with Thor and Deborah,
have indeed been devoured by Julia.[9]

The Tangled Web of Family

We first meet the Corbett family when everyone gathers at the house
outside of Newcastle, in the village of Benstone. Jonathan Corbett has
had a stroke. He dies with Cassandra by his bed. This is an unwelcome
and unwelcoming return home, into childhood, into old roles that Julia
and Cassandra have cast off in their adult lives.

As I have suggested, Corbett family life was not easy; both parents
were activist Quakers, often away from home. Jonathan Corbett had
even been imprisoned for some of his activities. Cassandra recalls keenly
that, while her father did indeed love her, "she had had to share his love
with so much else: prisoners . . . refugees, lepers, delinquents, prosti-
tutes" (*G*, 40).

Julia's own family both rejects and reproduces some of the character-
istics of the Corbett family. Self-centered Julia is unable to sympathize
with her teenage daughter Deborah or with her social activist husband.
Granted, there is a driven, pathological quality to Thor's altruism, but
Julia's response is to ignore it rather than to deal with it. Deborah, who
admires Cassandra, is at the difficult adolescent stage of feeling constantly at war with her mother. Julia, reproducing her relationship with
her own father, keeps Deborah at arm's length, insisting that her
daughter call her by her given name rather than "Mother"—she can't
bear for people to think that she is old enough to have a teenage daughter. Moreover, as Julia becomes more involved in London life, the gap
between her own ambitions and her husband's work and aspirations
grows wider: Thor hopes to go to Africa to do missionary work.

Cassandra has two versions of "family" to contend with in her life:
the Anglo-Catholic community to which she belongs, headed by Father
Rowell, and the academic family of her Oxford college. However, neither family, much like her original family, is able to help Cassandra deal
with her depression and growing alienation.

The Imagination, the Novel—and Television

The novel opens with two parallel scenes in which Julia and Cassandra watch Simon on television in their respective homes. Byatt carefully embeds these episodes in the routines of the two sisters' lives, routines that are to be forever shattered by Simon's return from the Amazon.

We first meet Julia as she and Thor say goodbye to dinner guests in a scene that has the bright surface of a scripted television commercial; people seem determined to have fun. Afterward, Julia's insecurities about her role of hostess and her husband's indifference to socializing are revealed, along with the kind of relationship that wife and husband have evolved over the years. Thor's role is to support Julia and her desires: "Julia—be a little peaceful, sometimes. Don't mind things so much. It isn't good" (*G*, 8). Her dependence on him is made obvious. It is at this point that Julia turns on the television, just in time to watch the first of a series of programs on the Amazon—with Simon Moffitt as "host" in his own "home"—or better, his own habitat. We thus meet Simon for the first time filtered through a TV camera.

We next watch Cassandra cope with "meeting" Simon on television after all these years. But first we look over her shoulder as she writes in her rooms at Oxford:

> We shall do better . . . to think of chastity as purity, a scrupulous purity and to associate it with innocence, if we are to apprehend at all the moral force either of Lancelot's sin or of Galahad's virtue in the *Morte d'Arthur.* Chastity as the supreme virtue is not an automatically acceptable idea. Most of us would preserve our brother's life before a maiden's maidenhead, or decide, if faced with the alternative of the immediate suicide of not only one but twelve ladies that the preservation of our virtue in these circumstances is perhaps a little selfish and a little prudish. We shall do better if we think of "that which the maiden would never have again" as an original innocence—and extend the meaning of "intact" to the whole spirit, uninvaded and complete. If we remember that to a true Christian death is not dreadful, we shall face Lionel's death with greater equanimity, even before we discover that is an illusion of the fiend. (*G*, 15)

This passage is worth quoting in its entirety, for it reveals the workings of Cassandra's intellectual imagination and foreshadows her own predicament as she becomes more irrational and obsessive. For this is how we learn that Cassandra is a virgin, "intact"—in other words, completely isolated both physically and emotionally. Cassandra then goes down to the Common Room where her colleagues are gathered around the TV, and she sees Simon.

In both these scenes, television controls what Julia and Cassandra see and subsequently feel. In this way, television becomes implicated in Byatt's meditation on the imagination in the novel. We will return to this idea shortly.

The literary scholar Jane Campbell says that *The Game* "presents and demonstrates contrasting uses of the imagination and shows the impossibility of its ever fully taking in the world, the difficulty of breaking out of private worlds into communication, and the devastation that can result from the misuse of imagination."[10] Instead of presenting us with a single universalized imagination, Byatt provides a multifaceted picture throughout the novel. Cassandra has a dangerous sort of imagination; it is too often turned unhealthily inward. She writes of "nightmares and fears" in her letter to Father Rowell (*G*, 16) and later paints them. Cassandra's imagination is also tied up in her scholarly work: "It is no accident, Cassandra told herself, that I chose a field of study where the great images are those of unsatisfied desire, formalized, made into a mode of apprehension" (97). Cassandra's predicament is one that is not unique to her. In a curiously tripled voice—narrator, Cassandra, and perhaps Byatt herself—we are told that Cassandra's "own generation, deprived of . . . inept experience, had had time to become aware of what was possible, of the subtleties of passion, through the imagination" (17). However, and partially because Julia took Simon from her when they were girls, Cassandra never crosses over from the imagination of passion into its reality.

Julia possesses a bright, hard imagination; she is clearly intelligent, but she lacks passion. She thinks to herself: "I don't . . . use my imagination enough, and [Cassandra] uses hers too much" (*G*, 122). She is unable to range far from her own biography when she writes and tends to cannibalize the lives of those around her for material. Her imagination is reductive, derivative.

We meet the imagination under other guises as well: Thor has what one might call a utopian imagination, and Simon Moffitt has an eloquent and often morbid imagination that he uses to bring the Amazonian jungle to life for TV viewers. In this respect, Moffitt is a precursor to Adamson in *Morpho Eugenia* and reflects Byatt's own interest in the natural world—one of the many legacies, perhaps, of those Romantics and Victorians who set out to record, if not to conquer, the phenomenal world.

As in *Possession: A Romance* and *Morpho Eugenia*, Byatt here explores the uses of the imagination by developing texts-within-texts, including the extant rules of Cassandra and Julia's game, Cassandra's journal and bits of her scholarly work, Julia's novel, and the reviews of her novel. In *The Game*, the reader is able to observe a novelist (Byatt) creating a novel in which a novelist (Julia) is writing a novel. This wheels-within-wheels effect is the defining stamp of the postmodern and aligns Byatt with other contemporary British novelists, such as Julian Barnes and John Fowles. In fact, one could generalize and say that all of Byatt's novels are concerned with the position of the writer both outside and inside the text. At one point, as Julia plans the novel that will ultimately be the death of Cassandra, she is aware of the pattern of her narrative falling into place, a pattern of which "one took possession and in the same movement" from which one "detached oneself" (*G*, 123). Here, the writer—Byatt, certainly, but also Julia—invites the reader to *watch* her fashion her fiction.

Television also becomes part of this wheels-within-wheels pattern in the *The Game*—it can almost be treated as a "text" in itself. It seems as if Byatt, steeped as she is in the literary imagination, is also trying to come to terms with the effects of what was then a new medium: regularly scheduled TV programs had been on the air for only about ten years when Byatt began writing. In a way, what Campbell says about the imagination in *The Game* can also be applied to the medium of television: it, too, is unable to represent the world completely and without distortion; it, too, has the potential for "devastation" precisely because of this inability to capture the truth of things.

By taking up the subject of television, Byatt deliberately complicates her meditation on the imagination. She suggests that TV is a different way of seeing, capable of both stifling and stimulating the imagination. For example, Byatt writes about how the camera is able to control the point of view—the watcher's gaze. As Julia watches Simon on TV for the first time, she thinks about the "smooth rapidity of the camera-work" and, her eye "bewildered by a series of changes in focus," notices how "the sun occasionally burst in long, white, hissing stars which rested on the leaves—a phenomenon the camera can hold, as the eye can not. It was alien and enveloping, in no way pretty" (*G*, 11).

Part of the Julia-Simon-Cassandra relationship exists in hyperspace, for both sisters interact with Simon *through* TV. The narrator tells us that, for Cassandra, "since the television appearances, which gave his pronouncements the illusory appearance of privacy and intimacy, Simon had become again accessible to the imagination, to dispute, to thought, to dreams" (*G*, 90). Julia, on the other hand, dwells upon Simon's physical appearance; she notes that he has "a long, mournful face. . . . His expression was both pompous and deprecating, as well as in some way secretive; he had changed, he had changed, but Julia remembered that look" (13). Both sisters' memories of Simon are reconstituted, refantasized, within the confines of the small screen. Thus, there are two Simon Moffitts in *The Game*: one is the real person whom Julia and Cassandra know and interact with, in the past and in the present; the other is the Simon Moffitt who is the commentator on life in the Amazon jungle.

Byatt explores the medium of television as a kind of parallel to reading a literary text. The camera, Byatt seems to suggest, is very much like a novel's narrator: both may seem "invisible" at times, but then each may reveal its presence at certain crucial points in order to remind the reader/viewer of the artifice behind the art. For example, Julia and Cassandra, as they watch Simon on TV, talk about how Simon appears to be alone; there seems to be no camera at all. They realize that any given scene may appear to be natural but is in fact carefully staged and edited (*G*, 51). Simon also understands how the camera is implicated in its subject. In his TV persona he intones, "Our picture of reality is never fixed but can always be elaborated and made more accurate. And this changes us" (22). Our reading—or viewing—thus moves between absorbing the narrative that is the result of artifice and examining the artifice itself. In *The Game*, Byatt wants us to see imagination from both the inside and the outside.

Cassandra's Journal and Julia's Novel

Perhaps it is not immediately obvious that representing the creative imagination has a long *gendered* history in Western art and literature; we might think that imagination transcends such categories as male and female. Yet this is not the case. As Byatt puts it, "Female visionaries are poor mad exploited sibyls and pythonesses. Male ones are prophets and poets" (*SS*, ix). It is precisely the gendered imagination that concerns Byatt; after *The Shadow of the Sun*, she says, all her novels have been about "the problem of female vision, female art and thought" (xiv). (Actually, one could argue that *The Shadow of the Sun* is about the *absence* of female vision.) Thus, when we examine Byatt's work as a whole, we discover a series of explorations of female vision not only in her earliest work but also in later texts, such as *Possession: A Romance* and the more recent short story "Artwork."

Cassandra and Julia are no exception. Each sister represents different aspects of female vision—not necessarily in opposition to each other, but different enough to indicate a range of possibilities rather than simple stereotypes. The scholar Giuliana Giobbi suggests that Byatt has rewritten Jane Austen's *Sense and Sensibility*, another tale of two sisters—Elinor (who represents sense) and Marianne (sensibility). Giobbi says that "Elinor's self-restraint and Marianne's indulgence in sensibility are shown as equally possible and plausible female attitudes."[11] Byatt may be rewriting Austen; however, Cassandra and Julia, for all *their* "possible and plausible female attitudes," are much more desperate than Austen's imaginary sisters.[12] Byatt remembers that the scholar Dame Helen Gardner told her that "a woman had to be dedicated like a nun, to achieve anything as a mind" (*SS*, ix). Cassandra is the embodiment of this philosophy. Julia is decidedly not "dedicated like a nun," and this is both her strength and her weakness as a novelist. Whatever their differences, both women turn their creativity into writing.

Even more than her scholarly writings, Cassandra's journal is her great work, idiosyncratic and mad though it is. She has kept a journal for most of her life—and Julia has surreptitiously read it all *her* life. The journal is detailed, obsessive, consuming:

> [Cassandra] was occasionally distressed by the extent to which the events and solid objects around her were only remarkable in so far as she "collected" them for her journal. . . . And once the journal had been only raw material for some large imaginative work—something finished and formed, which would, like a magnet, polarize all these unrelated scraps so that they lay in concentric circles or stood and pointed all one way like fur. (*G*, 23–24)

For Cassandra, life must be observed and then written down to be experienced. As she gets older, the journal spins out of control and becomes simply the record of the "tyranny of objects" (137). This fear of the material world is also revealed in the paintings and drawings Cassandra makes in the months before her suicide (142).

At one point in her journal, Cassandra muses on her name and its implied doom as embedded in myth: the original Cassandra refused Apollo's advances; he then cursed her by ensuring that no one would ever believe her prophecies. Given to Agamemnon at the fall of Troy,

Cassandra was taken back to Greece, where she was killed by Agamemnon's wife Clytemnestra. Cassandra writes: "Cassandra. Not Cassandra Austen, sisterly supporter of the expressive Jane. Cassandra who was Apollo's priestess, and—since she refused intercourse with the Lord of the Muses . . . incapable of communication . . . like myself, like myself, a specialist in useless knowledge" (G, 141).[13] Cassandra writes, in part, about her relationship to Julia here, creating an inverse parallel between the Corbetts and the Austens. Her "useless knowledge" will become much too useful to Julia, who exposes—and distorts—the relationship Cassandra has finally achieved with Simon in her book.

Julia's exploitation of her sister's life begins innocently enough. After their father's death, Julia writes to Cassandra, asking to visit her at Oxford. She speaks of a restlessness, saying: "I've got to dig deeper and spread wider. I want to write something with a few symbols and a Message" (G, 106). Her visit to Oxford provides Julia with the material she thinks she needs to "dig deeper": just as she had stolen Cassandra's story so long ago, she now steals Cassandra's words, "a sense of glory," for the title of her novel—and then steals Cassandra's very life (102).

Julia's intention is to write "a novel about the dangers of imbalance between imagination and reality. . . . It would mean coming to grips with the Game . . . with what's frightened me . . . with Cassandra" (G, 122–23); it would be "about the way Cass sees Simon—intensely meaningful, unreal" (136–37). Along the way to achieving this goal, Julia exposes the dark side of English university life through her fatally accurate and cruel pictures of Cassandra and her friends. (Compare this episode with Dorothy Sayers's picture of academic life in her mystery *Gaudy Night* [1936]). Julia's lack of imagination is made obvious; once again, she is unable to depart from her real-life subjects, and the characters in *A Sense of Glory* are all too recognizable.

Cassandra hears about the book indirectly from one of her colleagues, who clearly takes a malicious pleasure in telling her about it. She begins to prepare herself for suicide; not even Simon's appearance in Oxford can deter her. The narrator says: "Like certain reptiles [Cassandra] had learned to survive by leaving in Julia's hand the dead stump of the tail by which she had been grasped" (G, 222). By killing herself, in some perverse way, Cassandra "survives," leaving Julia to cope with what she has wrought. Cassandra has won the game.

But there is another way to read the conclusion to Byatt's novel. As an ironic coda to *The Game*, I quote the ending of Christina Rossetti's famous poem "Goblin Market":

> For there is no friend like a sister
> In calm or stormy weather;
> To cheer one on the tedious way,
> To fetch one if one goes astray,
> To lift one if one totters down,
> To strengthen whilst one stands.[14]

Just as Byatt makes Charlotte Brontë's poem "Retrospection" into a dark commentary on the relationship between Cassandra and Julia, I invoke Rossetti's poem in order to make one final point about the Corbett sisters. In "Goblin Market," Laura and Lizzie are each necessary to the survival of the other; they exist in a symbiotic relationship. Their final closeness is the reward for successfully uniting against the forces of evil (sexual or otherwise) that the goblins represent. In a way, Cassandra and Julia are like Rossetti's sisters, for each is incomplete without the other; each lacks what the other possesses in overabundance—just like Jane Austen's sisters. Together, they form a gestalt, a whole picture of realized female vision. Yet in Byatt's novel, it seems that one sister must be sacrificed in order to preserve the other. Julia has won the game.

Thus, the final meaning of *The Game* is left unresolved. This doubleness of meaning surfaces in a crucial conversation that Cassandra has with Simon about Julia's book. She says that *A Sense of Glory* (Cassandra's very words, remember) must be about "what Dr. Johnson called 'the hunger of the imagination that preys incessantly on life.' . . . So I'm peculiarly vulnerable to—to the imagination" (*G*, 225). Ironically, though Cassandra is referring to her own "hunger" and her own lack, she captures something essential about Julia's insatiable, mimetic imagination, which "preys incessantly on life." Neither sister has won the game.

However, *The Game* seems to accept the impossibility of any final resolution. Here, as in her other novels, Byatt takes very seriously Murdoch's dictum that, "since reality is incomplete, art must not be too much afraid of incompleteness" (20).[15]

Chapter Three

Short Stories

Byatt's short stories appear in two collections: *Sugar and Other Stories* (1987) and *The Matisse Stories* (1994). Both collections, especially *The Matisse Stories*, can be read as a sequence: that is, while each story stands on its own, each can be read in connection with the others. However, Byatt's tales may be distinguished from other, more formal short-story sequences in that characters are not carried over from one story to the next, such as in Hemingway's *Nick Adams Stories* and Jamaica Kincaid's *Annie John*. Rather, what holds the stories together in Byatt's collections is a repetition of emphasis and theme.

To foreground certain thematic links, I have grouped the eleven stories in *Sugar* in twos and threes instead of discussing them sequentially as they appear in the text (though my groupings do often follow the order in which they were published). *The Matisse Stories* contains only three stories ("Medusa's Ankles," "Art Work," and "The Chinese Lobster"); these are much more consciously linked together than those in *Sugar*, and I take them up in the order in which they appear.

Sugar and Other Stories

"Racine and the Tablecloth" and "Rose-Coloured Teacups"

"Racine and the Tablecloth" is about the slow smothering of female intellect under the weight of societal disapproval. It is hard to resist reading it as a piece of alternative autobiography. That is, this story of a curious and able girl, forced by cultural and historical circumstance to suppress her intellectual ambitions, could have been Byatt's story. In fact, "Racine" may well be the story of Byatt's mother, who, like so many women before the 1960s in the United States and in England, was forced to sacrifice meaningful work for husband and children.

There are three main characters in "Racine and the Tablecloth": Emily Bray, the schoolgirl who is our heroine and protagonist; the headmistress Martha Crichton-Walker, who functions as "the clash of principle, the essential denial of an antagonist";[1] and the "Reader," Emily's imaginary, objective—and therefore presumably just—audience. The narrator, another important presence, often directly addresses her own "reader"—that is, us—as she develops the narrative.

Emily is a brilliant student who arrives at an exclusive and expensive private boarding school at midyear—timing that serves to set an already lonely and isolated girl apart. She is shy, unhappy, and, if the schoolmistress Miss Crichton-Walker is correct in her criticisms, rather grubby—very much like Anna Severell in *The Shadow of the Sun*. But as the child of working-class parents, Emily is also like Oliver Canning in *Shadow*. She comes to the school on scholarship and is very self-conscious about the class differences between herself and her classmates. Emily's passion is the work of the 19th-century French poet Racine; her reading of his works transports her, takes her away from her trying existence at school.

Miss Crichton-Walker is neat, severe, judgmental, "firmly benign and breastless" (*SOS*, 2). The lines of battle are drawn between Emily and the schoolmistress, who seems intent on breaking what little spirit Emily reserves to herself. (Crichton-Walker is based, says Byatt, on a teacher she knew, "a destroyer, knocking down academic success.")[2] The narrator describes an early confrontation between the two: "Emily Bray saw that there were two outsiders in the room [of students]. There was herself, set aside from the emotion that was swimming around, and there was Miss Crichton-Walker, who wanted them all to be sharing something" (3). Though the headmistress is grudgingly respectful of Emily's intellectual gifts, she finds ways to criticize her, as in her description of the girl's handwriting as "aggressive" (5).

Just as a younger girl might invent an invisible companion for herself, someone to play with, Emily imagines an "ideal Reader" (*SOS*, 6). "He was dry and clear, he was all-knowing but not messily infinite. . . . Emily was enabled to continue because she was able to go on believing in the Reader" (6). She imagines this Reader, not the headmistress or her other teachers, as the true audience for her work: "In another place, the Reader walked in dry, golden air, in his separate desert, waiting to weigh her knowledge and her ignorance" (29). Emily is much better equipped to come to terms with the Reader's judgments than she is with Miss Crichton-Walker's, whose opinion of Emily's scholarship is so colored by her own feelings.

Toward the end of the story, the narrator directly addresses the reader: "Who won, you will ask, Emily or Miss Crichton-Walker, since the Reader is mythical and detached, and can neither win nor lose?"

(*SOS*, 30). We learn that Emily marries "young and hastily" and settles down to the small rewards and trials of homemaking, raising two "clever daughters" (30). But Emily is not able to evade the Crichton-Walkers of the world, for the pattern of her school life is repeated in her daughter Sarah's life. Sarah wants to study French and mathematics, yet an adviser at her school tries to discourage her and attempts to enlist Emily in his plans. The story ends with the following comment: "What Sarah made of herself, what Sarah saw, is Sarah's story. You can believe, I hope, you can afford to believe, that she made her way into its light" (32).

There is a lurking malevolence in "Racine and the Tablecloth," embodied in Miss Crichton-Walker and the deputy head at Sarah's school. This evil permeates all the small rituals of public-school life, based as many are on class and privilege. (What we call private school in the United States is called public school in England.) Moreover, this evil is gender-biased: Emily, and then her daughter, are expected to fit into roles fixed by gender rather than by ability and inclination.

But "Racine" does not foreground the issue of gender; rather, it reads like a parable, a story with a hidden message. For example, the narrator tells us of an April Fool's joke in which Emily and her classmates, in concert with the boys at the neighboring school, switch their assigned pews in church. This is certainly a harmless prank by today's standards, but it is rich in meaning for the story, in which gender is so proscribed. In a way, "Racine" is a variation on the story Byatt tells in *Still Life*, in which she explores the split future of two sisters: Stephanie, who stays home, and Frederica, who goes off to Cambridge.

"Rose-Coloured Teacups" is another story of women who are squeezed out of their ambition and their rightful place in academe. Byatt builds her narrative on three levels: the central character, Veronica, imagines her mother at university in the 1920s, then remembers herself there in the 1950s, and goes on to imagine a future when her emphatically modern daughter Jane will attend the same university. Both Veronica and her mother attended university in high hopes; both gave up their ambitions once they married. Will Jane break this chain of despair?

The story opens with a scene in which three women are drinking tea from pink luster cups in their college rooms. This scene is "imagined not remembered" by Veronica, who escapes into this picture of peace when her own domestic life threatens to overwhelm her (*SOS*, 38). Moreover, it is, as the narrator says, "a curious form of mourning, but compulsive, and partly comforting" (36). Veronica mourns her mother, and her own lost ambition.

Like rose-colored glasses, which soften the harshness of reality, the teacups symbolize a period of innocence, of hope, in the insulated world of the university—"a safe place" (*SOS*, 38). Veronica is aware of her romanticizing of her mother's past when, in reflecting on the scene she has imagined, she feels that she is "overdoing the pink." "She did not like pink," we are told (36). The truth is that "her mother had wanted her to be at the college and had felt excluded, then, by her daughter's presence there, from her own memories of the place. The past had been made into the past, discontinuous from the present. It had been a fantasy that Veronica would sit in the same chairs, in the same sunlight and drink from the same cups" (37).

The teacups also come to be associated in Veronica's mind with her mother's "miserable disappointed face" and her own feeling at university as, in a "daze of defeat and anguish," she carelessly packs up the cups, thus breaking them. The reason for her violent feelings is long forgotten, however important it may have been at the time (*SOS*, 37). Two cups and one saucer are all that remain.

This story—imagined, remembered, experienced—of three generations of women ends with a very masculine intrusion into the 1920s room of Veronica's mother. Several "young men in blazers and wide flannels, college scarves and smoothed hair, smiling decorously," come to tea (*SOS*, 38). One of these men is Veronica's father. The present, the story suggests, is irrevocably bound up in the past, and the choices of one generation resonate into the next.

"Loss of Face," "On the Day E. M. Forster Died," and "Precipice-Encurled"

"Loss of Face," "On the Day E. M. Forster Died," and "Precipice-Encurled" are loosely linked by the fact that the main characters are writers. Each writer—a literary scholar in the first, a novelist in the second, and Robert Browning in the third—reflects intensely on writing itself and on writing as a vocation.

In the first story, a Milton and George Eliot scholar, Celia Quest, attends an academic conference in an unnamed Eastern country. Confined to a hotel for the most part of her stay—the city is, at the moment, in "fear of turbaned terrorists"—Celia feels disoriented, out of touch, as if she has not left her Western home at all (*SOS*, 113). I use the word *disoriented* deliberately, for Byatt, from the beginning, plays with the word *orientation* and its connotations of "East" and "direction." For example, the hotel and its elevators are compared to an "orientation maze"—it seems to be uniquely non-Western and therefore rather bewildering (112). Byatt gave a number of lectures in India, China, Korea, and Hong Kong in the early 1980s. She may well have drawn upon her experiences in these places for this story; we might imagine that, like Celia, she felt cocooned in a self-conscious Westernness.

One of the themes in "Loss of Face" is the collision of cultures. For example, how can people from different backgrounds come to a common understanding of a literary text? What happens when one culture reads the canonical texts of another's and for good or ill assimilates some of the values inherent in such texts—and in the privileging of such texts? Byatt is aware of an Anglophone audience for her work beyond England and has commented on the difficulties of crossing cultural barriers: "I am a European writer as well as being a local English one. I am at the moment exercised by the problem of communicable detail—can an Italian or a Californian or an Indian take any interest in or appreciate the nuances of an English bus queue? How many readers will have read Milton's *Paradise Lost* or . . . *The Aeneid*? How many who have not will be annoyed to find them in my books?" (McTighe, 71).

These questions are Celia's as well: how can her non-English-speaking audience "hear Milton's transitions from Latinate complexity to Anglo-Saxon plain speech?" (*SOS*, 114). But Byatt does not have to go far from home in order to worry about readers being able to read Milton: Celia's own English students, we learn, are stubbornly resistant to *Paradise Lost*.

At one point, Celia visits the "Folk Village"—a static representation of how life used to be in this imaginary Asian country: "Here was collected everything that was poised silently to vanish away" (*SOS*, 120). By including this episode, Byatt seems to be drawing a parallel between this monument to the past (romanticized as it may be) and the "monuments" of canonical English literature (Celia, we are told, thinks of art "as a work of rescue" [120]). "Loss of Face" is of two minds: it criticizes Western notions of cultural superiority at the same time that it upholds the innate greatness of English literature.[3]

The title "Loss of Face" is double-pronged, first as a metaphor signifying the loss of status through defeat or humiliation, and second as a reference to the unfortunate inability of many Westerners to distinguish differences in Asian faces. Asians literally "lose" their faces in Western eyes. However, the narrator tells us that Celia can distinguish a Chinese face from a Japanese, and that she realizes that the "uniformity of the black hair, to Western eyes, creates an illusion of greater similarity"

(*SOS*, 115). In fact, after spending time in China, Celia "found herself seeing her compatriots as unfinished monsters, pallid meat topped by kinky, lusterless, unreal hair" (115). In spite of this, at the end of the tale, Celia "misreads" an Asian face, which results in her own loss of face.

After Celia gives her lecture on Milton, on his figures of virtue ("Milton was very sure what virtue was" [*SOS*, 113]), an Asian scholar, Professor Sun, politely and inexorably disagrees with her interpretation. She is interested in a uniquely English aesthetic, while he is more interested in a materialist, contextualized reading that would problematize this aesthetic by introducing class into the mix. Later, at the official conference banquet, after Celia has had quite a long conversation with her dinner companion to the left, she "made the mistake of asking his name" (126). She has failed to recognize this same Professor Sun.

The professor is understandably hurt and angry. He had broken a characteristic reserve—and taken quite a risk, given the political situation of his country—to declare that "I think perhaps we should be studying Third World Literature. We should think about imperialism" (*SOS*, 125). Celia had replied: "I am told I should [study Third World Literature]. But Milton and George Eliot are my roots, I do not want them to vanish from the world" (126).

At the end of "Loss of Face," as Celia broods on her mistake, Byatt expands the metaphor of face to include culture and cultural relativism: how does one move from "sketched universals" to the "exact particular" (*SOS*, 126)? How does one achieve a balance between the universal and the particular? What do we lose when we exalt one over the other?

"On the Day E. M. Forster Died" opens with a declaration: "This is a story about writing. It is a story about a writer who believed, among other things, that time for writing about writing was past" (*SOS*, 129). The narrator—an explicit "I"—says further that "it seems worth telling this story about writing, which is a story, and does have a plot, is indeed essentially plot, overloaded with plot, a paradigmatic plot which, I believe, takes it beyond the narcissistic consideration of the formation of the writer, or the aesthetic closure of the mirrored mirror" (130).

Mrs. Smith, the main character, is a writer, wife, and mother. She believes (as she has been taught) that the novel is indeed "salvation," that the "bright books of life were the shots in the arm, the warm tots of whisky which kept her alive and conscious and lively" (*SOS*, 130). Surely this is Byatt speaking as well. The moment of the story is, as the title indicates, the day in 1970 when E. M. Forster died. The location is the

London Library; as Mrs. Smith contemplates her next writing project, "a fantastically convoluted, improbably possible plot reared up before her like a snake out of a magic basket" (132). In an excited, expansive mood after outlining her novel, Mrs. Smith (we never learn her first name) walks down Jermyn Street, reads the headlines, and learns that Forster is dead. Her immediate reaction: "Now I have room to move, now I can do as I please, now he can't overlook or reject me" (135). Of course, she realizes that he did not know that they were in any sort of competition; in fact, it is not a real competition, but an expression of Bloomian anxiety of influence. (See *Still Life* [129ff] for an account of Frederica Potter going to a tea party over which Forster presides.)

"On the Day E. M. Forster Died," written by a writer about writing, about a writer writing, is crossed with another story of "deathly music-machines and lethal umbrellas" (*SOS*, 145). Mrs. Smith encounters Conrad, a friend of a friend, who commandeers her into coffee. She does not like him very much. But Conrad appeals to Mrs. Smith because he is full of information "about things she knew too little about" (137). He recently has had a conversion experience and become a music student. Mrs. Smith sees him as "a man submitted to a new discipline . . . for the sake of an ideal vision," and because of this ideal vision, because of the music, Mrs. Smith forgives him much (139–40).

However, on this day, the day E. M. Forster died, she notices that he looks sick and is rather dirty—that he smells "of mortality" (*SOS*, 141). He tells a tale of danger and espionage and asks for her help. He is obviously afraid and agitated, and Mrs. Smith becomes afraid of his madness. She thinks: "How precarious it was, the sense of self in the dark bath of uncertainty, the moment of knowing, the certainty that music is the one thing needful" (145). Mrs. Smith, of course, has her own version of the "one thing needful": her projected novel. Conrad's madness serves as a kind of warning or foreshadowing of what can happen to anyone when something unexpected rears up and displaces one's true work.

The narrator adds a coda to the story: we learn that, after her encounter with Conrad, Mrs. Smith discovers that she has cancer. Her response, part denial, part mourning for what is not to be written, is to stare "out of the window and [try] to think of short tales, of compressed, rapid forms of writing, in case there was not much time" (*SOS*, 146).

"Precipice-Encurled" begins realistically, with a description of a woman sitting in a window overlooking a canal in Venice: "She is a plump woman in a tea gown. She wears a pretty lace cap and pearls." However, we next read: "These things are known, highly probable" (*SOS*, 185). Byatt, as she does in *Angels and Insects*, thus begins to weave a story around real Victorians. The narrator tells us that this woman (who remains unnamed until the end of the story) "is the central character in no story, but peripheral in many, where she may be reduced to two or three bold identifying marks" (186). But Byatt gives her a story in which she can emerge more fully into our imagination—and a story in which the imagination is a central theme.

The woman, an actual historical person, is Katherine Kay Bronson (Mrs. Arthur Bronson), who met Robert Browning in 1880. They remained close friends until Browning's death. He dedicated his last book of poems, *Asolando* (1889), to her. Mrs. Bronson often took his social affairs in hand when he stayed in Venice and lent him the use of her palazzo. She is, the narrator tells us, "an enthusiast: she collects locks of hair, snipped from great poetic temples" (*SOS*, 186). Mrs. Bronson, interested in Browning's comfort, solicitous of his welfare, also collected whatever bon mots fell from his lips in order to record them for posterity. Here, locks of hair and famous words are given equal weight.

This is one thread of the story. Another is the tale of the imaginary scholar who finds a letter of Sarianna Browning, Robert's sister. Following a ghost of a trail of evidence, the scholar speculates that Browning, at 77 (the last year of his life), might have begun to fall in love with Mrs. Bronson, the accomplished cultivator of poets and society. The (unnamed) scholar, like Mrs. Bronson, is also a sum of hypothetical scenarios: we see him "*perhaps* turning over browned packets of . . . notes" (*SOS*, 187, emphasis mine). He believes that a "good scholar may permissibly invent, he may have a hypothesis, but fiction is barred" (187–88). It is Byatt, of course, who invents—as she invents the scholar himself—and who lets loose the possibilities of fiction. She takes her cue from the epigraph to the story, lines taken from Browning's *The Ring and the Book*:

> What's this then, which proves good yet seems untrue?
> Is fiction, which makes fact alive, fact too?
> The somehow may be thishow (185).

The categories of fiction (Byatt's story) and fact (the particulars of Robert Browning's and Mrs. Bronson's lives) are thus intermixed, effectively destabilizing both.

Mrs. Bronson's story, and the story of the scholar who pursues her, wraps around yet another story, that of Juliana Fishwick and the painter Joshua Riddell, in which is embedded the portrait of Browning, the heart of "Precipice-Encurled." Here, Browning ruminates on his life, acquaintance, and accomplishments—or rather, Byatt creates a Browning to ruminate so (*SOS*, 188–94, 212–14). "The best part of my life, he told himself, the life I have lived most intensely, has been the fitting, the infiltrating, the inventing the self of another man or woman, explored and sleekly filled out, as fingers swell a glove" (191). In other words, Browning believes he has lived most intensely when he is creating fictional characters. We are told that "writing brought to life in him a kind of joy in greed" (192). Byatt transfers her own comments about herself as a "greedy reader" to Browning—who is, of course, one of the writers she has read so greedily (see chapter 1). Browning's meditations establish a genealogy for Byatt's own forays into fiction writing.

The Fishwicks provide the context for the excursus on Browning. They have rented the Villa Colomba and invited young Joshua Riddell and Browning to visit. Their daughter Juliana is goodhearted but not a beauty; she is too plump, the narrator tells us, for that year's fashions. She is innocent, feeling love as "vaguely aflame, diffusely desirous" (*SOS*, 203). Joshua Riddell, intended by his family for "the Bar, the House of Commons, the judiciary," has plans of his own: "He meant to be a great painter. He meant to do something quite new, which would have authority. He knew he should recognize this, when he had learned what it was, and how to do it" (196). Joshua, as we see, has a different kind of innocence.

Juliana and Joshua begin to fall in love, but like Browning's and Mrs. Bronson's relationship, it is never to be: Joshua goes to the mountains to paint and, absorbed alternately in Ruskin and in Juliana, ignores the signs of a coming storm and falls to his death. The Fishwicks give up the villa, and Browning's visit is put off. Browning heads back to London and never sees Mrs. Bronson again.

The title, taken from Browning's "De Gustibus" ("What I love best in all the world/Is a castle, precipice-encurled") is in part an allusion to Riddell's precipice and to the villa itself, perched as it is in the mountains. But "precipice" is also a symbol: Riddell teeters on the dangerous edge of commitment, either to art or to love. Through Joshua, Byatt develops a meditation on an aesthetic with an emphasis on the visual, on the representation of light and color. John Ruskin is pressed into service, for according to him, "clarity of vision was the essence of truth, virtue, and good art" (*SOS*, 206). The "clarity of vision" Joshua experiences on the mountain leads him to reject Juliana. Monet is invoked as well; the narrator tells us how, in *Vétheuil in the Fog*, Monet "had painted, not the thing seen, but the act of seeing" (210). Once again, Byatt makes a metaphor for her own writing.

At the end of "Precipice Encurled," one theme that emerges is that of loss, of possibilities and potentialities never realized. Joshua's death is described as "the vanishing between instants of all that warmth and intelligence and aspiration" (*SOS*, 211). The story of Joshua is, in a way, a nonstory, a story that didn't happen—in both real life *and* in fiction. The stories of Mrs. Bronson and Juliana, who never marries, are nonstories as well: "An opportunity has been missed. A tentative love has not flowered" (214). In essence, "Precipice Encurled" is a path not taken.

"The Changeling," "The July Ghost," "The Next Room," and "The Dried Witch"

In spite of Mrs. Smith in "On the Day E. M. Forster Died" (she is "a writer who believed, among other things, that time for writing about writing was past"), "The Changeling" is a *mise-en-abîme*, in which Henry James both influences Byatt's writing and, through her, Byatt's imaginary author. It is a Gothic tale that evokes the ambiguity and darkness of *The Turn of the Screw*. Josephine Piper is a writer whose subject "was fear. Rational fear, irrational fear, the huge-bulking fear of the young not at home in the world" (*SOS*, 151). Her most famous book is *The Boiler-Room*, in which the central character, the disturbed and antisocial Simon Vowle, has created a sanctuary behind the furnace in his boarding school. In real life, Josephine sees many such troubled boys: she and her son "had tried to fill the bedrooms, surround the dining room table, with guests whom . . . they called the Lost Boys" (148).

At the urging of her friend Max, she takes in Henry Smee, who is, he says, very much like Simon Vowle. It seems to Josephine upon first meeting him that he does indeed look like the Simon she created in her book. He is silent and withdrawn, having, the narrator says, "a habit of stasis" (*SOS*, 150). Josephine begins to be afraid of him, "to listen in fear for his door to open again, for him to begin his slow, deliberate, desperate-seeming descent" (151).

The secret of the story, what remains hidden under the cover of Josephine's writing, is that Josephine herself is the one who is full of fear: she has crafted a life to suppress this fact. The exact nature of Josephine's fear is not made clear—it may simply be a fear of fear. Josephine's mother was agoraphobic; Josephine spent her childhood worrying that fear may be hereditary (*SOS*, 153). Her husband left her because, she

believes, "he had found her out"—he had seen through her defenses
(157). She had tried carefully to shield her son Peter from her fears, but
Josephine realizes too late that he may have had other, different fears
that she was too blind to see. Her son, instead of following in her foot-
steps to university, "spent all his time helping a group who brought
soup to ragged sleepers in parks and subways . . . who were not above
taking what they saw as necessities from supermarkets" (157). It is significant that Byatt names the son Peter, deliberately invoking Peter Pan:
Peter himself is truly Josephine's lost boy.

When Henry Smee reads *The Boiler-Room*, he asks Josephine: "How do
you *know* about Simon. . . . The world is more terrible than most people
ever let themselves imagine. Isn't it?" (*SOS*, 155). But she is afraid to tell
the truth about how she has come to her knowledge. One night, when
Josephine comes home, she finds Henry in her room, examining himself in
the mirror. She screams: "Get out, get out of my house, I can't bear any
more of this, I can't bear your creeping" (159). He reacts oddly, sinisterly:
he smiles "a small circumscribed and satisfied little smile"—as if he had
intended to push her to this point (159). When Henry leaves the house,
Josephine's writing block clears. He commits suicide several weeks later.

The theme of unhappy school days appears more than once in Byatt's
fiction. The imaginary Simon is based on Josephine's own school experience, for she often used the boiler room for sanctuary while in school:
"She had been saved . . . by the solitary and sensuous pleasure of writing
out her fear" there (*SOS*, 154). Before Josephine, Byatt herself fled to
the boiler room of her school in order to make space for writing (see
chapter 1). "Simon Vowle was an exorcism" (154), the narrator tells us.
The question is for whom.

Like the other stories in this cluster, "The July Ghost" centers on a
woman who lives alone. Its subject is genuine grief that is bottled up,
unreleased, and, when catharsis is offered, mediated through another's
experience.

Imogen is a woman too sensible to see her own son's ghost when he
appears in her garden; she can only be solaced by his presence secondhand. It is her lodger who can see the ghost. It is not so much that he
has an ability or a sense that she lacks; rather, she has too much grief to
be able to take comfort in such a visitation. It took Byatt herself many
years before she could write about her son and his death. She transmutes
some of her own powerful feelings into this tale.

The story begins with the voice of the (unnamed) lodger: "I think I
must move out of where I am living" (*SOS*, 40). He then proceeds to tell

the story of the ghost to an American woman he meets at a party. This conversation, part flirtation, is a frame-story for the story of Imogen and her son. In fact, he met Imogen under similar circumstances: he had said these exact words to her at a different party weeks earlier. His lover, Anne, had just left him, and he could not stand to be in the flat they had shared. Imogen had invited him to stay with her.

At Imogen's house, the lodger sits in the back garden to read and write. He is often disturbed by the children who have taken over the Commons on which the garden wall abuts. They lose their balls over the wall and scramble to the top to retrieve them. Imogen tells him that "there aren't many safe spaces for children, round here," and that the Commons is "an illusion of space. . . . Just a spur of brambles and gorse-bushes and bits of football pitch between two fast four-laned main roads." She adds, "No illusions are pleasant" (*SOS*, 43).

These remarks prepare us for the appearance of a very particular boy in the garden. The lodger first notices him sitting in a tree (*SOS*, 44). As the boy returns day after day, the lodger begins to converse with him, though the child never replies. However, when the lodger meets him coming out of the kitchen door, he decides he must tell Imogen. She explains that the boy might be a friend of her son's, who was killed in a car accident while trying to reach the Commons two years earlier. Once he describes the boy's physical appearance, including his clothes, she reacts oddly. In a "precise conversational tone," she says that "the only thing I want, the only thing I want at all in this world, is to see that boy" (46). She sits down "neatly as always," and faints. For the boy is her son. While she thinks she is "too rational" to see ghosts (46), she says, "I can't stop my body and mind waiting. . . . I can't let go" (47).

However, the version of this tale that he tells the American woman has no ghost; he talks about a boy who was *like* Imogen's dead son and begins to explain their relationship in terms of a mutually shared grief—his for Anne, hers for the boy. He revises the truth because "there was a sense he could not at first analyse that it was improper to talk about the boy—not because he might not be believed . . . because something dreadful might happen" (*SOS*, 49).

The lodger comes to like the boy more and more; he asks him if there is anything that he can do for him. The boy, it seems, does try to tell him something. It seems that "what he required was to be re-engendered, for him, the man, to give to his mother another child, into which he could peacefully vanish" (*SOS*, 52). The lodger realizes he could be mistaken: "The situation was making him hysterical. . . . He could not spend the rest of the summer, the rest of his life, describing non-existent tee-shirts and blond smiles" (52). When the lodger comes to her bed-room, Imogen seems to understand his intent and acquiesces. However, once they begin to make love, she cannot: "Sex and death don't go. I can't afford to let go of my grip on myself" (54). The boy is obviously grieved by this failure.

The story ends with the lodger returning to Imogen's house to collect his things. When he goes to his room, the boy is sitting on his suitcase. The lodger tries to explain to him why he must leave, saying "I can't get through. Do you want me to stay?" At this, "as he stood helplessly there, the boy turned on him again the brilliant, open, confiding, beau-tiful desired smile" (*SOS*, 56). We are left wondering what the lodger will do next.

"The Next Room" is about a woman who had set out on her career, her gladly chosen lifework, but put her dreams and ambitions aside for 20 years in order to care for a demanding, selfish, invalid mother. Joanna Hope's work as a surveyor in Third World countries required that she travel; however, after her father died and her mother became ill, she had to stay in the London office. Once her mother dies, however, the 59-year-old Joanna discovers that she has not really broken free, for she keeps hearing the voices of her parents in the next room, querulous, angry, and constant.

The story opens with Joanna attending the cremation of her mother, feeling "an emotion to which, firmly and with shame, she put a name. It was elation" (*SOS*, 58). Joanna returns home, begins gingerly to plan her new life, and reflects on the presence and absence of both her parents: a hairbrush, a dressing gown, a gardening jacket, a tweed hat. Joanna's way of remembering her parents, her organizing image, is what she calls "the jigsaw": "a set of images, strip-cartoon pictures, patches of colour, she seemed to snip out with mental scissors and fit together awkwardly with overlaps or gaps, labelling this for reference 'my mother'" (61).

Joanna's relationship with her father, we are told, was mediated through her mother, who was "a great requirer" (*SOS*, 62). Because of this, Joanna feels that she never really knew or understood him. His place in her mental jigsaw is more ambiguous: "There were things now, that constituted sharp corners and jagged edges, that she had never brought out to look at. . . . Many of these pieces were to do with her vanished father, who had begun to vanish long before he had in fact choked gently to death" (62). But examining this and other memories that make up the jigsaw makes her uncomfortable. As her mother so often did, Joanna switches on the television, in time to listen to a Native American describe his people's relationship with the dead: "We can hear the spirit-voices of our ancestors, close to us, not gone away, in the grass and trees and stones we know and love. You send your ancestors away in closed boxes to your faraway Heaven" (65). The TV, instead of deflecting her thoughts, only gives shape to the question of, "Where had her mother gone, particles and smoke?" (66).

We next learn that Joanna's mother had told her about a curious state she would often find herself in between waking and dreaming, in which she heard her own parents "quarrelling dreadfully in the next room, ever so close . . . they might turn on me and draw me into it at any minute . . . they are waiting for me—I almost said, lying in wait, but that would be an awful thing to say" (*SOS*, 71–72).

These two incidents make explicit what Byatt has been hinting at all along: that the border between the living and the dead is more permeable than we think. It is no surprise, then, when Joanna begins to hear voices in the next room, in her fitful sleep induced by painkillers. She hears "aggrieved voices, running on in little dashes like a thwarted beck clucking against pebble-beds. . . . They had the ease of long custom and the abrasiveness of new rage" (*SOS*, 74). Even when the realtor comes, "the voices hissed and jangled. It was as though these brick walls were interwoven with some other tough, indestructible structure, containing other rooms, other vistas, other jammed doors. Like a dress and its lining, with the slimmest space between" (75).

Joanna escapes to Durham on business and stays at a hotel reputedly haunted by two ghosts. But her own familial voices are all that she hears, for they "were attached . . . to her own blood and presence" (*SOS*, 83).

I group "The Dried Witch" with these stories because, in spite of its very different setting, it has certain generic similarities to them. It is a British version of Shirley Jackson's "The Lottery," in which a small village holds a ritual lottery in order to choose a scapegoat each year. In Jackson's story, the scapegoat is then stoned to death. "The Dried Witch" owes its ambiance to the fairy tale in which the figure of the old crone is capable of inspiring fear, respect, and pity. The place and time of the story are never specified, but certain Asian resonances and the un-English names of the characters signal that the story occurs "once upon a time" and far away.

A-Oa (a name that hints at "Alpha-Omega") is an aging widow who, frustrated by the restrictive customs of her village and her own "dryness," becomes a witch. The villagers turn on her and condemn her to a painful death. "The Dried Witch," like all fairy tales, can be read allegorically: it is the story of anyone who deviates from the norms of his or her community and of the price that must be paid.

More specifically, this story is a fable about women who are seen as transgressing social boundaries. In many cultures, the old woman is viewed as frightening—as taboo—because she has lost her sexual attractiveness and ability to bear children. She is a threat because she no longer has a place in the hierarchy. At the same time, she is often a repository of lore that can benefit the whole community. Such a woman is often labeled a witch, "a term invented for women who contest the patriarchal orders of theological or medical knowledge."[4] And finally, "The Dried Witch" is an allegory of the artist, the writer—the woman writer—who cannot win for losing: she suffers when her gifts dry up; she is penalized by the community when her talents are too much in view.

A-Oa suffers from dryness—a literal, physical dryness, and a figurative, spiritual, or creative dryness. "There was an age when a woman might become a jinx, and she had perhaps arrived there" (SOS, 86). But A-Oa was not always old and dry. In the early days of her marriage, in her hope for children, in her "running blood," A-Oa had viewed the elder village witch "with a mixture of repugnance, fear, and something approaching pity." For "the old woman, in her . . . dry black cloths seemed unnecessary, waste, fragile." But now A-Oa herself is "waste, fragile," and seeks a charm against dryness.[5] The elder witch promises "power over wet and dry, to heal or, if need be, to harm. You will be respected and feared. Unless you come against some more powerful magic" (93).

The "more powerful magic" is that of the shopkeeper Kun, who represents male power and retribution. He is a great extorter and blackmailer; he knows secrets about the villagers, and "how to make himself necessary" (SOS, 88). A jinx, on the other hand, is not "necessary" in the conventional sense; she is feared, able to "dry up a child, or cause crops to fail, or pigs to be barren. A jinx could cause a tree to burst into flames" (88).

As A-Oa begins to work small cures, she gains respect and a title: "Mother." A young man of the village, "the beautiful, gleaming Cha-Hun," comes for a love charm (SOS, 97). He stands on her doorstep, asking permission to enter. "'I am too old to forbid you,' said A-Oa drily, meaning that there would have been a time when it would have been

sinful and punishable for him to enter a house alone with a woman who
was no kin of his, but that now it was not, for she was no woman, she
was something else" (98). This passage illustrates the rigid hierarchies
that govern village life. Cha-Hun desires his absent brother's wife. He
says he will give his life to possess her. But it is A-Oa who will be put to
death if the pair are caught in adultery. And it is very likely that they
will be caught, for Kun follows Cha-Hun wherever he goes. A-Oa realizes that he is sexually interested in the boy, as he was in her own miss-
ing husband. (Most of the men were conscripted into the army years
ago.) A-Oa, in spite of the danger, agrees to provide the potion, because
of "the force of his youth . . . [and] the girl's youth, that blazed and
would not be denied" (101).

Of course, A-Oa is caught and punished. The motif of dryness takes
on a frightening reality as the villagers chant: "We sun the jinx. We put
the jinx to dry in the sun" (*SOS*, 107). She is bound to a tree stump and
left to die. What follows is an excruciating description of her suffering,
and how she comes to accept it. At the very end, in a final gathering of
will and affirmation, she sets the thorn trees alight around her.

"In the Air"

Mrs. Sugden is a retired schoolteacher who watches too much TV and
feels guilty about it. Her most meaningful human contact is her daily
call to get the recorded weather forecast. Otherwise, her main companion is a sheepdog named Wolfgang. "In the Air" is a dismal story about
one woman's obsession with "the man"—a stalker of women on the
Common where Mrs. Sugden walks Wolfgang every day (*SOS*, 162).
"The man," we learn, exists only in Mrs. Sugden's imagination: "He was
black, he was white, he was brown, he was dirty grey, he was a thin
youth with acne or an ageing bullet-headed stroller in leather jacket and
trainers. He carried a briefcase, a plastic bag of junk from rubbish bins, a
knife" (163). He is, in sum, potentially anyone. "Every day," we are told,
"she feared him a little more, every day the mental encounter took
another step into the vividly realised" (163).

At first, one might be tempted to dismiss Mrs. Sugden's unhealthy
fantasies as a projection outward onto "the man" of her own fears about
sexuality, her body, and its natural aging. Byatt/the narrator is aware of
this possibility. However, Mrs. Sugden represents a point, extreme as it
may be, on a scale along which most women are ranged in society. "Mrs.
Sugden, a sensible woman, knew he was an obsession, but did not know

how to exorcise him." She is aware of very real assaults on women in her neighborhood. "Why should he not wait for, or at the least, accidentally notice her too?" (*SOS*, 163). She wonders: "Were little girls always violated and old women struck down in their thin blood, or is it more now, is it really more, and different?" (167–68).

One day, Mrs. Sugden watches a blind woman being stalked by a gangling young man in a blue track suit. He circles her, making grotesque gestures ("'mopping and mowing,' said Mrs. Sugden's fairy-tale vocabulary to her" [*SOS*, 173]). This brings Mrs. Sugden out of her isolating fear: she must reach out and help someone else who is in danger and literally blind to it. She introduces herself to Eleanor Tillotson, and they walk together. Eleanor tells Mrs. Sugden: "There isn't much I could do, if I was worried. Just live a little less, in a smaller circle" (177). The young man, Barry, stops to ask the time; he is intrusive, asking questions of Eleanor too directly, Mrs. Sugden feels, and getting himself, along with Mrs. Sugden, invited to Eleanor's for tea.

We see Barry through Mrs. Sugden's eyes: "Gold curls, damp or greasy, clustered on his forehead. His features were all exaggerated, like his movements. His mouth was large. . . . His nose was full and snuffing, with curling nostrils and huge dark holes" (*SOS*, 175). Mrs. Sugden feels he is playing with both of the women; he knows her fear, but he is blocked by Eleanor's fearlessness. At one point in Eleanor's flat, he suggests to Mrs. Sugden that one could move the furniture around: "She'd be all over the place, wouldn't she, she wouldn't know what to do with herself?" (182).

What is fascinating about the crafting of this story is how the reader's initial doubts about Mrs. Sugden and her fears are gradually turned into real alarm. While we pity Mrs. Sugden at first for her loneliness, we finally identify with her helplessness. The story ends ominously: as Barry and Mrs. Sugden stand on the sidewalk after tea, he takes out a knife and begins to play idly with it. He says, "Goodbye then. We'll see each other again, for sure. Up and down. I'm around a lot. I'll look out for you specially" (*SOS*, 184).

"Sugar"

Proust provides the intertext for "Sugar," which reads like a remembrance of things past in Byatt's own life; this feeling is enhanced by her use of an unnamed first-person narrator. Byatt has always made known her admiration for Proust. As she says in the 1989 introduction to "Sugar," she appreciates his ability to "narrate what was his own life . . . because what he wrote contained its own precise study of the nature of language, of perception, of memory, of what limits and constitutes our vision of being" (*PM*, 16). This indeed is the theme of "Sugar."

The fulcrum of the story is a hospital room in Amsterdam in which the narrator's father lies dying of cancer. From this locale—spatial and mental—the narrator ranges backward in time and place as she reflects upon her family: her mother, who "was not a truthful woman" (*SOS*, 215); her father, a judge, a Yorkshireman, "a late-convinced Quaker, a socialist-turned democrat" (217); and her father's father. The narrator recounts bits of history about her father's family. Her grandfather owned a candy factory and expected his children to follow him into the business. The narrator's father, however, saved his money and defiantly went to Cambridge to read law—as did Byatt's own father, who refused to go into his father's candy business.[6]

Byatt examines the idea of family myth, of tradition and history, and how such things are altered by family members. The narrator says, as she sits by her father's sickbed, that she "needed an idea of the past, of those long-dead grandparents" (*SOS*, 219). This idea, she knows, can never be the result of an absolute truth, but only a result of the truth that belongs to memory, defective and self-serving as it is.

Her mother, for example, seemed to want to alter memory; she "lied in small matters, to tidy up embarrassments, and in larger matters, to avoid unpalatable truths" (*SOS*, 215). At one point, the narrator gives the following example of her mother's art: "My mother's accounts of my grandmother's selflessness were like pearls, or sugar-coated pills, grit and bitterness polished into roundness by comedy and my mother's worked-upon understanding of my grandmother's real meaning" (229). This passage is worth taking apart: the narrator/daughter can learn only at secondhand about her grandmother, who died when the narrator was young. Her mother mediates the meaning of her grandmother's life. Her mother, however, often shaped her "accounts" into polished narratives, each with an internal logic of its own. Through long use and retelling, these stories have accrued layers of significance that drain the original moments of their pain or embarrassment. The pearl, begun as a grain of irritation in an oyster shell, is an apt and vivid image of these stories and their layers. It also invokes the notion of pearls cast before swine—which, of course, cannot appreciate their worth. The sugar-coated pills point to the title and to the family business, as well as serving as a parallel to pearls.

The mother is not the only player in this familial collusion, which is both painful and necessary, as the daughter realizes, "for the sake of peace" (*SOS*, 215). At one point, she asks her father, "Have you ever thought . . . how much of what we think we know is made out of her stories? One challenges the large errors. . . . But there are all the *little* trivial myths that turn into memories" (240–41).

We might see "Sugar" as strategically placed at the end of Byatt's collection of short stories as a commentary on the deeply personal that these stories often represent—and often do *not* represent. As the narrator of "Sugar" observes: "After things have happened, when we have taken a breath and a look, we begin to know what they are and were, we begin to tell them to ourselves" (*SOS*, 248). However, any such telling involves a certain amount of self-deception. This particular story began, Byatt says, "as a kind of temptation. I had been thinking about the problem of the relations between truth, lies and fiction all my life" (14). This problem is well illustrated by the title of the story: "Sugar" resonates beyond the particular memories the narrator/Byatt has of the candy factory and becomes a sign for art itself: "I saw that much of my past might be [my mother's] confection" (240), the narrator says. She/Byatt goes on to say that "I have inherited much from her. I do make a profession out of fiction. I select and confect. What is all this, all this story so far, but a careful selection of things that can be told, things that can be arranged in the light of day?" (241).

It is hard to resist the clear sound of Byatt's own voice here, as if she has dropped the mask of the narrator. Compare this statement to Byatt's scholarly voice in her commentary on the story: "If fiction does not eat up life, reality, truth, it rearranges it so that it is forever unrecognisable except in terms of the fixed form, the set arrangement" (15). Byatt captures the essence of "Sugar" and of her fiction generally in this statement. Whatever the autobiographical origins of her work may be, they are always transformed into art. Byatt retains a sense of ambivalence about these metamorphoses: "the relations between truth, lies and fiction" are continually problematized, a process that is both exhilarating and exhausting.

The Matisse Stories

"Medusa's Ankles," "Art Work," and "The Chinese Lobster"

The Matisse Stories is Byatt's tribute to Henri Matisse's method and to his palette. Matisse, we are told, is Byatt's favorite painter; she aspires to write in the same way that he painted (Kellaway, 45). According to one reviewer, "Byatt is attempting literally to paint with words, to convey physical sensations from the taste of food to the weight of heartache."[7] Indeed, Byatt says she has a vivid visual sense: "I see any projected piece of writing or work as a geometric structure: various colours and patterns"—quite like, one might add, Matisse's later collages.[8] Matisse experimented with translating pure color into form; in *The Matisse Stories*, Byatt uses color in much the same way. In each story, colors often serve as objective correlatives to both theme and character.

In "Medusa's Ankles," a middle-aged woman's routine visit to her hairdresser becomes anything but routine. Susannah is to be interviewed on TV and has more than her usual share of anxiety about her aging looks. She had initially chosen Lucian's shop because of the Matisse on the wall, a reclining voluptuous nude—which has since been replaced by contemporary black-and-white photographs of models. However, Susannah continues to see Lucian because she has come "to trust him with her disintegration" (*MS*, 7). Apparently, the fact that Susannah is intelligent, a successful academic with a specialty in classics, provides no protection against the effects of age. In the strange between-world of the beauty parlor, in which one becomes disconnected from one's identity on the way to arriving someplace—or becoming someone—else, Susannah contemplates her face, both itself and symbol:

> She looked at her poor face, under its dank cap and its two random corkscrews, aluminum clamped. She felt a gentle protective rage towards this stolid face. She remembered . . . looking at her skin, and wondering how it could grow into the crepe, the sag, the opulent soft bags. This was her face, she had thought then. And this, too, now, she wanted to accept for her face . . . this greying skin, these flakes, these fragile stretches with no elasticity, was her, was her life, was herself. (19)

In a reversal of the usual relationship between hairdresser and client (patient?), Susannah does not confide in Lucian; he, however, tells her all about his personal life. On this particular day, Lucian tells her about making the decision to leave his wife for a younger woman. Susannah, married herself, identifies with Lucian's wife throughout his chatter—an identification that the narrative of "Medusa's Ankles" suppresses, only to foreground it at the very end of the story. At one point, Lucian says: "I don't want to put the best years of my life into making suburban old dears presentable. . . . I want something more." Susannah is, of course, one of the "old dears." To make matters worse, he complains about his wife: "She's let herself go. It's her own fault. She's let herself go altogether. She's let her ankles get fat, they swell over her shoes, it disgusts me, it's impossible for me" (*MS*, 21).

When Lucian's assistant does something disastrous to Susannah's hair, she flies into a rage: "She could only see dimly, for the red flood was like a curtain at the back of her eyes, but she knew what she saw. The Japanese say demons of another world approach us through mirrors as fish rise through water, and, bubble-eyed and trailing fins, a fat demon swam towards her, turret-crowned, snake-crowned, her mother fresh from the dryer in all her embarrassing irreality" (*MS*, 23). "'It's horrible,' said Susannah. *'I look like a middle-aged woman with a hair-do.'* She could see them all looking at each other, sharing the knowledge that this was exactly what she was" (24). The result is worth quoting at length:

> Susannah seized a small cylindrical pot and threw it. . . . It burst with a satisfying crash and one whole mirror became a spider-web of cracks, from which fell, tinkling, a little heap of crystal nuggets. In front of Susannah was a whole row of such bombs or grenades. She lobbed them all around her. Some of the cracks made a kind of strained singing noise, some were explosive. She whirled a container of hairpins about her head and scattered it like a nailbomb. She tore dryers from their sockets. . . . She broke basins with brushes. . . . She silenced the blatter of the music with a well-aimed imitation alabaster pot of Juvenescence Emulsion, which dripped into the cassette which whirred more and more slowly in a thickening morass of blush-coloured cream. (25–26)

Lucian is astonishingly understanding and soothing about the whole incident. When Susannah goes home, and before she washes her new hairdo out—and this is the twist of the story—her estranged husband comes home and notices her for the first time in years: "And he came over and kissed her on the shorn nape of her neck, quite as he used to do" (28).

In this story, Susannah has tapped into the power of Medusa, the woman-monster out of mythology whose hair is a mass of deadly writhing snakes and who is capable of turning to stone anyone who looks at her. As such, Medusa is traditionally viewed as ugly and repugnant—all that is the opposite of youth, beauty, and desire. She also symbolizes, via Freud, the threat of castration and the power of woman. In a way, Medusa, here with the "fat ankles" of middle age, lies latent within the *Rosy Nude* of Matisse that Lucian initially hung in his shop.

The French feminist Hélène Cixous, in her famous essay "The Laugh of the Medusa," turns the Medusa figure into something positive and affirming for women: "And she's not deadly. She's beautiful and she's

laughing."[9] By doing so, Cixous contests the power men have traditionally wielded through their control of myth and challenges women to
rewrite myth in their own "true" image. As *Possession: A Romance* makes
clear, Byatt has read Cixous; we might read "Medusa's Ankles" as a
response to Cixous, in which Byatt accepts Cixous's revision of Medusa
but wants to keep—and honor—the terrible aspect of her beauty and
the edge to her laugh.

"Art Work" begins with a meditation on Matisse's *Le Silence Habité des
Maisons* ("the inhabited silence of the house"). In this painting, a mother
and child sit at a table while the child turns the pages of a book. Byatt
asks of the painting, and of her readers, "Who is the watching totem
under the ceiling?" (MS, 32).

Byatt goes on to create her own vision of the "inhabited silence" of a
contemporary London household: the Dennison house, filled with
domestic sounds, including washing machine, dryer, television, the elec-
tric train that son Jamie plays with, and the suppressed sound of pop
music coming through "the earphoned head" of daughter Natasha,
whose "face has the empty beatific intelligence of some of Matisse's
supine women" (MS, 34). At this point, we step into another Matisse
painting: Natasha's bedspread "is jazzy black forms of ferns or seaweeds
on a scarlet ground, forms that the textile designer would never have
seen without Matisse. Her arms and legs dangle beyond the confines of
the ruffled rectangle of this spread, too gawky to be an odalisque's, but
just as delicious in their curves" (34–35).

Debbie, mother, wife, design editor of a women's magazine, sits at
her typewriter writing about new colors in kitchen plastics, such as the
one she describes as a "peculiarly luscious new purple, like bilberry juice
with a little cream swirled in it" (MS, 38). Debbie has given up her own
artistic ambitions as a wood engraver to allow her husband Robin to
pursue his painting. The narrator tells us that Debbie's "fingers remembered the slow, careful work in the wood, with a quiet grief that didn't
diminish but was manageable. She hated Robin because he never once
mentioned the unmade wood engravings" (54). Robin, who at first
seems to be the main candidate for the "watching totem under the ceiling" in the Dennison vignette, presides over the third floor, converted
into an art studio. He has appropriated the best space and light in the
house—and colonized his family's lives as well; their desires are always
made subordinate to his.

However, it is Mrs. Brown, the black housekeeper from Guyana, who
is the central character and the true totem of the house—and of art. We

first meet her as she moves a vacuum cleaner "up and down the stairs, joining all three floors" (*MS*, 38). Sheba Brown is thus seen as one who can cross over from one milieu to another. She is a genius of juxtaposition in other ways as well: "Mrs. Brown's clothes were, and are, flowery and surprising—jumble-sale remnants, rejects and ends of lines, rainbow-colored pullovers made from the ping-pong-ball-sized unwanted residues of other people's knitting" (40). When Robin fails to interest the Florimel Gallery in mounting an exhibit of his works, it is Mrs. Brown who succeeds. The Dennison family discovers that her sartorial confusions are just a prelude to the larger collages she makes out of the discards of other people's lives. If we see her against a larger canvas than that of the Dennison family, Sheba Brown can be imagined as a recycler of culture, reversing the flow of Western appropriation of the Third World.

Sheba Brown and Robin are locked in an allegorical battle over the possession of culture in small: Robin constantly complains about what he sees as Mrs. Brown's cleaning interferences in his studio. At one point, Mrs. Brown had apparently gathered the detritus of her cleaning—paper clips, a dead flower, matches, and so on—and placed it in a decorated ceramic bowl that Robin was using as a model for color. In fact, Robin has several such "fetishes" that serve as his inspiration for color—a tin soldier, a butter dish, and other such miscellaneous items. Mrs. Brown tends to rearrange these things; Robin is compulsive about what can and cannot be touched. The colors must be arranged just so. These fetishes are the way Robin attempts to come to terms with what he feels is the crushing obligation to live up to the magisterial color in Matisse's paintings.

Robin, an exacting neorealist, hates Mrs. Brown; he sees her as "chaotic and wild to look at" and thinks that she represents "filth" (*MS*, 58). Mrs. Brown obviously has none of Robin's inhibitions about color as she goes about in her "magenta and vermilion coverall over salmon-pink crêpe pantaloons, or in a lime-green shift with black lacy inserts" (59). Her philosophy, diametrically opposed to the classically trained Robin's, is that "they're all there, the colors, God made 'em all and mixes 'em all in His creatures, what exists goes together somehow or other" (60).

Debbie, trying to manage family, a self-absorbed husband, and a job that stifles her own creativity, depends upon Mrs. Brown to keep her house running smoothly. It is clear to her, the mediator in the battle between Robin and Mrs. Brown, that Robin makes "resolute attempts to unsettle, humiliate, or drive away Mrs. Brown, without whom all Debbie's balancing acts would clatter and fall into wounding disarray"

(*MS*, 54–55). Debbie also knows that "Mrs. Brown has her own modes of silent aggression," and that the battle is not one of Robin's imagination (48).

When Debbie sees Mrs. Brown's exhibit at the Florimel Gallery, quite by accident, it is as if the gallery had been transformed into a "brilliantly colored Aladdin's cave" (*MS*, 77). Here are all the castoffs that Mrs. Brown has collected and now rearranged into tapestries and soft sculptures—including clothing from Debbie's own family. Her work is highly symbolic. Made up of the bits and pieces of domestic life, it serves as a running commentary on women and their subjugation. For example, she has made a mulberry-colored dress that once belonged to Debbie into the scales of a huge dragon that threatens a woman rag doll, bound and chained with twisted bras and petticoats.

Debbie feels betrayed. She also feels "a kind of subdued envy that carries with it an invigorating sting" (*MS*, 82). As a result, Debbie goes back to her woodcuts and achieves commercial success with them. Robin turns his grief and his rage at Mrs. Brown into art and begins painting differently, with a "loosed, slightly savage energy" (90). In the work of both husband and wife, Mrs. Brown's face appears—as good and bad fairies in Debbie's woodcuts, as Kali the Destroyer in Robin's. But Kali, the Hindu goddess of death, has her positive aspect as well, for out of death new life is born.

"The Chinese Lobster" is, in part, a meditation on Matisse's place as a painter in a world vastly different from the one in which he painted. While Matisse's greatness is never in doubt in the tale, how one might appreciate or appropriate his paintings is. The argument about Matisse centers on gender—his own exploitation of the women in his family, his representation of women in his art, and what it is like to "read" his paintings as a woman and as a man.

Professor Gerda Himmelblau, dean of students at a London college, must investigate a charge of sexual harassment brought by a female student against Peregrine Diss, a famous and imposing art critic who is a visiting professor at the school. Perry Diss is the quintessential older male professor, passionate about "his" art (he lays claim to most of the great Western tradition) and unable to cope with a postmodern world that seems intent on destroying everything he loves. Gerda Himmelblau attributes his eloquent crankiness to "the possibly crabbed view of a solitary intellectual" (*MS*, 98). She also recognizes—and for her this is more important—that he "loves [paintings], like sound apples to bite into, like fair flesh, like sunlight" (98).

Gerda herself has a strong aesthetic sense, as we learn in the narrator's description of her clothes: she wears "suits in soft, dark, not-quite-usual colours—damsons, soots, black tulips, dark mosses—with clean-cut cotton shirts, not masculine . . . in clear colors: palest lemon, deepest cream, periwinkle, faded flame" (*MS*, 99).

The student peggi nollet (she spells her name entirely in lower case) is a different picture altogether. She is writing her dissertation, titled "The Female Body and Matisse," and she is also engaged in the studio work required for graduation. In the stained and rumpled letter she sends to Gerda about Perry Diss, she writes that he "is a so-called EXPERT on the so-called MASTER of MODERNISM, but what does he know about Woman or the internal conduct of the Female Body, which has always until now been MUTE and had no mouth to speak?" (*MS*, 100). Peggi recounts a conversation that she had with him: "He said Matisse was full of love and desire toward women (!!!!!) and I said '*exactly*' but he did not take the point" (102). One of her pieces is titled *The Resistance of Madame Matisse*, which peggi describes as showing Madame Matisse and her daughter "being *tortured* by the Gestapo in the War whilst *he* sits by like a Buddha cutting up pretty paper with scissors. They wouldn't tell him they were being tortured in case it disturbed his *work*. I felt sick when I found out that. The torturers have got identical scissors" (104). She goes on to relate how Diss comes to her studio to see her work-in-progress. He does not like it, of course. According to peggi, Diss said she had too many clothes on, and that she ought to wear brighter colors—and then he "began kissing and fondeling me and stroking intimate parts of me" (104; peggi's spelling is atrocious throughout this missive). Peggi is also suicidal, and this incident pushes her into deeper despair. What is more, after the reader gets Perry Diss's account of the incident, one might conclude that she is delusional as well.

Just as peggi and Gerda Himmelblau differ in taste and appearance, so do Perry Diss and peggi—a fact that aligns Himmelblau against peggi and seems to substantiate his denial of harassment. He is elegant, with a head of white hair and startling blue eyes. Himmelblau thinks of him as "both fastidious, and marked by ancient indulgence and dissipation" (*MS*, 109). Peggi, on the other hand, is described by Diss in far less respectful terms: "Her skin is like a *potato*, and her body is like a *decaying potato*. . . . I do not think her hair can have been washed for some years" (115). She reworks prints of Matisse by changing the outlines of the female bodies with some unknown substance, which Diss thinks is blood or feces. How could he be interested in her sexually if she creates such desecrations of Matisse?

As we learn more about peggi, it becomes rather clear that Diss is innocent. However, sexual harassment is not about attraction; it is about power. We might imagine that, if Diss can assert his physicality against peggi's—and her physical body can be extended to include her art— perhaps Diss can ensure that his own aesthetic values triumph.

Gerda Himmelblau and Perry Diss have a conversation over a Chinese lunch, which serves as a kind of visual and sensual counterpoint to their conversation. The two share an aesthetic, highly stylized visual and gastronomic experience as they proceed slowly from course to course. This makes them almost conspiratory—or at the least, members of the same club that excludes the peggi nollets of the world. Peggi's greatest sin, for both Perry and Gerda, is that she cannot *see* Matisse. Why Matisse? asks Perry. Answers Gerda: "Because he paints silent bliss. *Luxe, calme et volupté*" (*MS*, 121). In other words, Matisse is everything peggi is not. But this sympathetic union also causes Gerda to identify against peggi when Diss calls her a "poor little bitch" (109). Gerda, in the midst of investigating a sexual harassment charge, cannot or will not confront this; she can only manage, "in her head, wincing," to think, "Don't say 'bitch'" (110).

This story, only partially about sexual harassment, real or imagined, is complicated further by the fact that Gerda also identifies against the disturbed and suicidal peggi in another, more fundamental way. Gerda's best and only friend, Kay, the only person she has ever really loved, committed suicide a few years before. Her daughter killed herself as well: "Over the years Kay's daughter's pain became Kay's, and killed Kay" (*MS*, 127–28). Gerda now feels that "she is next in line" (129).

The very issue that might incline Gerda toward peggi instead strengthens the bond she has with Perry Diss. She notices scars ("well-made *efficient* scars" [*MS*, 130]) on his wrists; she becomes aware of an undercurrent in their conversation; both know, and know the other knows, the despair that leads one to suicide. Finally, "Gerda Himmelblau sees, in her mind's eye, the face of Peggi Nollett, potato-pale, peering out of a white box with cunning, angry eyes in the slits between puffed eyelids. She sees golden oranges, rosy limbs, a voluptuously curved dark-blue violin case in a black room. One or the other must be betrayed" (132–33).

In the end, Gerda Himmelblau decides to pass peggi on to another adviser and hopes the charge of sexual harassment will evaporate. It is an ambiguous compromise for peggi, but out of it comes a tentative reprieve for Gerda. As she and Perry Diss part, she realizes that "something has happened to her white space, to her inner ice, which she does not quite understand" (*MS*, 133). Perry Diss has touched her, both through their shared but unspoken grief and through his assertion of a shared aesthetic.

Chapter Four

The Virgin in the Garden and Still Life

People may well be overly fond of quoting Tolstoy's observation in *Anna Karenina* that "happy families are all alike; every unhappy family is unhappy in its own way." However, it cannot be denied that unhappy families make the best fiction. Byatt's novels *The Virgin in the Garden* (begun in 1972 and published in 1978) and *Still Life* (1987), provide compelling, if sometimes painful, reading about one unhappy family in particular. These two novels comprise the first half of a planned tetralogy. *Babel Tower* is the third, published in the spring of 1996, too late to be considered in this study. Just as *The Virgin in the Garden* and *Still Life* render British life in the 1950s in meticulous detail, *Babel Tower*, set in 1960s England, is both a fond but vexed memoir and a critique of an age.

Byatt has referred to this group of novels as her "Powerhouse Quartet." "Powerhouse" describes a family in which, as the narrator says in *Still Life*, "the principles and even the practices of the parents are so liberal, so rational, so acceptable that any necessary rebellion against their authority must take the form of absurd gestures, petulant or violent."[1] Byatt says that her friend the American psychoanalyst Marynia Farnham first introduced her to the term as a way to describe Byatt's own "good and liberal" family.[2]

A major theme of *The Virgin in the Garden* and *Still Life*, then, is family relationships of the dysfunctional kind. But Byatt has other stories to tell as well—of the interior lives of women and of women's attitudes toward their culturally bound roles in 1950s England. At one end is Winifred Potter, cowed into submission by her domineering husband Bill, and at the other is Winifred's daughter Frederica, who is about to embark on a very different life from that of her mother, in academe and beyond.

Byatt is also interested in examining that thin line so celebrated by the Romantics between madness and the creative imagination, and she does so by grafting Vincent Van Gogh's peculiar genius onto Marcus

Potter, a math savant with perfect pitch who is prone to disturbing hallucinations. But there is more: Byatt weaves two distinct subgenres into her sequenced novels. *The Virgin in the Garden* is, in part, a "theater novel": Byatt mixes the personal dramas of the main characters in with the long preparation for and rehearsal of a play based on the life of Elizabeth I. (The way she weaves scenes and quotations from this imaginary text into the novel looks forward to *Possession*.) *Still Life* is, in part, an academic novel: Byatt continues to explore the life of the young woman scholar at Cambridge, a theme she first took up in *The Shadow of the Sun*. What ties all these themes together is Byatt's exacting passion for language and what she calls "the life of the mind."

The Virgin in the Garden

The Potter family—Stephanie, Frederica, Marcus, and their mother Winifred—is ruled over by the despotic, opinionated Bill, head of the English Department at Blesford Ride School in North Riding, Yorkshire. Owing to Bill's influence, the Potter siblings are rather stunted emotionally; this fact will dominate their lives and their relationships with others throughout both novels.

The novel focuses on how the three children attempt to make room for themselves in the stifling atmosphere created by their father. Frederica begins the personal and intellectual journey away from the family and into academic life; her sister Stephanie becomes involved with Daniel Orton, the stolid but socially passionate curate; and Marcus, painfully shy and clearly in the early stages of schizophrenia, becomes involved with Blesford's science teacher, Lucas Simmonds, who is highly unstable and a prototype of the contemporary New Ager, though more dangerous.

The time of *The Virgin in the Garden* is 1953, the coronation year of Elizabeth II. In the novel, Elizabeth's accession to the throne is emblematic of a renewed postwar belief in the future: "People had simply hoped," the narrator tells us, "because the time was after the effort of war and the rigour of austerity."[3] Elizabeth must live up to both her father's reputation and that of her namesake, Elizabeth I, who so dominated her age that it came to be named for her.

Alexander Wedderburn, an English teacher at Bill's school, has written an allegorical verse-drama, *Astraea*. It is to be part of the yearlong coronation festivities and staged as a grand outdoor pageant on the grounds of Long Royston, home of Matthew Crowe. Crowe, an entrepreneur and patron of the arts (Byatt imagines him as a Prospero), plans to turn over Long Royston to the New University—an egalitarian adult education college sponsored by Cambridge University—after the close of Wedderburn's play. Frederica, not for her talent but through sheer force of will and intensity of demeanor, is cast as the young Elizabeth I in Wedderburn's play. She, along with Stephanie, has a crush on Wedderburn. Stephanie outgrows it, but Frederica single-mindedly pursues him; he responds but often ambivalently.

Elizabeth II is never a player in the novel, but she does make one appearance, tiny on a flickering gray television screen, the light of which throws into relief the Potter family ranged round the TV in a domestic vignette of seeming serenity. This scene foreshadows the final scene of the novel, in which Frederica and Daniel sit, watching Stephanie and Marcus on the sofa: "That was not an end, but since it went on for a considerable time, is as good a place to stop as any" (*VG*, 428).

Still Life

Still Life follows Frederica into Cambridge University. Stephanie copes with a new baby, Daniel's querulous and self-centered mother, Daniel himself, and her brother Marcus, all of whom are crowded into council housing (English low-income housing). One of the most harrowing sections of *Still Life* is Byatt's account of gynecological and obstetrical practices in the 1950s, a time when it was thought that pregnancy ought to be treated as if it were a disease, and that it was unhealthy for women to spend time holding and cuddling their newborns.

Marcus, after his relationship with Simmonds came to an ignoble end, refused to stay in the same house with his father and has sought refuge with Stephanie. He slowly begins to come out of his depression when he gets involved with the parish's youth group and interested in natural history. As in *The Virgin in the Garden*, Alexander Wedderburn, now a successful author and television personality, is a principal character whose life continually intersects with Frederica's and her family's. Just as Byatt weaves Wedderburn's play about Elizabeth into *The Virgin in the Garden*, she works his next play, *The Yellow Chair*, into *Still Life*.

Byatt moves both a part of her novel and Alexander's play from England to the south of France, to Van Gogh country. The characters in *The Virgin in the Garden* literally step from one canvas to another and are transformed by the light of Provence. Frederica, who is working for a summer as an au pair—and not a very dedicated one—meets Alexander as he starts his play and helps him crystallize his thoughts. Frederica remembers that she loves Alexander; he, on the other hand, rather testily regards his feelings for her as "a temporary dramaturgical folly" (*SL*, 68).

The central tragedy of *Still Life* is Stephanie's death: she is electrocuted by her refrigerator while her brother Marcus stands by, immobilized by the sight. The Potters, whose identity as a family is fragile under the best of circumstances, find that their center cannot hold and subsequently fracture into their private griefs.

An Excursus on the Two Titles

The titles of both novels have clear associations with art: *The Virgin in the Garden* seems borrowed from an allegorical tableau; *Still Life* suggests the contrived, static arrangements of fruits and flowers that were so often painted in a hyperrealistic style in the 18th and 19th centuries. Realism is Byatt's preferred mode, though it is always a realism shaped by postmodern notions about the slipperiness of language. Moreover, the realism that characterizes both novels is, paradoxically, painterly in its detail and metaphoric language.

The Virgin in the Garden opens at London's National Portrait Gallery in 1968, 16 years after the events in the novel take place. Frederica has asked Alexander Wedderburn and Daniel Orton to meet her at the gallery to see a famous actress perform Queen Elizabeth I. *Still Life* opens at the Royal Academy of Arts in 1980 (some 20 years after the events of the novel), at an exhibit of post-Impressionist art. In both prologues, we begin with Alexander's point of view before working our way around to the Potter family. These scenes at a gallery contextualize the painting metaphors that structure the two novels. It is Frederica who arranges the meetings; it is Alexander who voices Byatt's awareness of the symmetry of these beginnings (Frederica, he muses, has set into motion a "form of repetition, deliberate, contrived, and aesthetic" [*SL*, 2]). By gathering Alexander and Daniel together at the beginning of *The Virgin in the Garden*, Frederica effectively returns them all—and us—to the past; she does the same when she arranges the same rendezvous in *Still Life*.

In each case, the choice of subject and of artist (we can call the actress who performs Elizabeth I an artist; the production, after all, takes place in the National Portrait Gallery) signals Byatt's intentions. Elizabeth I was and is a powerful icon, not only for those in her time but for anyone looking back on the English Renaissance. The "reality" she represents is multilayered, metaphoric—Spenserian—and so is *The Virgin in the Garden*. Van Gogh's work dominates the Royal Academy exhibit. The change is significant, both for Byatt's characters and for Byatt's art. Alexander has changed subjects, from Queen Elizabeth I in his play *Astraea* to Vincent Van Gogh in *The Yellow Chair*. Along with Alexander, Byatt has taken up the problem of representation from a different perspective: she is a realist who understands, as Alexander says about the difficulties of writing his play, that "language is against" her; she has moved from the emblematic and the allegorical to a different mode of capturing "the thing itself" (*SL*, 2).

In a way, *Still Life* is a quarrel with *The Virgin in the Garden*, a quarrel that is embedded in small in these titles. A "virgin in the garden" has endless possibilities—such an image is always and overtly pointing to meaning elsewhere. But a "still life," at least at first sight, attempts to assert the thing itself as its subject.

While *Virgin* is an exuberant celebration of metaphor, *Still Life*, by contrast, was designed to be spare and exact. Byatt says: "I wanted to write about birth and about death and sex. . . . I wanted my thoughts, my descriptions, to move between simply naming like Proust's 'clear and usual' images, and the kind of mental icons which are [Van Gogh's] Sunflowers" (Kenyon, 78). It is a "failure," Byatt says in her essay "Still Life/Nature Morte," because she was unable, in the end, to "forego metaphor," to eschew "myths and cultural resonances" (*PM*, 3).

In "Van Gogh, Death and Summer," Byatt admiringly quotes Van Gogh praising the Dutch, who, he says, "paint things just as they are . . . let's do as they did." As we try to reconcile our memory of a Van Gogh painting with this declaration, we come to realize that "things" may well have no single, fixed aspect—as Van Gogh's own still lifes demonstrate. He also says that "we can paint an atom of the chaos, a horse, a portrait, your grandmother, apples, a landscape" (*PM*, 273). *The Virgin in the Garden* and *Still Life* are attempts to capture a few of these atoms before they pass completely out of reach.

Portraits and Players

"I started thinking about *The Virgin in the Garden*," says Byatt, "when a student asked why no one could write a novel like *Middlemarch* now. I listed the elements we've lost: large numbers of characters, wide cultural relevance, complex language" (Kenyon, 54; see also Dusinberre, 187).

In a way, Byatt fuses all three elements together in both novels: most of her characters possess an enormous talent for talk, and this talk is rich, sophisticated, highly allusory, and thoroughly engaged with the serious intellectual questions of their day. Francis Spufford says that "Byatt's people are not mechanical, or predictable, though they are rather more coherent than most fictional characters. In that, they resemble the novels as a whole, in which extremity sometimes seems as much to enable coherence as coherence is used to indicate extremity" (23).

Winifred is one character who cannot talk and cannot use language to mediate the world; the narrator tells us that Winifred "preferred things unstated and undiscussed" (*VG*, 210). Marcus is another character who remains quite silent; he bypasses the verbal and experiences the visual instead. Stephanie, Frederica, and Alexander, on the other hand, tend to interpret the stuff of their lives in terms of Shakespeare or Donne or Eliot—both George and T. S. For example, Stephanie, as Kenyon says, "is able to use Romantic literature to interpret the world. For Stephanie (and Byatt) literature illuminates mental concepts and articulates spiritual longings" (64).

Frederica, even more than Stephanie, turns everything into language: "She had never, she realised, looked at a picture or a carving or even landscape without some immediate verbal accompaniment or translation. Language was ingrained in her" (*VG*, 104). For example, when Frederica takes a bus trip, she uses the time to meditate on Shakespeare and Racine and contemplates the Alexandrine line: "The actual form of your thought was different, if you thought in closed couplets, further divided by a rocking caesura" (202). This is not the typical stuff of adolescent daydreams.

This habit is a problem for some readers who criticize Byatt's characters for seeming more intent on producing the correct literary quotation for the moment than on expressing their true feelings. The point that Byatt wants to make, however, over and again in her fiction, is that living the life of the mind, being steeped in literature, art, and philosophy, can only intensify one's experience of everyday life. In what follows, I focus on the three Potter siblings in both novels in order to illustrate their intense inner lives.

Marcus: Visionary

Byatt says that in Marcus she wanted "to create someone for whom the world comes unmediated" (Kenyon, 69). He is, she says, "largely me" (Conroy, 9). One way to understand what this means is to read Marcus in the context of Byatt's essay "Van Gogh, Death and Summer." Byatt began by reviewing four books on Van Gogh but ended up writing an excursus on Van Gogh and his connection to, and embodiment of, larger questions having to do with art, passion, and religion. She is sympathetic to Van Gogh and his elevation in the pantheon of art and calls him "the uncomprehended sufferer" and the "flaming and bloody visionary" (*PM*, 265). These words can be applied to Marcus as well: he lacks the ability to filter out a pure apprehension of the surrounding physical world.

The youngest of the Potter children, Marcus apparently is protected by no barriers whatsoever between himself and his sense perceptions, a condition that makes daily life terrifying. (The inability to shut out and off incoming sensory data is reminiscent of the problems of autistic children.) Emblematic of this lack of boundaries is Marcus's assay into acting at Blesford Ride: in *Hamlet*, he plays Ophelia. He so enters into the character that he thinks he will not be able to get out again. While everyone else is impressed with what they perceive as his superior acting ability—talk begins about Marcus's possible future in the theater (he has been so quiet and aimless up to this point)—Marcus knows better: he can never take on the character of another again, not if he wants to keep his own personality.

Marcus's father Bill is insultingly insensitive to his son's problems, and his sisters, though they often experience brief nagging worries about Marcus, are too caught up in their own lives to see how deeply troubled he is. His mother, who probably knows him best of all and shares in some of his suffering, is so beaten down by life with Bill that she suppresses her knowledge, preferring to imagine Marcus as a perpetual infant. Lucas Simmonds, who takes an unhealthy interest in Marcus and his visions, is also insensitive to Marcus's suffering.

Like Van Gogh, Marcus has "flaming and bloody" visions: he is able to apprehend what might be called the underlying geometry of the universe, and he often glimpses fire and light dancing at the periphery of his vision (rather like the "aura" epileptics perceive before having a seizure). Consider, for example, Marcus's private game, which he refers to as "spreading himself":

> This began with a deliberate extension of his field of vision, until by some sleight of perception he was looking out at once from the four field-corners [of the playing-fields], the high ends of the goal-posts, the running-wire top of the fence. It was not any sense of containing the things he saw. Rather, he surveyed them, from no vantage point, or all at once.

> . . . Sometimes, for immeasurable instants he lost any sense of where
> he really was, of where the spread mind had its origin. He had to teach
> himself to find his body by fixing the mind to precise things. . . .
> . . . He learned early to be grateful for geometry, which afforded grip
> and passage. . . . Broken chalk lines, the demarcation of winter games
> crossing summer ones, circles, parallel tramlines, fixed points . . . were
> lines to creep along, a network of salvation. (*VG*, 27–28)[4]

Marcus, raised in Bill's agnostic household, has a healthy skepticism
when it comes to things spiritual and supernatural. However, when
Lucas Simmonds begins to pay attention to Marcus and seems to understand the source of his difficulties, Marcus gradually finds himself agree-
ing to aid in Simmonds's attempts to transcend the "physico-chemical
soma," as he puts it (*VG*, 61).

Marcus "sedulously avoid[s] thought," because it is so dangerous,
because it opens up the abyss (*VG*, 62). It is precisely this "abyss" that
Simmonds wants to exploit for his own purposes. He "diagnoses" Marcus: "You do have direct access to thought forms, the patterns, that
inform and control us. What you need, and I can provide, indeed, by a
providential coincidence have come here to offer to provide, is the spiritual discipline to make all that safe and evolving" (64). Simmonds is the
closest thing that Marcus has had to a friend in his life; Simmonds's
acceptance of what sets Marcus apart from others is, at first, a great
comfort to the boy. However, the relationship soon becomes stifling and
takes a number of bizarre twists before it finally crashes. In the end,
Marcus is frightened by Lucas Simmonds's sexual advances—though it
must be said that Lucas is even more frightened of his own desires. Marcus begins a long process of healing at the end of *The Virgin in the Garden*—a process that continues throughout *Still Life*.

Stephanie: Persephone

Both Frederica and Stephanie are naturally bright and well educated,
with unconventional looks that can be taken for beauty under certain
circumstances. Stephanie is more reticent than her often tactless sister;
Frederica, stubborn and headstrong, is better able to get what she
thinks she wants. It becomes clear early on in *Still Life* that each could
use some of the qualities of the other: one sister's emotional shortcomings are the other's strengths.

Initially, we may wonder why Stephanie does not pursue an academic
career after her Cambridge days, for she seems well suited to it. Instead,

she returns to Blesford to teach at the local girls' school, waiting, it seems, for some outside fate or force to take charge of her life. When we realize that her father also wishes an academic career for her, we understand her hesitation as grounded in an opposition to her father's will.

Daniel Orton is the outside force that takes over. Through sheer force of will, Daniel has become a clergyman. He does not have a traditional religious vocation, but he is dedicated to helping others and decided that the Church is the best way to do so. Daniel does not have Stephanie's recourse to literature: he plods his way doggedly through *King Lear* (a tale that has its parallels in the story of the Potter family) and lives implacably in the very literal present. In spite of Stephanie's initial resistance and the hostility of her father, Daniel determinedly courts and marries her. Throughout *A Virgin in the Garden*, we watch Stephanie try to deal with "her surprise at falling in love, her fear of loss of intellectual life" (Kenyon, 73). Byatt says that "Daniel represents Dis, the god of the underworld. He is warm, dark, physically strong. He carries off Stephanie, who is seen in terms of whiteness, passivity, feminine sensuality and spring flowers. She and Daniel form a unity" (Kenyon, 62).

Stephanie is the sexually experienced one who has had a number of "Cambridge encounters." She goes to bed with the virgin Daniel in his cold and impersonal room in the vicarage. It is an awkward business, "not very successful, a disorganised arhythmic flurry. . . . Daniel, overexcited and wild, did not know, half the time, whether he was in or out, coming or going" (*VG*, 184–85). Intercourse is more important to him both symbolically and literally than it is to her—though she does assume that now that she has slept with Daniel that she must love him.

Before Daniel and Stephanie have a chance to get used to each other, she becomes pregnant and, indeed, seems altogether done in by her life at the end of *The Virgin in the Garden*. Stephanie sits on the sofa "like some unnatural and ungainly Pietá, looking out . . . with what seemed like unseeing patience" (*VG*, 428). It seems that Stephanie will fulfill her mother's fears for herself when she first married; Winifred remembers how she "had been most afraid of living like her mother, too many children, too little money, mastered by a house and a husband which were peremptory moral imperatives and steady physical wreckers" (86).

Byatt says of *Still Life*: "I wanted at least to work on the assumption that order is more interesting than the idea of the random . . . that accuracy of description is possible and valuable. That words denote things" (*PM*, 5). How might one attain such goals, not in art, but in life? In a way, Stephanie's life embodies this ambition. Trained at Cambridge under the influence of F. R. Leavis—like Byatt herself in reality—Stephanie has a keen intelligence and an appreciation of language and literature and of how they come together in her life. In *Still Life*, not altogether reconciled to what she has lost in marrying Daniel, she takes up a life of domestic responsibilities along with the added duties of being a curate's wife. Her goal is to bring order and accuracy and beauty to the everyday. Away at Cambridge, Frederica worries: "Surely, surely, it was possible, she said to herself in a kind of panic, to make something of one's life *and* be a woman. Surely" (*SL*, 198). However, it is Stephanie who faces the more difficult task of living with often-competing identities: wife, mother, daughter, sister—*and* woman. Her senseless death (however it may make "sense" in Byatt's overall scheme) leaves questions about the woman Stephanie might have become forever suspended.

The bizarreness of Stephanie's death is located in its sheer banality: danger lurks in the mundane—in a household appliance.[5] The kitchen, so often the symbol of complacent domesticity, contains within it the seeds of despair and grief. It is hard to resist the moral that this particular story wants to make.

Frederica: Wise Virgin

We often grow embarrassed for Frederica as she attempts to navigate the adult world into which she has been admitted but for which she has not been prepared. In *The Virgin in the Garden*, the close, intoxicating world of theater people, the often erotic charge of literary engagement, only throws into stark relief the dreary goings-on of village life and the stifling influence of her father. In *Still Life*, it is not quite clear whether Frederica is to represent, as Olga Kenyon thinks, the modern "liberated" woman, or whether she is caught up in a world of men over which she has small control (75).

What Olga Kenyon refers to as "the virgin's hatred of the burden of desire" (71) has special resonance for Frederica, who wants to be grown-up and sophisticated before her time. Yet at the moment she is to achieve her desire—her will—with Alexander, she bolts, afraid that he will discover her virginity and laugh at her.

She goes off with Edmund Wilkie, an urbane, witty, and self-involved Cambridge undergraduate. Frederica is not romantic, though she is passionate; her very passion for Alexander drives her away from him. With

Wilkie, however, she harbors no illusions. He says: "Now . . . listen. I'm a scientist. I'm going to tell you how all this works, and what gives women pleasure, and what gives me pleasure, and then you won't be frightened, and I shall enjoy myself, if we go along gently and carefully. O.K?" (*VG*, 419). As unromantic as this is—and selfish and sexist, in Edmund's assumption that female pleasure is invariable from one woman to the next, while his own is central—it is, perhaps, the rite of passage Frederica needs: "She was grateful to him for seeming so matter-of-fact and secure" (410). However, Frederica bleeds profusely after intercourse (the chapter title is "Seas of Blood"). Wilkie is just the man to deal with the situation, with towels, sheets, and padding. The reader realizes that the fastidious and elegant Alexander would have been quite at a loss. The passion that existed between Frederica and Alexander, their professions of love, would not have stood up to such pressure. Their love remains idealized, confined in the garden of their imaginations.

In *Still Life*, Frederica goes to Cambridge and finds it "a setting for cocoa, toasted crumpets, tea parties," while what she wants is "wine, argument, sex" (*SL*, 119). Frederica is greedy for experience of all sorts, and for her, Cambridge is a time for putting off her North Yorkshire habits and provincial ways: "She . . . was vulgar and clever and arrogant and frightened, uncertain of tone and well-meaning," the narrator tells us (123). Frederica makes many social mistakes—including sexual ones. However, the narrator tells us, "she had a great deal of energy. She was prepared to pay" for her knowledge and experience (124).

Frederica continues her interest in the theater, playing the chaste Lady (as did Byatt herself at Cambridge) in John Milton's *Comus*. One evening, a number of her ex-lovers and current objects of desire attend the performance all at once; for them, the disjunction between Frederica's stage persona and her private life is a cause for amusement. Frederica feels, and rightly, that she has been set up. Afterward, she defensively asserts that chastity is "personal *integrity*—that's what it's about" (*SL*, 275). Indeed, Frederica has a good deal of personal and intellectual integrity and is a casualty of the cultural paradox that young men are expected to acquire heterosexual experience but young women are not. Frederica is often frustrated by the closed circle of men she meets and by her own position on the margin: "The world was their world and what she wanted was to live in that world, not be sought out as a refuge from or adjunct to it" (*SL*, 138).

Frederica thinks of Cambridge men as birds "wanting one thing, if not only one, lavish, nervous, posturing, inhibited, bright, brilliant, manipulative, vanishing behind protective coloring" (*SL*, 213). The apparent exception to this vision is Nigel Reiver, who has been courting her in a push-pull way. When they finally make love, he says to her, "Stop fighting . . . stop fighting" (347). At the end of the novel, she apparently has.

Byatt's 1950s Cambridge is the time of her own undergraduate days there; Frederica's experiences may well parallel her own. It is tempting to identify the following passage with Byatt herself, reflecting on the young girl she was and the woman she has become. Both Antonia and Frederica, as it turns out, were to follow the same trajectory:

> There were two hypothetical future Fredericas—one closed in the University Library writing something elegant and subtle on the use of metaphor in seventeenth-century religious narrative, and one in London, more nebulous, writing quite different things, witty critical journalism, maybe even a new urban novel like those of Iris Murdoch. The trouble was, she sometimes thought, that the two Fredericas were really indissolubly one. The Ph.D. writer would have died of aimlessness and spiritual vertigo without the drive of the worldly one; the worldly one would have felt like a creaking, varnished carapace without an abundant inner life. (*SL*, 304)

Alexander Wedderburn's Astraea

Byatt says:

> When I began *The Virgin in the Garden* I was studying seventeenth-century metaphor and narrative, and images relating to mind and matter. The world of the spirit and the fallen world of the senses. The subject developed through various Renaissance images of the virgin in a bower and Spenser's Garden of Adonis. Here the seeds lie quietly before they take on bodily form. I'm addicted to the *Faerie Queen* because of its narrative shape. (Kenyon, 59)[6]

In *Astraea*, Byatt has written a play whose rich, complex language and iconic power hark back to Renaissance England and to the language and imagery of Shakespeare, Ralegh, and the others who circled Elizabeth and her court. She says: "The play in my novel, and the novel itself, are nostalgia for a *paradis perdu* in which thought and language were naturally and indissolubly linked" ("Still Life/Nature Morte," 3–4). By creating a temporal disjunction between 1950s England and the Renaissance,

Byatt is able to exploit the dominant tropes of both periods: metaphor in the Renaissance and realism in the 20th century. Both metaphor and realism construct the garden, the controlling image of the novel.

Throughout the novel, characters wander in a surfeit of gardens, both literal and metaphorical. Early on, Frederica tells Alexander that the motto for her school is "Knowledge is now no more a fountain sealed." "A fountain sealed," a symbol of virginity, is found in the garden in the Song of Songs. This fountain and garden are revisited throughout medieval and Renaissance literature and then, as Byatt has Frederica point out, recycled in Tennyson's chaste all-woman academy in his poem *The Princess* (*VG*, 102). From the beginning, then, Byatt asks her readers to read allegorically and intertextually.

The staging of *Astraea* in the garden at Long Royston may be the actual *mise-en-scène,* but this locale slips easily into the metaphoric as the cast members fall under the spell of Wedderburn's play and the garden becomes a midsummer night's dream of flirtations and affairs. Other gardens are drawn into this one: the garden of Eden, the garden of the Beloved in the Song of Songs, the garden in *The Romance of the Rose*, Chaucer's and Spenser's gardens, the doubled garden-within-a-garden in which Elizabeth I walks—the historical figure and Wedderburn's character simultaneously—and the "garden" of Marcus's soccer field and his countryside wanderings. Moreover, Long Royston's mock Tudor garden and the school's biology lab are intended to be, according to Byatt, parodies of gardens (Kenyon, 62).

The literary garden is traditionally designed to contain a virgin, and Elizabeth I is the quintessential virgin in Byatt's. Elizabeth I serves as an icon for Byatt's ongoing preoccupation with the relation between real life and literary life. She is a wonderfully ambiguous figure: "the archetypal virgin," as Byatt says, "with power." As a "paradoxical female figure"—an androgynous or hermaphrodite virgin, both virgin and not-virgin—Elizabeth contains within her the contradictions inherent in language itself (Kenyon, 61).

Byatt's novel is full of "virgins" who parade endlessly in a *mis-en-abîme* of gardens. They are, for the most part, innocent of sexual experience and innocent of the world. For example, Kenyon describes Marcus as "virginal" in that he is "untouched by knowledge" (70). But there are virgins who live a contradiction: though Alexander is experienced sexually and considers himself to have made a number of important conquests, he remains untouched by his own desire and the desire of others. Alexander, the narrator says, "was a man whose personal life, though occasionally exigent, never became a siren song" (*SL*, 75). "I am a very private person and I think the artist has to be private even though her work becomes public," says Byatt. "That is perhaps why Alexander remains a slightly shadowy figure in *The Virgin*; it is his play which is real" (Dusinberre, 191). His desire is subordinated to and sublimated in his art.

In *Still Life*, Frederica is another contradictory virgin. Sexually ignorant, she has experienced only the erotic in the novels and poetry that make up the meaningful web of her life. She consequently possesses a knowing air mixed with fleshly innocence.

Changing Canvases: Alexander Wedderburn's *The Yellow Chair*

Byatt is a realist novelist who questions the project of realism; at the same time, she is also a postmodern novelist who questions the postmodern project. Byatt says: "I am afraid of, and fascinated by, theories of language as a self-referring system of signs, which doesn't touch the world. I am afraid of, and resistant to, artistic stances which say we explore only our own subjectivity" (*PM*, 5). As we read *Possession: A Romance*, for example, we can identify a number of opinions expressed in that novel as Byatt's own, but we must do so only tentatively in the face of *Possession*'s emphatic postmodernity. However, in *The Virgin in the Garden* and *Still Life*, Byatt and the narrator are more in sync, making it easier to imagine the narrator and the characters as speaking for/with Byatt. In *Still Life*, says Olga Kenyon, Byatt "wants to make the reader trust the tale *and* the teller" (55).

In the prologue to *Still Life*, when Alexander reflects on how he had hoped to "write a plain, exact verse with no figurative language, in which a yellow chair was the thing itself, a yellow chair, as a round gold apple was an apple or a sunflower a sunflower," he voices Byatt's own ambitions (*SL*, 2). However, in a quotation from Proust that serves as one of the epigraphs for *Still Life* ("Les mots nous présentent des choses une petit image claire et usuelle"), Byatt indicates that she knows that "the thing itself" is never just that. Instead, things are freighted down with meaning that is endlessly circulated and refashioned. In *Still Life*, Alexander and Byatt speak together: "It couldn't be done. . . . Metaphor lay coiled in the name sunflower, which not only turned toward but resembled the sun, the source of light" (2).

Therefore, as we watch Alexander work out the problems of writing *The Yellow Chair* (about "madness, destruction, and death" [*SL*, 335]), we watch Byatt work out her problems with writing in a realist vein while remaining true to the instability of language, which is always trying to turn the everyday into something else. One can take this further, for within this novel-writing plot, in which is nested a play-writing plot, is another plot: Van Gogh's struggle with painting and representation. Alexander takes as his subject for *The Yellow Chair* the many quarrels about art in which Vincent Van Gogh and Paul Gauguin embroiled themselves when they stayed together at Van Gogh's Yellow House at Arles. He steeps himself in Van Gogh's letters and Gauguin's memoir, *Avant et Après*, and bakes in the same sun they did as he worries out a way to dramatize talk about art.

In Provence, he stays at Crowe's house in a room right out of a Van Gogh painting: "white-washed, double-doored, with a yellow wooden bed, a green-shuttered window, a woven rug, a writing table, two yellow-stained rush-bottomed chairs, and a bookcase" (*SL*, 70–71). The yellow chairs in his room are related to Van Gogh's originary chair in his painting and share in its history. Van Gogh, Alexander thinks, had "authority," which allowed him to "both paint and name a chair, and bring into play his own terror and hopes and, behind it, the culture of Europe, north and south, the church itself" (75). To both "paint and name" is Alexander's true desire, made all the more seductive by its impossibility.

In this chapter, I have tried to capture the sense of process, of becoming, that informs *The Virgin in the Garden* and *Still Life*. Byatt has indeed lived up to the challenge of George Eliot and Marcel Proust, creating out of her own experience, memory, and passion a lesson for the way we live now.

Chapter Five

Possession: A Romance

Every so often, a novel one thinks will attract only a small, specialized audience crosses over and lodges in the popular imagination. A. S. Byatt's *Possession: A Romance* is such a work. Part academic potboiler, part suspense story, part romance, it is a virtuoso postmodernist exercise that weaves together many strands: a contemporary story of academic conflicts, rivalries, and discoveries; a 19th-century chronicle of ill-fated love; and a meditation on the imagination and creativity. *Possession* is, Byatt says, "like the books people used to enjoy reading when they enjoyed reading."[1]

Byatt shuttles her readers back and forth from the present-time narrative to the middle of the 19th century through a number of texts, including, most crucially, the letters and poetry of Randolph Ash and Christabel LaMotte, composite figures of real-life 19th-century poets; the journal of Ash's wife Ellen; the journal of Blanche Glover, Christabel's lesbian companion; the standard biography of Ash; and a number of scholarly articles about the poets. Every one of these texts-within-the-text is, in fact, a stunningly convincing invention of Byatt herself.

Possession: A Romance has elicited a number of admiring comparisons with the novels of such writers as David Lodge, John Fowles, and Umberto Eco, all of whom are recognized as postmodern writers. What the critic Marc Blanchard has to say of postmodernism in general can be specifically applied to Byatt's novel, which "seek[s] constantly to rehistoricize the present by retreading the past, adapting to circumstances, while also recasting one's entire perspective in a new way."[2]

A remarkable and compelling example of historical metafiction, *Possession: A Romance* represents a shift for Byatt from her earlier novels. But *Possession* is also a novel Byatt has been working toward all her writing life. For example, we can find the beginnings of many of the ideas and strategies she uses in *Possession* in her first novel, *The Shadow of the Sun*, which is at once a coming-of-age story and a meditation on the artist's creativity and on the inevitable tensions an artist faces in balancing that creativity with his or her—especially her—life. In a way, Cassandra in *The Game* is a precursor of Christabel, though Byatt's Victorian poet is much more sane.

In *The Virgin in the Garden* and *Still Life*, Byatt explores the workings of the imagination; imagination and creativity are abiding concerns in *Possession*. Reading Byatt's work chronologically constitutes a study of the developing artist—the developing *female* artist—in search of new models and new myths. In fact, Byatt says that her novels are concerned with the "problem of female vision, female art and thought" (*SS*, xiv).

Byatt constructed *Possession: A Romance* so that the reader can shift between a number of critical perspectives—historical, textual, psycho-analytical, New Critical, structuralist, deconstructive, new historicist. But *Possession* can be read without these critical filters, and has been by any number of people who prefer to pass over the often dense discussions of literary criticism and concentrate instead on the gossipy academic infighting and the tangled love story. Such readers may well dwell on the affinities between *Possession* and the classic drugstore romance. It may be an "academic" version of such romances, but *Possession: A Romance* is capable of satisfying in the same sort of way.

The novel begins with Roland Mitchell, a research assistant at the British Library. He is busily hunting down material for a scholarly edition of the works of Randolph Henry Ash, a Victorian poet Byatt has invented. During his research, Mitchell finds a few letters Ash wrote to the equally imaginary poet Christabel LaMotte. Up to this point, it has not been known that the two knew each other. As he pursues this connection, Roland meets the feminist scholar Maud Bailey, who is related distantly to Christabel and whose specialty is LaMotte's poetry. Roland and Maud make a series of discoveries about Randolph Ash and Christabel LaMotte that lead them on a number of adventures, which come to parallel the lives of the poets they are pursuing. At one point, Roland, "with precise postmodernist pleasure," thinks "that he and Maud were being driven by a plot or fate that seemed, at least possibly, not their plot or fate but that of [Ash and LaMotte]. . . . Might there not, he professionally asked himself, be an element of superstitious dread in any self-reflexive, inturned postmodernist mirror-game or plot-coil that recognises that it has got out of hand?" (*PR*, 456).

By comparing notes and sharing information about Ash's and La-Motte's poetry and correspondence, Roland and Maud begin to assemble evidence that Ash and Christabel had a love affair—and a child named Maia. These events affect not only their lives but their poetry as well. Following a trail of clues that often entails unraveling obscure allusions in the poets' works, Roland and Maud discover a cache of love letters in a doll's bed in Christabel's old room, untouched since she died (92ff).

In a climactic scene, the principals of the story converge on the gravesite of Randolph and Ellen Ash. The end of *Possession: A Romance* is deliberately reminiscent of a Shakespearean "all's well that ends well" conclusion, in which family wrongs are righted, lovers are united, and conflicts are resolved. We learn that Maud Bailey is the great-great-great-granddaughter of Christabel LaMotte and Randolph Ash. Maud and Roland admit that they love each other and take the first tentative steps toward establishing a relationship.

The Main Characters

Byatt's characters have always been introspective, couching their very real dilemmas in the language of literary allusion and philosophical musings. Readers of her earlier novels who have criticized Byatt for creating such characters feel that too many intellectual layers distance readers from her books and insulate her characters from a real engagement with their lives. Francis Spufford speaks to this problem at the same time that he absolves Byatt: "If at times one cannot believe, quite, in the normality of her characters, their disease is that useful ailment, a disease of lucidity" (22). (Byatt's position is made clear when she has the narrator say that "natures such as Roland's are at their most alert and heady when reading is violently yet steadily alive" [*PR*, 511]). While Byatt creates inward-looking characters in *Possession: A Romance*, she does so with a much lighter hand than in the past. While it would be too reductive to draw strict parallels between Byatt's 19th-century characters and her present-day ones, we can discern, I think, a pattern of repetition, of intertextual relations, between the two sets of characters.

Christabel LaMotte is a composite of Emily Dickinson, Christina Rossetti, and Elizabeth Barrett Browning, with a dash of George Eliot and the Brontës thrown in. Our first introduction to her comes through a letter that Roland Mitchell discovers in the library. "I know you go out in company very little," Ash writes to her (*PR*, 7). Ash sees Christabel as "distant and closed away, a princess in a tower" (301). These are small details, but ones that will take on significance later as the nature and consequences of Christabel's isolation become clearer.

When Roland tries to discover more about Christabel, he finds a "brownish, very early photograph" of the poet, in which she is "veiled under a crackling, translucent page." He observes that "her clothes were more prominent than she was; she retreated into them, her head, perhaps quizzically, perhaps considering itself 'birdlike,' held on one side . . . [the

photograph] was generic Victorian lady, specific shy poetess" (43–44).
There is something deliberately voyeuristic about this scene; it is almost
as if Roland wishes he could peel back that veil and peer beneath those
too-big clothes in order to see the "real" Christabel, who will remain,
both for her "readers" in the novel and for us outside of it, mysterious
and unknowable.

As befitting a conventional heroine in a romance, Christabel LaMotte
is fair-skinned. Ash notes "the whiteness of her" and "the green look of
those piercing or occluded eyes" (*PR*, 301). The narrator also describes
Christabel as "very fair, pale-skinned, with eyes . . . of a strange green
colour which transmuted itself as the light varied" (298).

Christabel's greatest work is a long poem titled *The Fairy Melusina*
(see *PR*, 314ff, for an extended excerpt). She also rewrites a number of
Breton fairy tales, published as *Tales Told in November*. Her reputation,
much like that of the real Victorian poet Christina Rossetti, has grown
through the efforts of 20th-century feminist scholars intent on recovering the work of women artists of the past.

The literary giant of his day, *Randolph Ash* is a cross between Browning and Tennyson, with bits of Wordsworth, Arnold, Morris, Ruskin,
and Carlyle. His imaginary poetry is Browningesque not only in style
but in subject as well: Ash writes a number of monologues, poems about
obscure but engaging real and imaginary personages. Ash is handsome,
with brown hair and a beard "the colour of horse-chestnuts." The narrator also tells us that "his brow was expansive, the organ of intellect well-
developed, though he was equally well-endowed with bumps of com-
passion and fellow-feeling. . . . The mouth [was] firm and settled—a
face, one might think, that knew itself and had a decided way of taking
in the world" (*PR*, 298). Here, the narrator/Byatt uses the language of
phrenology, the "science" of reading one's personality from the configu-
ration of bumps on the skull, in vogue in the 19th century.

The reviewer Michael Dirda is probably right in identifying the affair
between Ash and LaMotte as "roughly mirror[ing] George McLean
Harper's reconstruction of Wordsworth's youthful love for Annette Val-
lon," adding that it "also owes something to the rumored passion of
Rossetti for the married poet W. B. Scott."[3]

Christabel has a friend, *Blanche Glover*, an artist who paints in the pre-
Raphaelite style and with whom Christabel shares a small house in the
country. Blanche is in love with Christabel, though it is not clear
whether they have had a sexual relationship. In her anger and jealousy
over Christabel's relationship with Ash, Blanche goes to Ash's wife and

tells her about the affair. Ellen Ash remembers her as a "poor mad white-faced woman, in her neat, worn boots, pacing and pacing . . . clasping and unclasping her little dove-grey hands" (*PR*, 493). Blanche cries, "We were so happy . . . we were all in all to each other, we were innocent" (493). We learn about Glover's great work in a letter from Christabel to Ash: she is "engaged on a large painting of Merlin and Vivien—at the moment of the latter's triumph when she sings the charm which puts him in her power, to sleep through time. . . . 'Tis all veiled suggestion and local *intensity*" (190; cf. 53). Perhaps we are to imagine a parallel between Merlin and Ash, Vivien and Christabel: while Christabel is no temptress set upon destroying Ash (the usual antifeminist interpretation of the Merlin-Vivien relationship), she does indeed change his life. In fact, there is a very real and well-known paint-ing on the subject of Merlin and Vivien, *The Beguiling of Merlin* (1874), by the pre-Raphaelite artist Sir Edward Burne-Jones. This is the paint-ing reproduced on the front of the first hardcover and softcover editions of *Possession*. Blanche, in her despair, commits suicide by drowning, like Shakespeare's Ophelia (the subject of another pre-Raphaelite painting, by John Everett Millais).

Ellen Ash, helpmeet to her literary husband, is terrified of sexual intercourse and has been since their wedding night. Their marriage has never been consummated. (Ellen has a historical parallel in Jane Carlyle, whose marriage to Thomas Carlyle was never consummated.) They met when she was young but married late because her family would not con-sent to the marriage. At one point, Ellen meditates on how "a young girl of twenty-four should not be made to wait for marriage until she is thirty-four and her flowering long over" (*PR*, 499). She says to herself "in harsher moments" that her nature is "profoundly implicated in not knowing, in silence, in avoidance" (494). "I wanted to be a Poet and a Poem, and now am neither," she writes in her journal (136). In her pro-tectiveness toward her husband and his genius, we find traces of Caro-line Severell, the wife of the novelist Henry Severell in *The Shadow of the Sun*. She keeps the world at bay so Randolph Ash may write his poetry in peace; she vets most of his correspondence and controls his social cal-endar. It may be that Ellen Ash (along with Beatrice Nest, discussed later in this chapter) is the most difficult of characters to understand and to sympathize with: we are too enamored of Ash and Christabel, too fas-cinated by their ill-fated love story, to spare much attention for Ellen.

We meet *Maud Bailey* immediately after the episode in which Roland muses on Christabel's photograph. This juxtaposition is deliberate, for Christabel and Maud have much in common, intellectually, emotionally, and physically. In her poetry, Christabel is obsessed with thresholds and boundaries—and violations thereof. In turn, the scholar Maud writes *about* Christabel's thresholds.

Byatt gives the color green a good deal of play in *Possession*: emerald green, blue-green, silver green. It is the color of Melusine, the mythological half-woman, half-serpent that Christabel writes about; it is the color of the sea, home to so many of the legendary female figures we encounter in *Possession*; it is the color of glass and the color of mirrors. Christabel wears "emerald green" boots that match her eyes (*PR*, 299); when we first meet Maud, she is clothed in a "green and white length" and wears "long shining green shoes." Like Christabel, she is pale: she has a "clean, milky skin" (44). Like Christabel, she is reserved, self-contained. Maud is tall, her hair "wound tightly into a turban of peacock-feathered painted silk, low on her brow" (44). She teaches at Lincoln University, where she has an office at the top of glass-walled Tennyson Tower. Both women could have been painted by any number of pre-Raphaelite artists.

Sir George Bailey and his wife, *Joan Bailey*, related to Maud and to Christabel LaMotte, live in Seal Court, a Victorian house in Lincolnshire in which Christabel lived the last part of her life. *Maia Thomasine Bailey*, Ash and Christabel's daughter, was raised by Christabel's sister *Sophie* as her own child. Maia, who prefers to be called May, has not the slightest interest in poetry; we learn that she marries a cousin and has ten children.

Roland Mitchell is a 29-year-old scholar with a Ph.D. from the imaginary Prince Albert College, London. (His dissertation is titled "History, Historians, and Poetry? A Study of the Presentation of Historical 'Evidence' in the Poems of Randolph Ash.") Roland has been unable to secure a teaching job and works as a research assistant. He lives with *Val* in a moldy basement flat that smells of cat urine wafting down from the house above. They have been estranged in their affections for some time when the novel opens. He is described as "a compact, clearcut man, with precise features, a lot of very soft black hair, and thoughtful dark brown eyes. He had a look of wariness, which could change when he felt relaxed or happy . . . into a smile of amused friendliness and pleasure which aroused a feeling of warmth, and something more, in many women" (*PR*, 14). Roland is a modern Ash to Maud's Christabel; however, the elements of high drama and romance that characterize Ash and Christabel's relationship are transmuted into the daily cares of contemporary life, and into a self-consciousness *about* high drama and romance.

Even Val has an Ash-LaMotte connection: for her required essay (something like an American university senior thesis), she wrote a paper titled "Male Ventriloquism: The Women of Randolph Henry Ash." Val argues that Ash "neither liked nor understood women, that his female speakers were constructs of his own fear and aggression, that even the poem-cycle, *Ask to Embla*, was the work not of love but of narcissism, the poet addressing his Anima" (*PR*, 16). In this paper, Val is apparently working out some of her own feelings about Roland and about men in general. At the end of the novel, Val begins a relationship with *Euan MacIntyre*, a solicitor who is also her boss. Euan's "charm and enthusiasm," Roland notes with a mixture of sadness and relief, are capable of "smooth[ing] the resentment and sullenness out of Val's face" (477). Euan gets involved in the plot as Maud's legal representative.

Fergus Wolff is Maud's ex-lover and a brilliant deconstructionist critic. Intense and sensual, he is Byronic, and self-consciously so: Roland describes him as a "devourer" (*PR*, 550). He is, in part, a 20th-century version of the wolf at the door—that is, the Randolph Ash of Blanche Glover's journal whom she so fears will take Christabel away (54). Maud is half afraid of Fergus, of his sexuality and his brilliance, because of the havoc that he may unleash in her life; she is afraid of what she might lose if she were to lose control and give in to him. The narrator tells us that Fergus "had a habit which Maud was not experienced enough to recognise as a common one in ex-lovers of giving little tugs at the carefully severed spider-threads or puppet strings which had once tied her to him" (155). For example, when Fergus writes to Maud about his plans for a scholarly paper, titled "The Queen of the Castle: What Is Kept in the Keep?" he means it as an offensive aimed at Christabel and her poetry and, by extension, at Maud herself. In fact, he calls it his "siege-paper." (And while Fergus speaks metaphorically, there is indeed a very material secret in the "keep"—in Christabel's tower are hidden her love letters to Ash and his to her.)

James Blackadder, Roland's boss, has been editing Ash's works since 1951, and the end is not yet in sight (the novel is set in 1986). The narrator says of him that he "was discouraged and liked to discourage others" (*PR*, 13). Blackadder is a "stringent" scholar, and it is his very meticulousness that prevents him from finishing his edition of Ash's works. Along with the character Beatrice Nest, Byatt has created in Blackadder a fictional character who has all too many counterparts in the real academic world, for many a scholar is capable of suffering monumental writer's block. Blackadder and his staff occupy a cavelike set of basement rooms at the British Museum known as Blackadder's Ash Factory.

Mortimer Cropper is a rich American scholar at the imaginary Robert Dale Owen University in New Mexico. (Robert Dale Owen was a real-life 19th-century British thinker and social critic.) Cropper represents the worst kind of scholar-biographer: his main goal is to own Ashiana, not necessarily to further scholarship but to fulfill his own need to possess the life of his subject—Randolph Ash. He has acquired some of Ash's letters, manuscripts, and personal effects in the name of a charitable trust called the Newsome Foundation. He has stolen other materials, which he keeps in a sealed and locked room for his own private, fetishized viewing. He is the author of *The Complete Correspondence of Randolph Ash* and of the biography *The Great Ventriloquist*. This title, the narrator tells us, is taken from one of Ash's "teasing monologues of self-revelation or self-parody" (*PR*, 120). And ventriloquism is an important motif in the novel, as various characters speak through and for others— and as Byatt "speaks" for them all. Byatt provides us with a segment of Cropper's own biography, in which he tells us, in highly florid prose, that he comes from a long line of collectors: his house in New Mexico, pretentiously named Everblest, is filled with antiques and objets d'art from all over the world. He is extremely close to his mother, with whom he still lives. He apparently has other interests besides the academic and aesthetic, for he also owns "photographs of a large and varied collection—as far as it was possible to vary, in flesh or tone or angle or close detail, so essentially simple an activity, a preoccupation." He had, the narrator tells us, "his own ways of sublimation" (124). We never discover just who is depicted in these photographs—women? Men? Children?

Cropper is behind the plot to despoil the Ashes' grave in order to retrieve the mysterious papers Ellen buried with her husband. His accomplice is *Hildebrand Ash*, the heir to the Ash family title, and a rather disreputable and grasping relation he is. Both Cropper and Blackadder, for all their differences, have their counterpart in the "real" fictional world of the 19th century—the world of Dickens and Eliot and Trollope.

In George Eliot's *Middlemarch*, we meet a character named the Reverend Edward Casaubon, whose ambition it is to write a comprehensive history of world religions—one that he is destined to talk about but never begin. Christabel's father, *Isidore*, is a historian and mythographer, but more successful than Eliot's Casaubon.

Dr. Beatrice Nest works with Blackadder in the Ash Factory on an edition of the journal of Ellen Ash. Just as Blackadder feels compelled to hunt down every literary and historical allusion in Ash's poetry, Beatrice Nest hovers endlessly over Ellen Ash's journal and is no closer to completing it than Blackadder is his edition of Ash's poems. As a student, she fell in love with Randolph Henry Ash, recognizing his genius and the strength of his passion in his poetry. In spite of her obvious promise as a scholar, her adviser warned her off any serious work on Ash, shunting her off to do an edition of his wife's journal as an occupation more suitable to her gender. She accepted obediently and took a lectureship at Prince Albert. Never married, she is described as "indisputably solid, but nevertheless amorphous, a woman of wide and abundant flesh, sedentary swelling hips, a mass of bosom, above which spread a cheerful heart-shaped face, crowned by a kind of angora hat . . . of crimped white hair" (*PR*, 123).

Leonora Stern, a zaftig feminist and sometime lesbian from Tallahassee, is a friend to Maud. Her specialty is the work of Christabel LaMotte; she is the author of *Motif and Matrix in the Poems of LaMotte*. An example of her prose: "And what surfaces of the earth do we women choose to celebrate, who have appeared typically in phallocentric texts as a penetrable hole, inviting or abhorrent" (*PR*, 265). Leonora is clever, bighearted, expansive. One of the odder alliances in the novel is that which develops between Leonora and Blackadder. Both have been excluded from Roland and Maud's adventure, and they put aside their vast political and literary-critical differences in order to figure out what Maud and Roland are up to. In one scene, on the beach in Brittany, we are given a sartorial sketch that highlights the differences between them: "Leonora's hair was loose, and . . . was lifted in dark snaking ringlets. . . . She wore a Greek sun-dress in very fine cotton . . . held by a wide silver band of cloth above her ample breasts, exposing shoulders dark gold with the glare of no English sun. Her large and shapely feet were naked, and her toe-nails painted alternately scarlet and silver" (453–54). Blackadder, on the other hand, is dressed "in heavy shoes and a dark parka over dark creased trousers" (454). Along the way, this unlikely pair become lovers.

Ariane Le Minier is a professor at the University of Nantes, specializing in women's writings. She writes to Leonora to tell her about the work of *Sabine de Kercoz*, a 19th-century writer who created a feminized mythology based on the legends of her Breton heritage. Sabine is Christabel's cousin. Maud and Leonora discover that Christabel visited Sabine and her father in 1859—a fact that no LaMotte scholar was hitherto aware of. Maud and Roland visit Ariane and discover that Sabine kept a diary while Christabel was in Brittany. In fact, we learn, it was Christabel who encouraged Sabine to write in the first place. What had been an exciting and rather titillating literary game so far turns much more serious when they learn, through Sabine's diary, of the great pain and grief that Christabel endured on the lonely Breton coast during her visit, undertaken because she was pregnant and unable to speak of it to anyone. We get a taste of Sabine's Gothic predilections in her vivid descriptions of Christabel and her tribulations.

Finally, Cropper's great-grandmother, *Priscilla Penn Cropper*, was an early feminist and accomplished medium who made the family fortune by creating a patent medicine, "Priscilla Penn's Regenerating Powders." She wrote to Christabel LaMotte (and also exchanged letters with Ash), and Christabel's reply survives in Cropper's archives. In this letter, Christabel writes of *Mrs. Hella Lees*, the medium she visited after her return from Brittany. Our scholars reconstruct how Ash apparently attended one of Mrs. Lees's seances, at which he saw Christabel. (Ash's experience leads him to write the scathing *Mummy Possest*.) When Christabel cries out that "you have made a murderess of me" (PR, 543), a horrified and grieving Randolph thinks she is referring to their unborn child. The truth is that she is thinking of Blanche and her suicide. Ash and Christabel never see each other again, and they are left with this tragic misunderstanding between them.

The Significance of Names

Many novelists give their characters names with symbolic force, a practice Byatt herself has been following since her first novel, *The Shadow of the Sun*. Instead of accounting for every name in every novel, however, I want to concentrate on the names in *Possession*. My intention is not to interpret (though I do speculate here and there) but to suggest some of the sources for Byatt's characters' names.

In general, these names allude to characters in other literary texts or have meaning in other contexts. For example, in naming Christabel's father Isidore, Byatt has layered in an allusion to the early seventh-century compiler and encyclopedist Isidore of Seville. If we know about the historical Isidore, we can transfer that knowledge to Byatt's Isidore and thus enrich our understanding of this minor character. Leonora Stern is a good example of a name whose components have accessible meanings in other contexts. The reader may recognize that Leonora is derived from *leo*, the Latin word for "lion." Leonora is indeed a dominating force in the novel, fierce in her loyalties and in her passions. But Leonora is far from "stern" in the novel, of course; it is the very inappropriateness of her surname that should give us pause. It is an example of what rhetoricians call *antiphrasis*—the ironic use of a term when just the opposite is meant.

Mortimer Cropper's last name has a range of meanings derived from "crop" and "to crop." A "crop" can denote a kind of whip; "to crop" can mean to cut off. The British expression "to come a cropper" means to fall heavily or to fail miserably. Ellen Ash's first name is Anglo-Saxon for "brave"; her maiden name was Best. Blanche means "white," while Glover, as in "one who makes gloves," may suggest a covering-up of something. An "adder" is a snake, as in James Blackadder. Fergus Wolff resonates in a number of ways, the allusion to "wolf" being the most obvious. Fergus is the name of a character in Irish legend and is also reminiscent of a character in Scandinavian mythology: Fenris-wolf, the son of Loki and Angerbode.

Randolph Ash writes of his "namesake, the mighty Ash. It is a common and magical tree . . . because our Norse forefathers once believed it held the world together" (*PR*, 106). In a way, Ash's poetry "holds the world together"; it renders the truth of the human heart more real, as it were. Ash carries an ash-stick. Cropper calls this walking-stick "part of [Ash's] personal mythology, a solid metaphoric extension of his Self" (268). Another metaphor at work here is "ash," as in the burned embers of a fire—passion extinguished perhaps. Byatt's imaginary literary critics have not been able to agree on who Ask and Embla may represent in Ash's long poem *Ask to Embla*, but we learn that Ask is, in part, Ash, and Embla is Christabel. Ask and Embla are the names of the first man and woman in Norse (that is, Scandinavian) mythology—the real-life basis of Ash's poem.[4]

The last name Nest captures something about Beatrice's cubbyhole at the Ash Factory, in which, like a bird lining her nest with odd bits and scraps of paper, Beatrice has nestled herself; her first name is the name of Dante's beloved, whom he cites as the inspiration for his poetry. Maud is the title of a poem by Tennyson, in which a young man, in love with the unattainable title character, sinks into madness and death. (I should note that this bare summary does not do justice to the symbolic and philosophical underpinnings of the poem.) In fact, Roland recalls a few lines from *Maud* when thinking about Maud Bailey, who is, he thinks, rather like Tennyson's heroine: "icily regular, splendidly null" (*PR*, 549).[5] And Bailey, Maud's last name, is an archaic word that denotes the enclosing, protecting wall of a castle—a symbol of her own reserve.

Christabel's name is also taken from a poem: Samuel Taylor Coleridge's mysterious, unfinished poem of the same name. Surely the fact that the poem is unfinished, therefore resisting interpretation to a much greater degree than finished poems—is important to an understanding of Byatt's Christabel. LaMotte recalls the French *mot*, "word"—or even better, "answer to a puzzle"—and recalls another word favored by Byatt and her characters: *riddle*. More obscurely, a *motte* in French is a "mound," or high piece of ground. Most military fortifications are built on hills. Christabel writes of "my closed castle, behind my mott-and-bailey defences," both punning on her name and strengthening the connection between herself and Maud Bailey (*PR*, 545). (Even the name of the home to which Christabel retires is significant: Seal Court resonates as "sealed up, enclosed"—suggesting yet another bond between Maud and Christabel.) Finally, I think Byatt intends for us to hear the connection LaMotte-Shalott-Camelot, which is reminiscent of the rhyme scheme of Tennyson's "The Lady of Shalott," allusions to which occur frequently throughout the novel.

Roland has both medieval and Romantic antecedents; it is the name of the brave hero of the early 12th-century *Chanson de Roland* and occurs in Shakespeare's *King Lear*: "Child Rowland to the dark tower came" (III.iv.185). (In Middle English, "child" connotes what we mean by the word "knight.") The great early 19th-century romancer Sir Walter Scott repeats this line in *The Bride of Triermain*.

Mythic and Imaginary Women

A major structuring device of *Possession* is the repetition of scene, action, phrase, object, color, and even personae. Of the many concerns Byatt takes up, the making of story and the accretions and transmutations of myth are paramount. In this section, I'd like to concentrate on just one recurring myth, namely, that of the chained, imprisoned, or entowered woman. At the risk of oversimplifying the case, one might say that such physical constraints are metaphors for emotional, intellectual, and psychological oppression. For example, Joan Bailey is in a wheelchair; Beatrice Nest is hemmed in by file cabinets and notecards; a heroine in a fairy tale written by Christabel is closed into a coffin. As I mentioned above, Tennyson's poem "The Lady of Shalott," and the Lady herself, are invoked over and over throughout the novel. Tennyson's Lady is locked into a tower and observes the world reflected through a mirror. She weaves what she sees on a great loom but is "cursed" in some mysterious way so that she cannot look directly at the world or enter into it.[6]

As Leonora Stern says, "every archetype" is here (PR, 461). Throughout the novel, we find allusions, direct and oblique, extended and fleeting, not only to the Lady of Shalott but to Coleridge's Christabel; Tennyson's Maud; Keats's La Belle Dame Sans Merci; the medieval poet Jean D'Arras's Melusine; the Princess and the Pea, Rapunzel, and princesses in general (Blanche calls Christabel "Princess" [50]); the feminized muse and the psychic medium; witches, lamias, undines; the Little Mermaid; selkies, water-nixies, and sirens. There are yet more female figures: Ariadne, Arachne, Pandora, Proserpina, Pomona, Medusa, Maia; Malory's Vivien and Elaine; Eve, Martha, and Mary. One reviewer of the novel, impatient with this sort of excess, says that "so heavily stocked is the trout pond with paradigms for [Byatt's] enterprise that the fishing isn't much fun."[7] However, this plentitude is a signal characteristic of the postmodern, underscoring the impossibility of coming to any single interpretation of Possession: A Romance.

Byatt on Literary Criticism, Reading, and the Imagination

In chapter 1, we focused on a few of the more important intellectual influences on Byatt and her fiction. Byatt, as we have seen, possesses a kind of double vision in that she brings to her fiction the considerable insights and experience of one who has honed and practiced her novel-writing skills for over 30 years as well as the informed judgment of the literary critic. Possession: A Romance is the result of both points of view. It is indeed the result of a "good and greedy reading," as Byatt says of those writers who transmute their own reading experiences into new texts.

In Possession, Byatt not only displays the results of her own reading but also enacts different ways of reading, both her overarching narrative and the texts embedded within this narrative. The narrator may or may not "be" Byatt—we have no absolute way of determining when the narrator is expressing an opinion that Byatt expects us to attribute to herself. And we would be wrong to try to identify Byatt with one of her imaginary academics—does she ally herself with the feminism of Leonora Stern? The fine sensibilities of Maud? The power of Ash?

However, Byatt does fill in certain gaps, supplying some allusions and explanations for the reader, and it is this kind of authorial nudging or hinting that I will take up here. (Byatt has much in common in this respect with the Canadian novelist Robertson Davies [*The Cornish Trilogy, The Deptford Trilogy*], who also cannot resist an opportunity to explain the workings of his novels.)

Literary critics have come to understand that a work of fiction takes on a life of its own after leaving the author's hands, and that a text is capable of different and differing interpretations in the hands of various readers. Balancing the author's original intention and historical circumstances with the reader's experiences (experiences constituted by her or his own cultural context), or determining whether such a balance is even desirable or achievable, remains a subject of debate in academic circles. Yet whatever our experiences are that may shape our particular reading of *Possession: A Romance*, we can still discern something of Byatt's intentions. For example, the title of the novel and the two epigraphs combine to direct us one way rather than another. (As experienced readers, we are already alert to the meaningfulness of titles, and the title *Possession: A Romance* is certainly intriguing.)

In using the word *romance* in her title, Byatt suggests a way for us to understand what kind of novel she has written. To underscore her intention, she borrows a quotation from Nathaniel Hawthorne's preface to *The House of the Seven Gables* for her first epigraph:

> When a writer calls his work a Romance, it need hardly be observed that he wishes to claim a certain latitude, both as to its fashion and material . . . as a work of art, it must rigidly subject itself to laws . . . it sins unpardonably so far as it may swerve aside from the truth of the human heart.

Hawthorne's preface is famous not only for its insights into his own work but also for its commentary on the genre of romance itself. Romance has proved to be notoriously hard to define, for it covers a multitude of texts, ranging from Greek and Roman narratives of late antiquity through medieval Arthurian romance to the contemporary Harlequin romance. In this particular excerpt, Hawthorne argues that what we call "romance" has a particular history, and it is this particularity that allows us to recognize a romance when we see one: every romance shares in similar conventions, patterns, and predictable outcomes ("laws"). The author of a romance does not intend to abide by the principles of either realism or real life; an author, by writing a romance, asks the reader to accept the logic of a world that does not necessarily correspond to our experience of it. By beginning with this epigraph,

Byatt focuses our attention on fiction and fictionality—and on the possibility that she is taking up a stance that can only be described as integral to the fiction she is writing.

Byatt's second epigraph is an excerpt from one of Robert Browning's poetic monologues, "Mr. Sludge, 'the Medium.'" Mr. Sludge is an unabashed charlatan who is fully aware that his talents are illusory. In fact, illusion is his great gift. He is able to "veritably *possess*" such qualities as "genius, beauty, / rank and wealth," not having any of his own (emphasis mine). The semblance of possession is all that he can hope for—or better, conjure up. Browning has his Mr. Sludge compare his work as a medium to that of a writer:

> All as the Author wants it. Such a scribe
> You pay and praise for putting life in stones,
> Fire into fog, making the past your world.
> There's plenty of "How did you contrive to grasp
> The thread that led you through this labyrinth?
> How build such solid fabric out of air?
> How on so slight foundation found this tale,
> Biography, narrative?" or, in other words,
> "How many lies did it require to make
> The portly truth you here present us with?"

It is this aspect of Mr. Sludge that Byatt means to exploit. She encourages us to draw a parallel between Browning's commentary on his own art and the novel we hold in our hands. In fact, Ash's poem *Mummy Possest* is Byatt's reply to, or companion piece for, "Mr. Sludge." She says that in *Mummy Possest*, "the ideas about dolls and lies . . . are a game with the ideas and lies in *Mr. Sludge*."[8] Fiction and the making of fiction are implicated in these "lies": "We fabricate to demonstrate . . . Truth," says Byatt/Ash/the narrator of *Mummy Possest*—"Truth" being that of the spirit world—and

> I call it artfulness, or simply Art,
> A Tale, a Story, that may hide a Truth
> As wonder-tales do, even in the Best Book. (*PR*, 442)

In other words, a fiction writer is able to capture more truth in fiction than a historian may in an objective narrative of facts (440).

Once we move past "Mr. Sludge," we may begin to notice how the word *possession* recurs throughout the text; this repetition of the theme announced in Browning's poem serves as a good example of what I am calling authorial nudging. There is the scene in which Ash and Christabel set off on their trip to Yorkshire: "For months he had been possessed by the imagination of her. . . . Her presence had been unimaginable, or more strictly, *only* to be imagined" (*PR*, 301). And when Ash finally tells his wife Ellen about Christabel, he says, "I could say it was a sort of madness. A possession, as by daemons. A kind of blinding" (492). "I felt possessed. I had to know," says Roland about his act of stealing Ash's letters and embarking upon his investigation (527). And Maud, talking about her realization that both Ash and Christabel are her ancestors, says, "I feel they have taken me over" (548). Trying to explain why she keeps others at a distance, she also says, "People treat you as a kind of *possession* if you have a certain sort of good looks" (549). There is a clear continuum of feeling, from sexual and physical possession to academic absorption, throughout the novel. Excessive possession leads to the objectifying of the other, whether the other is a human being or a text. Can we ever really "possess" another, or another's feelings? Can we every really "possess" a poem, in the sense that we can capture some fixed meaning for all time? These are some of the questions Byatt raises in her title and in her novel.

The Fictional Works within the Fictional Work

Chapter 1 of *Possession: A Romance* begins with an excerpt from one of Ash's major poems, *The Garden of Proserpina*, in which the poet writes of how

> The dragon Ladon crisped his jewelled crest
> Scraped a gold claw and sharped a silver tooth
> And dozed and waited through eternity
> Until the tricksy hero Herakles
> Came to his dispossession and the theft. (*PR*, 3)

These lines serve as a fine example of the multiple layers of Byatt's practice. First of all, as an epigraph to the first chapter, the excerpt recalls the effect of the real (but fictive) words of Browning's Mr. Sludge, which stand as an epigraph to the whole novel. Byatt's lines, however, are not "real" in that no Randolph Henry Ash exists outside of her novel. Nevertheless, Ash and his poetry are real for the reader, as real as the (fictive) verse of any actual poet.

Second, Ash's poem is founded upon another text, the myth of Hercules and his seven labors, undertaken in order to purify himself after killing his wife and children in a fit of madness. In drawing upon myth, Byatt/Ash reproduces the very real practice of such poets as Wordsworth, Keats, Shelley, Tennyson, and a host of other 19th-century poets. In fact, *The Garden of Proserpina* is styled after certain poems of Tennyson's, such as "Ulysses," "The Hesperides," and "The Lotos-Eaters." (We also get pastiches of poems by Browning and others from the Byatt/Ash pen.) We begin to perceive wheels within wheels, fictions within fictions, echoing each other endlessly in what contemporary critics call a *mise-en-abîme*. (The French novelist André Gide uses this term to characterize his fiction.) It may have been borrowed from medieval heraldry, in which it described the ever-shrinking depiction of a scene painted on a shield. (Think of the woman depicted on the Land O Lakes box of butter holding a box of butter on which a woman is depicted holding a box of butter on which a woman is depicted holding a box of butter. . . .) Byatt uses the term herself when she/the narrator takes up the subject of reading and writing (*PR*, 511). *Mise-en-abîme* has become a useful way to describe the postmodern habit of creating an infinite regression of plots.

The excerpt from *The Garden of Proserpina* announces the theme of the first chapter. The narrative "reality" is that Roland is in the library in the first place because he is hunting down a source for the poem. Once Roland discovers the letters, we might then imagine him as a Hercules who is about to steal Ash's letters to Christabel (in the treasure-house of the British Library) in the same way that Hercules stole the dragon's treasure. That Hercules steals the treasure in order to purge himself resonates as well: we may think of Roland's very contemporary labors that will prepare him to become a poet at the end of the novel; we may think of Ash's self-purification in the fire of passion (and we may pun on his name once more); we may think of the "treasure" Ash "steals" from Christabel: her virginity and, more important, her heart and soul. Finally, the occurrence of the word *dispossession* in the poem is no accident and leads us back to a meditation on—or forward to an anticipation of—"possession," the overriding theme of the novel.

Toward the end of the novel, we revisit *The Garden of Proserpina* through Roland's rereading of it. The narrator/Byatt makes the following comment: "It is possible for writers to make, or remake at least, for a reader, the primary pleasures of eating, or drinking, or looking on, or sex. . . . They do not habitually elaborate on the equally intense pleasure of reading" (*PR*, 510–11). What is interesting is that the narrator/Byatt then goes on to do just that—to elaborate on the pleasures of reading, which, we learn, consists of recovering the texts (what is called the intertext) that underpin Ash's poem: "Think of this—that the writer wrote alone, and the reader read alone, and they were alone with each other. True, the writer may have been alone also with Spenser's golden apples in the *Faerie Queene*, Proserpina's garden . . . [and] Paradise Lost, in the garden where Eve recalled Pomona and Proserpina" (511). In other words, the reader who begins with a particular text in hand—here, Roland with Ash's poem—may also experience more than one writer's reading. We watch Roland recovering Ash reading Milton who is reading Genesis. As an added pleasure, we read Byatt *writing* Ash, who reads . . . and thus we come to an awareness of ourselves as readers and join the company of Byatt's characters, readers and writers all. And how readers read and writers write—that is, how they make meaning—is a central concern of *Possession: A Romance*. Rather than a description of reading, *Possession*, as I have suggested, is an *enactment* of reading.

By the end of the novel, Roland has begun the work of becoming a poet, after a "good and greedy reading" of Randolph Ash's poetry. This is one of the many intertextual moments in the novel in which Byatt makes the point, and in the most celebratory way, that poems arise out of poems, and books out of books.

As we can see from just this brief reading, Byatt's invented poetry (along with the fictional letters, journal entries, and even literary criticism) is designed to mesh with and enhance the narrative in an extremely intricate and sophisticated way. Byatt says that

> the poems [in *Possession: A Romance*] are an integral part of the text, which begins where it begins and ends where it ends, and were written where they come, as were the stories. The three exceptions are the small spider poem, which came to me quite early and the two long poems, *Swammerdam* (based on Michelet's *L'Insecte*, in part) and *Mummy Possest*. Both of these were finally written after the end of the book but were in place as skeletons—i.e. I knew their metaphorical structure . . . when I wrote what surrounded them.[9]

Grave Diggings and Gothic Endings

The climax of the novel involves high suspense and skulduggery as the players race to discover the final clues to the mystery that surrounds

Randolph Ash and Christabel LaMotte. Beatrice Nest overhears a plot
to dig up the Ashes' grave to retrieve "the box" (PR, 475ff), which, we
learn, contains Ellen's and Ash's letters; a sealed letter from Christabel
to Ash, sent when she had heard how ill he was (488ff); and a lock of
hair (which Ellen mistakenly assumes is Christabel's). Ellen could not
bring herself to destroy these things and buried them with her husband
(cf. 482ff).

Beatrice Nest, Maud, Roland, Val, Euan, Blackadder, and Leonora
plot to keep Cropper and Hildebrand Ash from disinterring the box, or
failing that, to make off with its contents themselves. Such scheming, as
Euan says, is like "the unmasking at the end of a detective story" (PR,
524). The two sets of conspirators descend upon Sussex, upon the small
graveyard at Hodershall where the Ashes are buried.

At the very moment when Cropper and Hildebrand Ash begin to dig
(observed by the others, concealed at various points in the churchyard),
Cropper feels "for a moment, very purely, a *presence*, not of someone, but
of some mobile *thing*" (PR, 536). And, the narrator tells us, "in that
moment, the great storm hit Sussex," a storm of howling wind and
whipping rain and debris, as if nature itself took offense at Cropper's
act. In fact, a tree falls on his Mercedes, and another tree blocks his path
when he tries to flee with the box of letters. At this point, Maud,
Roland, and the others materialize; they all return to the inn where
Cropper is staying to play out the final scene of discovery.

Discovery is also "the moment of dispossession" (PR, 522) for Roland
and Maud, as they begin to tell how they started on the trail—beginning with Ash's letters in the British Library, and moving on to the letters hidden in Christabel's turret and to Sabine's diary. The players in
Possession read Christabel's last letter together—and we do, too, peering
over their imaginary shoulders. We learn why Christabel chose to keep
Maia a secret: it was her own pride, and her fear that she would lose her
daughter to the Ashes (544). She says of her relationship with Maia:

> I have been *Melusina* these thirty years. I have so to speak flown about and
> about the battlements of this stronghold crying on the wind. She sees me
> as a *sorcière*, a spinster in a fairy tale, looking at her with glittering eye
> and waiting for her to prick her poor little finger and stumble into the
> brute sleep of *adult truth*. (544)

In between the denouement and the final conclusion is another sort
of ending, which is also a beginning. Maud and Roland become lovers.
The novel ends in paradox:

In the morning, the whole world had a strange new smell. It was the smell of the aftermath, a green smell, a smell of shredded leaves and oozing resin, of crushed wood and splashed sap, a tart smell, which bore some relation to the smell of bitten apples. It was the smell of death and destruction and it smelled fresh and lively and hopeful. (*PR*, 551)

"Ends" and "endings" are deceptive terms, however. In the first chapter of *Possession: A Romance*, we learn that Roland finds Ash's letters to Christabel tucked into Ash's personal copy of Vico's *Principi di una Scienza Nuova* (Principles of the New Science). This has significance beyond that of illustrating Ash's wide-ranging interests and his insatiable curiosity about the world. Giovanni Battista Vico (1668–1744) was an Italian historian who developed the theory that history is not linear and progressive, but circular and cyclical. The implications of such a theory have been reductively expressed as "history repeats itself"—with the implied admonishment that we ought to learn from past mistakes. More important for our purposes—and Byatt's—the notion of history as circular ensures that we never arrive at an end point or a denouement. I believe Byatt also means us to think of James Joyce's monumental novel *Finnegan's Wake*, which also begins with an allusion to Vico: "riverrun, past Eve and Adam's, from swerve of shore to bend of bay, brings us by a commodius *vicus* of *recirculation* back to Howth Castle and Environs" (emphasis mine).[10]

As if to underscore the impossibility of an ending, what follows the ending of the story of Roland and Maud is a coda, titled "Postscript 1868," in which the narrator steps out of her/his customary role and speaks of what none of the characters could know, either through their own experience or through their piecing together of various parts of the story. "There are things," the narrator says, "that happen and leave no discernible trace, are not spoken or written of, though it would be very wrong to say that subsequent events go on indifferently, all the same, as though such things had never been" (*PR*, 552). We read of a chance meeting between Randolph Ash and his little daughter May—more fully, Maia Thomasine Bailey. Ash recognizes both Christabel and himself in the child. She tells him of her aunt, who is "always telling me poems"—who is Christabel, living on the margins of her illegitimate daughter's life in order to avoid the scandal and heartbreak that would result if the true relationship were known (554).

Ash weaves a crown of flowers for May, and she gives him a lock of her hair in return (the lock that Ellen would mistake for Christabel's). He gives her a message: "Tell your aunt . . . that you met a poet, who was looking for the Belle Dame Sans Merci, and who met you instead, and who sends her his compliments, and will not disturb her, and is on his way to fresh woods and pastures now" (*PR*, 555). Ash alludes to the figure of the lady-temptress, best known in Keats's poem of the same name. However, "on the way home, she met her brothers, and there was a rough-and-tumble, and the lovely crown was broken, and she forgot the message, which was never delivered" (555).

And so the novel ends, poignantly, perhaps sentimentally, but moving nonetheless, for the message that was never delivered represents all the "what ifs" and "if onlys" of human relationships. Moreover, and more critically, the undelivered message represents the writer's dilemma, the difficulty of saying, finally, all that one sets out to say.

Chapter Six
Angels and Insects: Two Novellas

Both novellas in *Angels and Insects*, *Morpho Eugenia* and *The Conjugial Angel*, pick up and develop themes found in *Possession: A Romance*. As we follow William Adamson and Matty Crompton in *Morpho Eugenia* in their work documenting insect life surrounding Bredley Hall, we are reminded of the journey that Randolph Henry Ash and Christabel La-Motte take in Yorkshire. And the subplot of spiritualism in *Possession* is moved to center stage in *The Conjugial Angel*. Randolph Henry Ash's poems *Swammerdam* and *Mummy Possest* and assorted nature poems serve as intertextual links to *Angels and Insects*. Both novellas allow Byatt to continue exploring Victorian life and culture, which she sees as more all-encompassing than our own: "For the Victorians, everything was part of one thing: science, religion, philosophy, economics, politics, women, fiction, poetry. They didn't compartmentalize—they thought BIG. Ruskin went out and learned geology and archaeology, then the history of painting, then mythology, and then he thought out, and he thought out" (Stout, 14). Byatt thinks BIG in *Angels and Insects*, but she also adds a knowing sensibility to her excursions into science, natural history, and philosophy that the Victorians lacked. Michael Levenson explains her commitment to doing so as a feature of her postmodernity, which "finds its ground in something else, something older, namely an earnest attempt to get back before the moderns and revive a Victorian project that has never been allowed to come to completion. What you have in Byatt is an odd-sounding but perfectly intelligible creature, the post-modern Victorian."[1]

The titles are worth commenting on here. *Morpho Eugenia* is the name the naturalist William Adamson gives to a new species of butterfly he discovers. The butterfly is lavender-white in color; when William first sees Eugenia Alabaster, she is wearing a lavender-white dress. He thinks he is in love with Eugenia; naming the butterfly in her honor is part of his courtship ritual. *The Conjugial Angel* is a drama that takes its title from a tract by Emanuel Swedenborg, the 18th-century philosopher who advocated direct mystical communication between this world and the spiritual realm. In *The Delights of Wisdom, Concerning Conjugial Love*,

Swedenborg describes the true union of souls that can occur between two people, a union that is to be distinguished from the more pedestrian, common understanding of marriage. (Swedenborg's followers kept the unusual spelling *conjugial* [as opposed to *conjugal*] to emphasize the difference between the two states.)

The two novellas are linked under the rubric of *Angels and Insects*: insects are a central preoccupation of *Morpho Eugenia*, and angels of *The Conjugial Angel*. Moreover, as a game of anagrams illustrates, "angels and insects" is also "anguish and incest," a central part of the plot of *Morpho Eugenia*.

A series of conjunctions govern the structure and themes of both novellas: *Morpho Eugenia* and *The Conjugial Angel*, insects and angels, natural society and human society, the material world and the spiritual world, lust and love, the living and the dead, truth and deception, reality and seeming, presence and absence. The cover of the first edition of the book points to this yoking as well: against a sky-blue background is a shadowy winged female creature who is both angel and insect. One way to read the two novellas, then, is as a study in the *liminal*—the name anthropologists have given to any transitory state or threshold between one kind of knowledge or consciousness and another.

Morpho Eugenia

The year is 1859—the year Darwin published *Origin of Species*. William Adamson, naturalist and collector, has just returned from the Amazon to the civilities and conventions of English society. After ten years of virtual solitude, he is finding it hard to adjust. He has been invited to visit the Alabasters at Bredely Hall and stays to catalog the Reverend Harald Alabaster's collection of natural curiosities from around the world. Harald Alabaster is a benign variation on Mortimer Cropper in *Possession: A Romance*; like Cropper, he has used his wealth to collect voraciously and indiscriminately. For the critic Mary Hawthorne, Alabaster's "compulsive hoarding of nature" has its parallel in Byatt's own "appropriation of the past."[2]

Adamson marries Harald's daughter, Eugenia Alabaster, who is beautiful, distant, and passive. Life is not happily ever after, however. Though he cannot quite pinpoint the source, William Adamson is aware of friction between Eugenia's half-brother Edgar and himself. He attributes the problem to class difference: Adamson is the son of an overreligious Yorkshire butcher. He dreams of returning to the (classless) jungle: "There would be new species of ants, to be named perhaps adamsonii, there would be space for a butcher's son to achieve greatness" (*AI*, 12). Edgar, whose "existence was entirely without aim or value," according to Adamson (71), calls him "underbred" (73). The clash of class is usually cast in such Darwinian terms throughout the novel, reflecting both insect and human hierarchies. "I am as good a *man*," writes Adamson in his journal, "take me for all in all, as E. A. and have, I dare swear it, used my intelligence and my bodily courage to greater purpose. But how would that consideration weigh with any such family, constructed exactly to reject any such intr . . ." (16). The entry breaks off in just this way, emblematic of the "intrusion" Adamson indeed represents.

But William settles down contentedly enough; though he misses his work, he is satisfied to rely on his new father-in-law's vague promises to pay for a future expedition to South America. It is Matty Crompton, a dependent on the family (and keenly aware of her subordinate place in the rigid hierarchy of the household), who rouses William from his inertia and engages him in fieldwork again—this time, not in the jungles of the Amazon but on the lawns surrounding Bredely Hall.

Together with assorted Alabaster children and Miss Mead (another family dependent), they begin to observe and catalog the various species of ants and their interactions. Matty suggests to William that they write a popular natural history together. In true long-winded 18th- and 19th-century style, this history is titled *The Swarming City: A Natural History of a Woodland Society, its polity, its economy, its arms and defences, its origin, expansion and decline.* (In a way, Byatt has written a postmodern-day version of Bernard Mandeville's *Fable of the Bees* [1714], a political satire ostensibly based on bees' behavior in the hive.)

As their project progresses, Adamson finds himself drawn to Matty and her sharp wit and intelligence, especially since he feels so estranged from his wife, in spite of the rather active sex life they have together—that is, when she is not pregnant, which is often. We are told that William and Eugenia's children "bred true to stock" in that they are pale and white like all the Alabasters (*AI*, 82). The family name may symbolize both the family's fair complexion and their coldness of heart. Eugenia gives birth first to a set of twin girls, then to a boy, then to twin girls again. It is not for nothing that the family home is named "Bredley Hall."

Adamson is finally jolted out of his complacency—and his illusions—when he discovers Eugenia and Edgar in bed together. This discovery may well have been orchestrated by other members of the household—perhaps by Matty. The hints and clues he had ignored for so long crystallize into a realization that the sister and brother's relationship has gone on for years, before he ever came to Bredley Hall, and that Eugenia's children are not his. Moreover, up to this point, Adamson realizes that the entire house has been somehow complicit in covering up, if not condoning, the incestuous relationship. He books passage on a ship to South America and takes Matty with him to start a new life.

The Mating Dance

The novella opens with a scene at a ball given by the Alabasters at Bredley Hall. We see the scene through the eyes of Adamson, who in turn sees Victorian society through the filter of his recent experiences in the Amazon. He muses: "Nothing he did now seemed to happen without this double vision, of things seen and done otherwise, in another world" (*AI*, 7). We picture the contrasts between the human societies Adamson encountered in South America and the society before him as it swirls over the dance floor—and between the behavior of the many societies of insects that Adamson so meticulously observed and the behavior he sees now. The following passage illustrates his inability to take off this filter and his difficulty with entering into English society again:

> "Not much dancing in the jungle," stated Mr. Edgar Alabaster.
> "On the contrary. There is a great deal of dancing. There are religious festivals—Christian festivals—which occupy weeks together with communal dancing. And in the interior there are Indian dances where you must imitate the hops of woodpeckers, or the wriggle of armadillos, for hour after hour." William opened his mouth to say more, and closed it again. Didactic rushes of information were a great shortcoming in returning travellers. (3)

We are asked to make other, visual comparisons between insect society and human: when Byatt/the narrator describes the Alabaster daughters, Eugenia, Rowena, and Enid, as "all three pale-gold and ivory creatures," we are to imagine them as butterflies (*AI*, 4). Adamson thinks his tuxedo is rather similar in appearance—if not in function—to the black carapace of the beetle (8). In fact, in the context of the ball, it seems to the reader that tribal society, Victorian society, and insect society share in a similar impulse to incorporate some sort of mating dance into their respective rituals.

There is another detail in the opening scene worth noting: the image of Mrs. Gertrude Alabaster, who, in response to Adamson's "didactic rush," "moved some of her black silk rolls of flesh on the rosy satin of her sofa"—rather like a spider getting comfortable in the middle of her web (*AI*, 3). Mrs. Alabaster's portrait as a great swollen spider is added to throughout the novel; this and other such images often nudge aside the human in *Morpho Eugenia*. Indeed, Byatt intends for us to maintain the double vision that so plagues Adamson at the beginning of the novella and to continue to see the parallels (and the discontinuities) between insect society and our own.

The opening scene also furnishes us with the first clue to the relationship between Eugenia and Edgar, in the description of their dancing together: "[Edgar's] large feet moved quickly and intricately, tracing elegant skipping patterns beside Eugenia's pearly-grey slippers. They were not speaking to each other. Edgar looked over Eugenia's shoulder, faintly bored, surveying the ballroom. Eugenia's eyes were half closed" (*AI*, 5–6). We file this scene away, wondering why Byatt/the narrator wants us to pay attention to Eugenia and Edgar dancing, until we have been given enough hints to put together the truth.

Another way Byatt presses her parallels between insect society and human is in her description of the Alabaster household as a vast functioning organism in which everyone, from the reverend down to the kitchen maid, has a place, as in an anthill or a beehive. For example, the domestic population, including children, appears "like a cloud of young wasps from under the roof of the house" every morning to scrub and sweep (*AI*, 57). Adamson is an outsider to this organism but is gradually absorbed into the system. "Understanding daily life in Bredely Hall was not easy. William found himself at once detached anthropologist and fairytale prince trapped by invisible gates and silken bonds in an enchanted castle" (25). The silken bonds allude once more to the web that Mrs. Alabaster occupies.

Indeed, the household revolves around Lady Alabaster as she sits in her parlor: servants and children come and go, offering her sweets and dainties. "William felt that this immobile, vacantly amiable presence was a source of power in the household" (*AI*, 31). Later the image of the spider is exchanged for another when we read about the queen ant, who "is unable to fend for herself. [The ants] exist to lavish attention on her when she is in her prime, on her and her brood" (43). Adamson and his amateur naturalists observe that the queen of the wood ants, like other ant queens, is much larger than the other members of the

colony, and different in appearance: she is "swollen and glossy," with a
striped look, owing to "the bloating of her body by the eggs inside it,
which pushed apart her red-brown armour-plating" (45). We are
uncomfortably reminded of Mrs. Alabaster. At another point, Eugenia
is depicted in similar terms. William feels he "had no place inside the
female society of kitchen, nursery, or pretty parlor . . . his wife dozed
and sewed and her attendants fed and groomed her" (86). He is a
drone, relegated to the margins of this society devoted to the reproduc-
tion of the species.

However, lest we grow too complacent about our reading, Byatt
interrupts these extended parallels at one point. An unsettling leap from
observing certain species of slave-making ants to the American Civil
War leads William to assert, "Analogy is a slippery tool. . . . Men are not
ants" (*AI*, 116). Yet when he examines his own life, he finds that

> his visions of his own biological processes—his frenzied, delicious mat-
> ing, so abruptly terminated, his consumption of the regular meals pre-
> pared by the darkly quiet forces behind the green baize door . . . brought
> him insensibly to see himself as a kind of complex sum of his nerve-cells
> and instinctive desires, his automatic social responses of deference or
> required kindness or paternal affection. (116)

But there is more than this to William Adamson and to Matty Crompton, who have names and destinies to live up to. As "Adam's son,"
William carries on the task of naming the creatures of the earth that was
allotted to Adam in the Garden of Eden. And Matty's last name may
well be an allusion to John Crompton (a pseudonym), who wrote *Ways of
the Ant* (1954).

Byatt is a TV nature program devotee, and her abiding interest in
natural history is clearly evident; as her acknowledgments show, Byatt
read a number of natural histories in preparation for writing *Angels and
Insects*. But William and Matty's observations on insect life are based not
only on contemporary entomological research but on the journals and
books of those naturalists the Victorians read, and whose names are
sprinkled throughout *Morpho Eugenia*—Henry Walter Bates (1825–92),
for example, and Alfred Russel Wallace (1823–1913), Thomas Moffett
(1553–1604), and Georges Buffon (1707–88). Moreover, Byatt calls
upon such 19th-century thinkers as Robert Dale Owen (1801–77),
Andrew Ure (1778–1857), and William Whewell (1794–1866) to provide a picture of how the Victorians believed human society to be organized. Levenson suggests that a "natural history of the ant colonies is

what Adamson writes, but Byatt makes clear that a 'natural history' of humanity is what any strong novel must be" (42).

Intertexts and Insects

As in *Possession: A Romance*, other texts supplement the narrative, again demonstrating Byatt's ability to ventriloquize various Victorian voices. These include Alabaster's religious writings, in which he tries to defend God against Darwinism; Adamson's field journal; Matty's allegorical insect fable; and excerpts from the natural history Adamson and Matty write together.

Harald Alabaster is writing, he says, "the kind of impossible book everyone now is trying to write. A book which shall demonstrate—with some kind of intellectual respectability—that it is not impossible that the World is the work of a Creator, a Designer" (*AI*, 38). Adamson is drawn into friendly debate from time to time as an aid to his thinking. These passages, both conversational and written, are examples of Byatt's favorite kind of philosophical speculation and perhaps are presented more successfully here than in *The Virgin in the Garden* (38–42, 66–70, 84–85, 96–105).

Adamson has been keeping his journal for a long time, first recording his learned and harsh religiosity and rote excoriations against pride, and then, as he matured, expressing an ebullient Wordsworthian naturalism (*AI*, 10–11). He is given to close observation: "The world looked different, and larger, and brighter, not water-colour washes of green and blue and grey, but a dazzling pattern of fine lines and dizzying pinpoints, jet black, striped and spotted crimson, iridescent emerald, sloppy caramel, slime-silver" (11). In keeping a journal, Adamson, the narrator tells us, "had become addicted to the written form of his own language" (14). We can imagine that the meticulousness of close observation in nature is rather like the close reading one gives a text.

Adamson is a romantic. When he first meets Eugenia, he is reminded of a Ben Jonson poem in a collection he owns called *Choice Beauties of Our Elder Poets*. This poem, "Her Triumph," contains the lines: "O so white! O so soft! O so sweet is she!" But more significantly, Jonson asks, "Have you seen but a bright lily grow, /Before rude hands have touched it?" Of course, Adamson casts himself as the owner of the "rude hands," putting Eugenia on an impossible pedestal, and never imagining that Eugenia has been having sex with her own brother for years.

Matty's fable, "Things Are Not What They Seem," includes a secret garden, a magical feast, and a Lady/Circe character who has the remarkable name of Mistress Cottitoe Pan Demos (*AI*, 137–60). The tale is highly allegorical and serves as one of the clues to Eugenia's relationship with Edgar. We imagine William Adamson in the role of Seth, the adventurer whose friends are turned into swine, and Matty as Mistress Mouffet (of tuffet and spider fame), who helps him think his way out of danger. Matty says of the tale: "I am afraid I got rather *carried away*. . . . It was as though I was dragged along willy-nilly—by the *language*"—as was Byatt herself, no doubt (160). Adamson begins to realize that there is a hidden passion in Matty; indeed, things are not as they seem.

As Matty's fable suggests, there is an element of the fairy tale in *Morpho Eugenia*; Adamson even compares himself to a prince trapped in a castle (*AI*, 25). When Matty and Adamson first meet, she comments obliquely on his cataloging job: "It is odd, is it not, how *sorting* so often makes a part of the impossible tasks of the prince or princesses in the tales. There are a great many frustrated lovers who are set to sorting seeds" (50).

We can imagine the writer as a sorter of seeds as well: she takes on the impossible task of making meaning out of the many bits and pieces of her experience, her reading, and her imagination.

The Conjugial Angel

Byatt reprises a few of the themes that she first explored in *Possession: A Romance* and the short story "Precipice-Encurled" as she brings to life in *The Conjugial Angel* not only the Victorian world but real Victorians: Alfred, Lord Tennyson, his sister Emily Tennyson, and his closest friend, Arthur Hallam. These historical characters are surrounded by imaginary ones: a group of earnest Swedenborgians (whose musings often sound like a genteel version of New-Age-speak) who gather round a séance table.

Most of the action takes the form of interior monologues, reminiscences, and meditations—Browning's narratives cast as real speech. The tone of *The Conjugial Angel* is muted, infused with sadness and loss. The main reason for this tone is that the novella possesses such a strong intertext: Tennyson's *In Memoriam*. In this respect, the novella is reminiscent of Peter Ackroyd's *Chatterton* and Julian Barnes's *Flaubert's Parrot*, which are also fictions intertwined with the works of real-life authors. Literary criticism and fiction-making fuse in these texts to create a typically postmodern hybrid of genres.

Byatt's interest in 19th-century spiritualism and mediums is one of long standing, she says, and comes out of her work on Robert Brown-

ing's and Elizabeth Barrett Browning's "spiritualist affinities." Swedenborg and spiritualism had loomed large among Tennyson's interests as
well. She adds: "I also used to give a series of lectures on *The Blithedale
Romance*, *The Bostonians*, Henry James Senior, William James, and *The
Golden Bowl*. Jonathan Miller and I used to discuss Mesmer and Pod-
more and the history of psychic research."[3]

Byatt reviewed Alex Owen's study of 19th-century mediums, *The
Darkened Room: Women, Power, and Spiritualism in Late Victorian England*
(1989), after the publication of *Possession: A Romance*, in which spiritualism has a small part; however, Owen's book did have an impact on *The
Conjugial Angel*. In *The Darkened Room*, Owen traces the rise of spiritualism and the unique role women had in it. Many women were able to
make a name for themselves—and more important, a living—in this
popular movement. While many and more mainstream professions were
closed to them in 19th-century England, spiritualism gave women eco-
nomic security and a sense of self-worth. In a way, the characters Lilias
Papegay and Sophy Sheeky embody Owen's thesis. Byatt/the narrator
says that "Mrs. Papegay was an intelligent, questioning kind of woman,
the kind who, in an earlier age, would have been a theologically minded
nun, and in a later one would have had a university training in philosophy or psychology or medicine" (*AI*, 195). Lilias Papegay possesses an
intelligence constrained only by her particular historical and cultural circumstances. In spite of her lack of options as a woman who recently lost
her husband at sea, she manages to support herself and Sophy through
her communications with the other side.

We cannot discount the figure of artist-as-medium in *The Conjugial
Angel*, as Browning first suggests in his poem "Mr. Sludge" (see the discussion in chapter 5 of "Mr. Sludge" as an epigraph to *Possession: A
Romance*). As such, the artist is a liminal figure who moves easily from
one kind of consciousness to another, from the everyday to the
dionysian. Byatt is once again having her postmodern cake: she imagines "mediums" within the novella—Lilias Papegay, Sophy Sheeky,
Alfred Tennyson, Arthur Hallam—while she is the "medium" who creates the novella: "In conjuring up a time that engages her so intimately,
Byatt herself becomes a kind of medium—our conduit to a lost world"
(Hawthorne, 99).

Singular Characters, Intertextual Lives

Understanding the plot of *The Conjugial Angel* is best done through
understanding the characters. If *Morpho Eugenia* is a study of human

nature writ large, then *The Conjugial Angel* is a study of human nature particularized.

Lilias Papegay, "of imagination all compact" (*AI*, 187), is a professional medium and a mediating force in the very structuring and plotting of the story. It is Lilias who brings the other characters together; it is Lilias who, in a running interior monologue, provides commentary on them. We are told that "Mrs. Papegay liked stories. She spun them from bobbins of gossip or observation" (192). Her name, or rather, her husband's name, means "parrot" in Spanish. The name is suggestive: just as a parrot may repeat what it hears, so, theoretically, does a medium, relating "stories" from beyond. Lilias is a failed writer; in straitened means, she finds that her stories do not allow her to make a living: "stilted, saccharine rubbish," she calls them (193). As a consequence, she turns to spiritualism. The séances furnish some income and serve as a substitution for her stories: "She wanted *life*. . . . This traffic with the dead was the best way to know, to observe, to love the living . . . in their secret selves" (196–97).

Captain Arturo Papegay first appears at the end of *Morpho Eugenia*; he is captain of the *Calypso*, the ship that takes William and Matty to South America. In *The Conjugial Angel*, he is present through absence. Lilias mourns his loss. She misses his company and the security of having a husband, and she also misses the satisfying sexual life she shared with him. At the end of the tale, finally returned from the sea, he steps out from the dark into a pool of lamplight and "materializes" in his wife's arms. In counterpoint to the other dead, who hover piteously and greedily over the novella and its inhabitants, Arturo Papegay is, as he says, "Twice wrecked . . . once cast away," but makes a successful return from the otherworld (*AI*, 336). Life and flesh triumph over death. (We might read this subplot as a variation on the Orpheus-Eurydice myth.)

Mrs. Papegay's assistant and protegé is *Sophy Sheeky*. What Lilias must work hard at—out of a yearning of spirit combined with calculated legerdemain—Sophy comes to naturally, for she does indeed possess psychic powers. Byatt captures the essence of, and the difference between, the two in their responses to a sunset over the sea town of Margate: Lilias imagines it as "the Angel," for she "desires *so* to see the invisible inhabitants of the sky" (*AI*, 188). Sophy, on the other hand, "observes that it was indeed a spectacular sunset" (188).

The other characters, members of Lilias and Sophy's select circle, include *Mr. Hawke*, a deacon, the editor of the *Spiritual Leaflet*—and a sometime suitor of Lilias Papegay (who describes him as "a little round man, an *appley* man" [*AI*, 190]). "He was a theological connoisseur," the narrator tells us, who "had been a Ritualist, a Methodist, a Quaker, a Baptist, and now had come to rest, permanently or temporarily, in the Church of the New Jerusalem" (190–91). Thus, Hawke inclines toward spiritual excess, though he clearly has his own quite carnal interests at heart.

Mrs. Annie Hearnshaw is caught in a "rich violence of . . . grief" over the successive loss of five daughters in seven years—not a one lived to see her first birthday (*AI*, 192). She longs for assurance that her little girls are safely and happily in heaven and uses the séance as a sort of early warning pregnancy test: she hopes to have a child again, despite her sorrow. Lilias imagines to herself a possible conjugal scene between Mrs. Hearnshaw and her husband, "a little man, like a black wasp" (230). She is appalled by the prospect of Mr. Hearnshaw climbing atop his ample and passive wife and by the cruelty of his claim on the marital bed (231).

The retired *Captain Richard Jesse* and his wife Emily are also frequent visitors at Lilias's séances. Represented by the others as the hero in the stories of his past, he is shy, modest, and fearless. Captain Jesse is like Sophy in his balanced practicality; while others twitter on about the other side, Captain Jesse says of the spirit world that "we might just *not see it* because we haven't developed a way of thinking that allows us to see it" (*AI*, 209). It is a question, then, of epistemology, not romance.

Emily Tennyson Jesse, Tennyson's sister, was once engaged to Arthur Hallam, Tennyson's closest friend. He died suddenly at age 22 (in 1833) and was subsequently immortalized in Tennyson's *In Memoriam A.H.H.* (begun right after Hallam's death and published in 1850).

Byatt's Emily carries a burden of guilt and anger. "You are accompanied through life, Emily Jesse occasionally understood, not only by the beloved and accusing departed, but by your own ghost too, also accusing, also unappeased" (*AI*, 280). She loved Hallam once but never sustained the passion for him that her brother displayed his whole life: "Alfred's mourning had been long and steadfast. It had put hers, however fierce, however dark, however passionate, ultimately to shame" (255). It seems that her family and Hallam's expected Emily to spend her life mourning Arthur's death and were disappointed and resentful when she decided to marry nine years later. Emily thinks about how her brother "Alfred had been faithful, as she had not. He had given her away at her wedding, so quiet, so secret . . . and had gone on writing those chill, terrible little lyrics, accounts of loss, of defeat, of unappeasable longing" (269). Emily remembers this chill lyric in particular:

O what to her shall be the end?
And what to me remains of good?
To her, perpetual maidenhood,
And unto me no second friend. (270)

It is understandable why Emily "could never be wholly easy about the
way in which Alfred's mourning had overtaken her own. Had not only
overtaken it, she told herself in moments of bleak truthfulness, had
undone and denied it" (264).

The members of the group attempt to contact Arthur Hallam regularly, but with no success. Emily Jesse, however, has very ambivalent feelings about communing with her dead fiancé. The narrator comments:
"Like her brother Alfred, like the thousands of troubled faithful for
whom he partly spoke, she felt a pressing and threatened desire to know
the individual soul was immortal" (*AI*, 211). She does not necessarily,
however, want this fact confirmed by Arthur Hallam. Would he reproach
her for marrying Captain Jesse, as her brother so often seemed to do?

Arthur Hallam has his postmortem say in *The Conjugial Angel*. He
appears to Sophy when she is alone in her attic room. Sophy sometimes
recites poetry to herself to open her mind and spirit to the otherworld—
poems such as Dante Gabriel Rossetti's "Blessed Damozel." While
doing so, she often senses a presence, a young man, "anxious and elu-
sive" (*AI*, 283). This particular night, as she recites Tennyson's "Mari-
ana" and John Keats's "Eve of St. Agnes," she conjures up Arthur, who
materializes with the grave still clinging to him (289). Sophy realizes
that Emily and Alfred Tennyson's mourning "was painful to him. It
dragged him down, or back, or under" (289–90). The living must let go
of the dead. As Walter Kendrick says, Arthur "cannot wholly die
because the living love him too much."[4]

Sophy takes Hallam into her arms to comfort him, moldering corpse
and all. Kendrick says of this particular scene: "Objectively considered,
[it] is disgusting, yet Byatt's flawless prose renders it perversely beautiful" (136). Sophy is truly made a medium through her recitations of
poetry: as she continues to speak, she is able to see the living Tennyson
as he prepares for bed, and she communicates her vision to Arthur. He
observes that "poems are the ghosts of sensations" (*AI*, 291). Even when
dead, Hallam has the sensibility of the literary critic.

Arthur Hallam makes one final appearance in the novella, at the next
meeting of the group around the séance table. He wants Sophy to tell
Emily that he is waiting for her—"I triumph in conclusive bliss. We

shall be joined and made one Angel" (*AI*, 328). However, and to the surprise of her mild and generous husband Captain Jesse, Emily is finally able to renounce Hallam, saying: "It is hard to love the dead. It is hard to love the dead enough" (329).

Alfred Tennyson enters into *The Conjugial Angel* mediated, as we have seen, through Sophy's vision, but also more accurately through Byatt's imagination. We see him at the precise moment Sophy does, listening to "the buzzing of little flying fragments of language that hung around his head all the time in a cloud" (*AI*, 294). We eavesdrop on his thoughts as he meditates on Arthur and remembers bits of their conversations and their time together. Up to this point, we have been getting phrases and stanzas of *In Memoriam* through Sophy's recitations and rememberings of the poem; these bits are woven into Byatt's story so that Tennyson's poem comments on *The Conjugial Angel*, and vice versa (*In Memoriam* first quoted, 202ff; see especially 270–73 and 304–7). Once Tennyson appears, the poem is given back to him, and he carries the responsibility of interpretation.

Highly personal yet carefully crafted, *In Memoriam* has been judged over and again to be the greatest elegy written in English. It moves from Tennyson's private grief to a questioning of humanity's place in the universe. Byatt, asked to assess Tennyson for readers at the end of the 20th century, says that

> lately I have come to admire him most for a quality most critics in my time have denied him—his intelligence. Every time I reread *In Memoriam*, I am more struck by its variety and range—of images, of ideas, of moods, of subject-matter. It appears to move along so simply and lyrically and at random, and is in fact a wide-ranging meditation on life and death, in the shockingly particular and the movingly general. It can be savage and baffled and wise and limp within one lyric—quite deliberately, reflecting the way human beings are, in grief.[5]

Byatt particularly takes up the intense friendship between Hallam and Tennyson that lies at the heart of *In Memoriam*, and she suggests how complicated the bond between the two men must have been. If *In Memoriam* is any evidence, Tennyson never recovered from Hallam's death and never stopped loving him. Byatt's Tennyson thinks of *In Memoriam* as "Arthur's poems"—not only as dedicated to him, but as a poignant commentary on what Arthur could have been had he lived (*AI*, 304). The depth of Tennyson's feelings, *The Conjugial Angel* suggests, has more than a touch of the homoerotic.

One way we can approach this homoerotic possibility between Hallam and Tennyson is through Eve Kosofsky Sedgwick's *Between Men: English Literature and Male Homosocial Desire*.[6] According to Sedgwick, the "homosocial" covers a range of relations between men, from the most casual of social bonds to strong friendship to male-male sexual desire. By arguing that such feelings must exist on a continuum, Sedgwick is able to problematize male friendship and explore how such friendships (in a given literary text—her main focus) both shore up and subvert the patriarchal system and compulsory heterosexuality. She theorizes that, when men are unable to express their feelings—erotic or not—directly, they sometimes do so through the mediating body of a woman.

In our text, and according to this scheme, Emily would serve as the mediating body through which Hallam and Tennyson pursue their love for each other without public censure—and perhaps without private awareness, and therefore guilt, of the true nature of their friendship. Once Emily and Arthur married, Alfred would have had almost unlimited access to Arthur, all within the socially accepted bounds of family. Moreover, and perhaps more interestingly, Sophy serves as another female mediating body/spirit between the two after Hallam is dead. In Byatt's novella, Hallam and Tennyson's love defies death—just as the literary monument that is *In Memoriam* transcends the flesh.

In depicting Tennyson's roaming over the memories that he has honed into poetry, and drawing on what is known about the Tennyson circle, Byatt also suggests that the dangers of the homoerotic (that is, the dangers to a resolutely heterosexual society) were apparent to all concerned. Tennyson recalls the suspicions of Arthur's father, and his own equivocation about marriage; furthermore, he remembers how "it was true, it was true, he had called himself, over and over, Arthur's widow, but that was only in the spiritual sense" (*AI*, 299). Emily remembers a summer tableau in which the two men lounge on garden chairs: "There were the two fingers of their trailing, relaxed arms, touching earth, pointing quietly at each other" (263). It is a charged scene, and one that Tennyson revisits as well, evoking Michelangelo's God and Adam in close proximity (297). Ultimately, whatever Alfred Tennyson and Arthur Hallam may feel for one another, it is clear that the cost of male friendship is always high in a culture that enforces rigid gender roles and does not permit men to reveal their feelings.

In closing, we may well ask who the conjugial angel in the novella is intended to be. There are several answers. Mrs. Papegay's angel is

Arturo, who is able to come home to her. Arthur Hallam, the angel that others have burdened Emily Jesse with, finally dissipates into the ether of eased memory, where he belongs. She discovers that Captain Jesse is her true angel: "We have been through bad times in this world," she says to him, "and I consider it only decent to share our good times . . . in the next" (*AI*, 329). Tennyson's angel is indeed Arthur Hallam, who is diffused into poetry: Tennyson describes *In Memoriam* itself as "beautiful and alive and true, like an angel" (311).

Michael Levenson makes a thoughtful and insightful comment on the figure of Hallam in the reader's consciousness:

> The first instinctive mockery of those who see ghosts gives way to a second, less cozy recognition that we novel readers are always seeing ghosts. Whenever we lend solidity to the stories we follow, we are living proof of a visionary capacity almost always undervalued. Byatt's purpose is to push this fact into the foreground of consciousness, so that reading novels becomes the training of vision. (44)

In a way, the reader's conjugial angel is literature itself.

Chapter Seven

Conclusion: Byatt's "Ficticism"

Byatt's latest publication, a collection of fairy stories titled *The Djinn in the Nightingale's Eye*, returns her to the genre she explored as Christabel LaMotte in *Possession: A Romance*. (In fact, two of the stories are taken from *Possession*.) Throughout, the tone is knowing, like Matty Crompton's in *Morpho Eugenia* as she tells her insect fable, "Things Are Not What They Seem." Once again, Byatt's work is thoroughly informed by postmodern sensibilities; at the same time, she contests some of postmodernism's pessimism about the impossibility of storytelling, especially in "The Djinn in the Nightingale's Eye," the centerpiece tale (which is long enough to qualify as a novella).

In fact, one might argue that Byatt has been writing fairy stories all along. The reviewer Alex Clark says of *The Matisse Stories* that "the mundane, the trivial, people, houses, restaurants, are catalogued with a precision that at times appears pointless, as if it may be leading nowhere. Suddenly, the pattern reveals itself and the stories become fabular, universal."[1] It is this fabular, universal quality that informs all of Byatt's work. Quest and romance, loss and recovery, are Byatt's favorite themes. A motorcycle, a green leather glove, a butterfly, a basement apartment, a child's board game, along with all the other details one finds in her novels and short stories, possess a resonance that belies their status as simple material objects—and, on another level, as mere *names* for objects. Indeed, "things are not what they seem"; they are always more.

In addition, the range and ambition of Byatt's work, especially in the first two novels of the "Powerhouse Quartet" (*The Virgin in the Garden* and *Still Life*) and *Possession: A Romance*, ground her characters and the circumstances in which they find themselves in the realm of myth, where men and women live on a grander scale than that of the everyday and events have consequences beyond the confines of individual lives. In her essay on Van Gogh, Byatt quotes one of his letters: "I want to paint men and women with that something of the eternal which the halo used to symbolise" (*PM*, 274). The same impulse drives Byatt's own painterly method of characterization. Moreover, trained in the school of F. R.

Leavis but living in the world of a postmodern aesthetic, Byatt is uniquely situated to explore that *ubi sunt* note that Van Gogh sounds in his phrase "used to symbolise." Byatt reveals a nostalgia for a past (however illusory) in which novels had the power to teach and delight. At the same time, she is fully conscious of her own nostalgic desires yet holds fast to them as the only sane and ethical thing to do.

When Marilyn Butler argues that Byatt abandoned the pretense "that life is what she is imitating in favour of full-hearted literariness" in *Possession: A Romance*, she confirms my point: as steeped in the tradition of the realistic novel as Byatt is, her real interests are more clearly rooted in what she calls the "life of the mind."[2]

Butler also says that Byatt as a novelist "tended to sound like a critic; as an academic critic, like someone wondering if she wouldn't prefer to be a novelist" (22). It is true that critics have sometimes faulted Byatt for what they see as her didactic or lecturing style; however, it is a style that is not aridly academic, but alive and curious and philosophical. Byatt, as Butler says, "has not stayed with fiction precisely . . . but developed a form (ficticism?) which has allowed her to be herself" (22). The term "ficticism" is a wonderfully apt term to describe the hybrid of fiction and criticism that Byatt practices, a hybrid that is leaving a considerable mark on the development of the contemporary British and American novel.

At the beginning of this study, I quoted Byatt's description of herself as a greedy reader; I would like to end with another of Byatt's comments on this theme. Writing about George Eliot and her reworkings of "certain stories" in her novels, Byatt says that Eliot demonstrates "not parody, not pastiche, not plagiarism—but a good and greedy reading, by a great writer." A "good and greedy reading" is not new, she says. Neither is it negative; it simply "looks different in modern novels— because of the pressure of the past, because of the accumulation of literary criticism and because of the weight of anxiety as it shows itself in modern form" (*PM*, 149). This difference is one more way to understand the postmodern turn in Byatt's writing; it points to a self-consciousness that pervades her work and the work of many other contemporary novelists.[3]

Byatt's graduate training in Renaissance literature, her deep and abiding interest in the Romantic and Victorian poets, her reading of Iris Murdoch, philosophy, and a range of texts beyond belles lettres, all add

up to a rich mix that she stirs into her fiction. "Antonia is like a passionate butterfly collector showing you her collection," says the novelist
Nicholas Shakespeare (Stout, 14). Her "collection" is not her novels
alone, but the vast intertextual web that includes everything that she
reads and thinks and sees.

Notes and References

Preface

1. Caryn McTighe Musil, "A. S. Byatt," in *Dictionary of Literary Biography* 14, no. 1 (Detroit, MI: Gale Publishing, 1983): 200; hereafter cited in text.

2. C. Hugh Holman and William Harmon, *A Handbook to Literature*, 6th ed. (New York: Macmillan, 1992), 391.

3. Quoted in Olga Kenyon, "A. S. Byatt: Fusing Tradition with Twentieth-Century Experimentation," in Kenyon, *Women Novelists Today: A Survey of English Writing in the Seventies and Eighties* (New York: St. Martin's Press, 1988), 56; hereafter cited in the text.

4. Byatt repeatedly draws upon Van Gogh as a subject and as a metaphor in her nonfiction and fiction (see *Still Life* and "Sugar" especially). Her latest work, *The Matisse Stories*, depends upon a knowledge of Matisse's work. Another artist worth mentioning at this point is Samuel Palmer. He is not as well known as Van Gogh and Matisse, but it is his work on the cover of the Vintage edition of *Shadow of a Sun*. "Cornfield by Moonlight" (1830), with a man leaning on a staff walking across a harvested field, *is* Henry Severell on one of his visionary walks. Indeed, the light of the moon is, paradoxically, a "shadow of the sun," a reflection of a greater light—a theme that permeates the novel (see chap. 2).

5. A. S. Byatt, *The Matisse Stories* (New York: Random House, 1993), 52; hereafter cited in the text as *MS*.

6. Ihab Hassan, *The Postmodern Turn: Essays in Postmodern Theory and Culture* (Columbus: Ohio State University Press, 1987), 93–94.

7. Richard Pearce, "What Joyce after Pynchon?" in *James Joyce: The Centennial Symposium*, ed. Morris Beja, Phillip Herring, Maurice Harmon, and David Noons (Urbana and Chicago: University of Illinois Press, 1986), 43.

8. Terry Eagleton, *Literary Theory: An Introduction* (Minneapolis: University of Minnesota Press, 1983), 37. My discussion of postmodernism in the preface, and of Leavis and New Criticism in Chapter One owes much to Eagleton and to Chris Baldick, *The Concise Oxford Dictionary of Literary Terms* (New York, 1990).

9. A. S. Byatt, "Accurate Letters: Ford Madox Ford" in *Passions of the Mind: Selected Writings* (London: Chatto and Windus, 1991), 93–108; hereafter cited in the text as *PM*.

10. A. S. Byatt, "Sugar/Sucre," in *Passions of the Mind: Selected Writings* (London: Chatto and Windus, 1991), 15–16.

Chapter One

1.   Caryn McTighe, "A. S. Byatt," in *Contemporary Authors*, new revised series, vol. 33 (Detroit, MI: Gale Publishing, 1991), 71; hereafter cited in text.

2.   A. S. Byatt, introduction to *The Shadow of the Sun* (1964; London: Vintage, 1991), ix; hereafter cited in the text as *SS*.

3.   Quoted in Mira Stout, "What Possessed A. S. Byatt?" *New York Times Magazine* (26 May 1991): 15; hereafter cited in the text.

4.   A. S. Byatt, *The Game* (Harmondsworth, Eng.: Penguin, 1983), 71; hereafter cited in the text as *G*.

5.   A. S. Byatt, *Morpho Eugenia*, in *Angels and Insects* (New York: Random House, 1992), 11; hereafter cited in the text as *AI*.

6.   Quoted in Kate Kellaway, "Self-portrait of a Victorian Polymath" [interview with A. S. Byatt], *London Observer* (16 September 1990): 45; hereafter cited in the text.

7.   T. S. Eliot, "A Dialogue on Dramatic Poetry," in *Selected Essays 1917–1932*, 3rd. rev. ed. (London: Faber & Faber, 1951), 44.

8.   In interviews, Byatt is often asked about her relationship with Drabble. She says, "I've suffered quite badly from being thought of Margaret Drabble's sister, and therefore expected to write books like hers, which I don't do." Quoted in interview with Jennifer Foote, "Out from Sister's Shadow," *Newsweek* (21 January 1991): 61; hereafter cited in the text.

9.   Iris Murdoch, "Against Dryness: A Polemical Sketch," in *Encounter* 88 (January 1961): 16–20; hereafter cited in the text.

10.   A. S. Byatt, *Iris Murdoch*, ed. Ian Scott-Kilvert (London: Longman/British Council, 1976), 5; hereafter cited in the text. Byatt goes on to say: "It seems to me that the relationship between the kind of conceptual thought and the kind of fiction [Murdoch] writes has been unusually fruitful, very much part of the same search for ways of understanding, both historically and practically, the way human beings work" (6).

11.   See also Byatt's remarks on Proust in her essay "'Sugar'/'Sucre,'" in *PM*, 14–18.

12.   A 1991 poem, "A Dog, a Horse, a Rat," which begins with a quotation from King Lear ("Why should a dog, a horse, a rat, have life, and thou no breath at all?"), is a lament that also takes up this theme: mourning and loss touched with anger and disbelief.

13.   Quoted in Justine Picardie, "Women's Writing Is More than That" [interview with A. S. Byatt], *London Sunday Times* (5 April 1987): 55.

14.   Quoted in Francis Spufford, "The Mantle of Jehovah" [review of *Sugar and Other Stories*], *London Review of Books* (25 June 1987): 23; hereafter cited in the text.

15.   *Possession: A Romance* (New York: Random House, 1990), 14; hereafter cited in the text as *PR*. The pagination of the first American paperback (Random House/Vintage, 1991) follows this edition.

16. Quoted in Suzanne Cassidy, "How to Write a Novel: Start with Two Couples," *New York Times Book Review* (21 October 1990): 11.

17. A. S. Byatt, "People in Paper Houses: Attitudes to 'Realism' and 'Experiment' in English Post-war Fiction," in *PM*, 148.

18. A. S. Byatt, letter to the author, 9 August 1994. For Byatt's other remarks on her composing process, including reproductions of a few of her notebook pages for *Still Life*, see Musil, 200, 202–3.

19. From "Notes on Writing a Novel" (1945), quoted in Byatt's preface to Elizabeth Bowen, *The House in Paris* (Harmondsworth, Eng.: Penguin, 1976), 221.

20. A. S. Byatt, "Reading, Writing, Studying: Some Questions about Changing Conditions for Writers and Readers," in *Critical Quarterly* 35, no. 4 (1993): 3; hereafter cited in the text as "Reading."

21. She says that she is "afraid of solipsism, and find[s] it frustrating as a reading experience" (*PM*, xv).

Chapter Two

1. Byatt adds, "I wanted my harvest, both in my life and in my work" (*SS*, xvi).

2. "A Farewell to False Love," in *The Poems of Sir Walter Raleigh*, ed. Agnes Latham (Boston: Houghton Mifflin, 1929), 28.

3. R. D. Spector, *Book Week* (30 August 1964): 14.

4. At one point, the narrator peers over Margaret's shoulder while she puts on makeup in front of a mirror: "She was on show, to herself as well as to others, and liked to watch her face in strange mirrors and play to herself the fine lady that all little girls pretend to be and all women still imagine to be somewhere either in the future or some other surroundings, whose possibility is suddenly glimpsed again in . . . cloakrooms in restaurants, mirrors across the table at public dinners" (*SS*, 29).

5. *The Poems of Charlotte Brontë*, ed. Tom Winnifrith (Oxford: Shakespeare's Head/Blackwell, 1984), 184, lines 1–4.

6. Byatt says the title points to "gamesmanship, homo ludens [laughing man], above all the shared literary game of the Brontës" (Kenyon, 57).

7. We may even be tempted to pair *The Game* with Drabble's novel about sisters, *The Summer Birdcage*. In addition, Drabble takes up the subject of the 19th-century woman writer—as does Byatt in *Possession: A Romance*—in *The Waterfall* (1969). See Joanne V. Creighton, "Sisterly Symbiosis: Margaret Drabble's *The Waterfall* and A. S. Byatt's *The Game*," in *Mosaic* 20, no. 1 (Winter 1987): 15–29, for a fine discussion of the relationship between Drabble and Byatt, both textually and psychologically.

8. When Cassandra realizes that Julia has somehow gotten to know Simon, the narrator tells us that "she was prematurely resigned, indeed, almost indecently anxious, never to see him again. Her abdication was grim and complete" (G, 93).

9. See Creighton, "Sisterly Symbiosis," for a more sympathetic treatment of Julia than what is presented here.

10. Jane Campbell, "The Hunger of the Imagination in A. S. Byatt's *The Game*," in *Critique* 29, no. 3 (Spring 1988): 147.

11. Giuliana Giobbi, "Sisters Beware of Sisters: Sisterhood as a Literary Motif in Jane Austen, A. S. Byatt, and I. Bossi Fedrigotti," in *Journal of European Studies* 87 (September 1992): 242.

12. See Giobbi for a similar conclusion (246).

13. See Giobbi for a discussion of the Cassandra/Cassandra Austen parallel (244).

14. Giobbi uses this poem as the epigraph to her "Sisters Beware of Sisters."

15. Murdoch adds, "Literature must always represent a battle between real people and images" (20).

Chapter Three

1. A. S. Byatt, *Sugar and Other Stories* (Harmondsworth, Eng.: Penguin, 1988), 1; hereafter cited in the text as *SOS*.

2. Quoted in Sarah Booth Conroy, "The Magic Brew of A. S. Byatt" [interview], *Washington Post Book World* (29 November 1991): D9; hereafter cited in the text.

3. One narrative comment is especially telling in this respect. Conversation at the conference is apparently dominated by "serious oriental questions about Kristeva's views on Desire and Harold Bloom's map of misreading" (*SOS*, 112). This suggests, however inadvertently, that the "oriental" audience is able to ask questions only, that it cannot provide answers or incisive readings of Julia Kristeva and Harold Bloom. This is, the story seems to imply, partially the result of a repressive government, partially a cultural characteristic. Byatt's choice of literary theorists is interesting, for Kristeva's "views on Desire" focus on desire toward the other; in this case, the East as constructed as different or other. (The East as other and the problems that arise from such an equation dominate a good deal of postcolonial scholarship and critique.) And Bloom argues that certain poets must somehow get around or conquer their predecessors in order to avoid the paralyzing effects of what he calls the anxiety of influence. In other words, in order to find a voice, one must silence, or as he says, misread, those who have come before. Postcolonial discourse is especially concerned with critiquing, modifying, and/or replacing the aesthetic influences and conventions of Western European literature and art.

4. Griselda Pollock, *Vision and Difference: Femininity, Feminism, and Histories of Art* (New York and London: Routledge, 1988), 144.

5. Byatt's use of the word *dryness* recalls Iris Murdoch's critical essay "Against Dryness" (see chap. 1).

6. A. S. Byatt, interview with Juliet A. Dusinberre, in *Women Writers Talking*, ed. Janet Todd (New York and London: Holmes & Meier, 1983), 188; hereafter cited in the text.

7.   Sue Kelman, "The Painted Words of A. S. Byatt," *The Toronto Star* (19 March 1994): K12.

8.   "Still Life/Nature Morte," in *PM*, 7.

9.   Cixous's essay has been widely anthologized. First published in 1975, it can be found in *New French Feminisms: An Anthology*, ed. Elaine Marks and Isabelle de Courtivron, trans. Keith Cohen and Paula Cohen (New York: Schocken Books, 1981), 245–64.

Chapter Four

1.   A. S. Byatt, *Still Life* (New York: Scribner's, 1985), 131; hereafter cited in the text as *SL*.

2.   A. S. Byatt, letter to the author, 9 August 1994.

3.   A. S. Byatt, *The Virgin in the Garden* (New York: Random House/Vintage International, 1992), 241; hereafter cited in the text as *VG*.

4.   For a comparison of Marcus to Wordsworth and his particular poetic genius, particularly with respect to the idea of "spreading" (which occurs in *The Prelude*), see Olga Kenyon, who says that Marcus "has elements of the child-seer, but [is] bereft of religious blessing. . . . In a world without religion Marcus can only undergo, without illumination" (69–70).

5.   Byatt had a similar accident with a refrigerator, but her husband was there to unplug it (Conroy, 9).

6.   Byatt also says of *The Virgin in the Garden* that "it is—among other things—a response to T. S. Eliot's ideas of the history of poetic language and the nature of the poetic image" (*PM*, 3).

Chapter Five

1.   A. S. Byatt, telephone interview with Mervyn Rothstein, quoted in "Best Seller Breaks Rule on Crossing the Atlantic," *New York Times*, 31 January 1991, C17.

2.   Marc Blanchard, "'N stuff . . .': Practices, Equipment, Protocols in Twentieth-Century Ethnography," in *Yale French Studies* 81 (1992): 112.

3.   Michael Dirda, "The Incandescent Spell of *Possession*," *Washington Post*, 17 October 1990, C7.

4.   Byatt benefits from a linguistic fact in this identification of Ash/Ask: in modern English, we have a number of words called doublets; i.e., words that are derived from the same source but follow different paths. Both English and Norse are Indo-European languages and therefore share in the same word stock. Norse *skin* is cognate with English *shin*, Norse *skirt* with English *shirt*. While the words have different meanings in English now, when English and Norse speakers were first in contact, they would have meant the same thing—but the Norse speakers would have said "[sk]," and the English speakers "[š]." Therefore, one might imagine Ash/Ask in one, or both, of two delightfully contradictory ways: Ash/Ask is the same, or Ash/Ask has somehow bifurcated—split into two.

5. The full lines from Tennyson's poem are "faultily faultless, icily regular, splendidly null/Dead perfection, no more."

6. Byatt dedicates *Possession* to her friend Isobel Armstrong, a Victorian scholar and author of a recent and definitive article titled "Tennyson's 'The Lady of Shalott': Victorian Mythography and the Politics of Narcissism," in *The Sun Is God: Painting, Literature, and Mythology in the Nineteenth Century*, ed. J. B. Bullen (Oxford: Clarendon, 1989), 49–107.

7. Judith Thurman, "A Reader's Companion," *New Yorker* (19 November 1990): 155.

8. A. S. Byatt, letter to the author, 9 August 1994.

9. Ibid. See *PR*, 43, for the "spider poem." Byatt adds, "I typed [the poems] out in tears because the alarmed publishers were already talking about making me cut the poetry to almost nothing."

10. James Joyce, *Finnegan's Wake* (1939; New York: Viking Press, 1972), 3.

Chapter Six

1. Michael Levenson, "The Religion of Fiction," *New Republic* (2 August 1993): 41; hereafter cited in the text.

2. Mary Hawthorne, "Winged Victoriana," *New Yorker* (21 June 1993): 99; hereafter cited in the text.

3. A. S. Byatt, letter to the author, 9 August 1994.

4. Walter Kendrick, [omnibus review], *Yale Review* 81, no. 4 (October 1993): 135–37: 136; hereafter cited in the text.

5. A. S. Byatt, "One Hundred Years After," *Times Literary Supplement* (2 October 1992): 8.

6. Eve Kosofsky Sedgwick, *Between Men: English Literature and Male Homosocial Desire* (New York: Columbia University Press, 1985).

Chapter Seven

1. Alex Clark, "Artists and Models," *Times Literary Supplement* (14 January 1994): 21.

2. Marilyn Butler, "The Moth and the Medium," *Times Literary Supplement* (16 October 1992): 22; hereafter cited in the text.

3. This self-consciousness is also acknowledged in her preface to Elizabeth Bowen's *The House in Paris*. Byatt writes of the "disproportionate influence, both good and bad, on my ideas about the writing of novels and, indeed, about the nature of fiction," and she criticizes the "wrought, formalised 'modern' novel, a novel which play[s] tricks with time and point of view" (*PM*, 217).

Selected Bibliography

The bibliography of Byatt's fiction and nonfiction is comprehensive, listed by most recent first within each section unless otherwise specified. The bibliography of reviews of Byatt's work is selective and includes reviews published in most major newspapers, magazines, and literary journals in the United States and many in Great Britain. Authors and titles of reviews are supplied when specified and are in alphabetical order; all entries are as complete as the author has been able to determine.

PRIMARY WORKS

Fiction

Novels

Babel Tower. London: Chatto and Windus, 1996. New York: Random House, 1996. As historians squabble over revisionist history of the 1960s in the U.S., Byatt has been busy writing a sprawling, Trollopian novel set in the context of 1960s England: all the decade's icons are here, from the Beatles and Tolkien to pastiches of 1960s "types." We meet many of the characters introduced in the first two novels of Byatt's "Powerhouse Quartet (*The Virgin in the Garden* and *Still Life*); Frederica Potter, however, emerges as the principal character. As in her previous novels, characters in *Babel Tower* wrestle with ordinary concerns infused with an extraordinary urgency.

    The novel takes a Dickensian turn and interest in the intersection of law and society, and we are given two law cases: Frederica's divorce and custody battle, and the prosecution of an "obscene" book, *Babbletower*, by Jude Mason, a brilliant visionary who lives on the margins of English society, literally and figuratively. As in *Possession: A Romance*, Byatt weaves in texts written in different voices and styles, the most disturbing of which are bits from Mason's novel, a dystopic vision of communal living gone wrong.

Angels and Insects: Two Novellas [*Morpho Eugenia* and *The Conjugial Angel*]. London: Chatto and Windus, 1992. New York: Random House, 1992. Paperback, New York: Random House, 1994. *Morpho Eugenia* weaves together an unlikely love story with learned disquisitions on botany and entomology. Parallels between insect society and human abound. William Adamson returns to England after his Amazonian travels and falls in love with Eugenia Alabaster, daughter of Sir Harald, whose natural history collection William is cataloging. But Eugenia and her half-brother Edgar have an incestuous secret that prevents William from completely entering into his marriage and his wife's family. Once married, William begins to write a study of the ant colonies on the estate with Matty Crompton, a family dependent. The novella ends with William and Matty together, on their way to South America.

The Conjugial Angel is a foray into 19th-century English spiritualism. Emily Tennyson Jesse, once affianced to Arthur Hallam—the best friend of Alfred, Lord Tennyson—is now married to the jovial Captain Jesse. She belongs to a circle of amateur spiritualists led by Lilias Papegay and her companion, Sophy Sheekhy. Lilias's husband Arturo is the captain of the ship that takes William Adamson and Matty Crompton to America; he returns from being lost at sea at the end of the novella. Tennyson makes a cameo appearance.

Possession: A Romance. London: Chatto and Windus, 1990. New York: Random House, 1990. Paperback, New York: Random House/Vintage International, 1991. The novel begins with Roland Mitchell, a research assistant at the British Library, busily hunting down material for a scholarly edition of the works of Randolph Henry Ash, a Victorian poet Byatt has invented. (Ash is a cross between Browning and Tennyson, with bits of Wordsworth, Arnold, Morris, Ruskin, and Carlyle thrown in.) During his research, Roland finds evidence that Ash had an affair with the equally imaginary poet Christabel LaMotte (a composite of Emily Dickinson, Christina Rossetti, and Elizabeth Barrett Browning, with a dash of George Eliot and the Brontës).

Mitchell meets the feminist scholar Maud Bailey, whose specialty is LaMotte's poetry. Mitchell and Bailey make a series of discoveries about Ash and LaMotte that lead them on a number of adventures, adventures that parallel the lives of the poets they are pursuing.

Byatt shuttles her readers back and forth from the present-time narrative to the journal of Ash's wife Ellen; the journal of Blanche Glover, Christabel's lesbian companion; the standard biography of Ash; a number of scholarly articles about the poets; and finally, and most crucially, the letters and poetry of Randolph Ash and Christabel LaMotte. Every one of these texts-within-the-text is a stunningly convincing invention of Byatt herself.

Still Life. London: Chatto and Windus, 1985. New York: Scribner's, 1985. Paperback, New York: Macmillan/Collier Books, 1991. The second in Byatt's "Powerhouse Quartet," Still Life continues to chronicle the lives of the Potter family. Stephanie, Frederica, and Marcus take on the responsibilities of adulthood. The novel follows Frederica into Cambridge University. Stephanie copes with a new baby, her husband Daniel, Daniel's querulous and self-centered mother, and Marcus; in a freak domestic accident, Stephanie is electrocuted. Alexander Wedderburn, now a successful author and television personality, finds that his life continues to intersect with Frederica's and with that of the other members of the Potter family.

The Virgin in the Garden. London: Chatto and Windus, 1978. New York: Alfred A. Knopf, 1979. Paperback, New York: Random House/Vintage International, 1992. In this first installment of Byatt's "Powerhouse Quartet," the Potter family—Stephanie, Frederica, Marcus, and their mother Winifred—is ruled over by the despotic, opinionated Bill. The Potters' inability, due to Bill's influence, to connect with each other emotionally will dominate their lives and their relationships with others. Frederica begins the personal and intellectual journey away from her family and into academic life; her sister Stephanie becomes involved with Daniel Orton, a stolid but socially passionate curate; and Marcus, painfully shy and clearly in the early stages of schizophrenia, has a breakdown after becoming involved with the highly unstable Lucas Simmonds. Set in 1953, the coronation year of Elizabeth II, the novel includes excerpts from the allegorical verse-drama (invented by Byatt) of the character Alexander Wedderburn, a work based on the life of Elizabeth I.

The Game. London: Chatto and Windus, 1967. New York: Scribner's, 1968. Paperback, Harmondsworth, Eng.: Penguin, 1983. Sisters Cassandra and Julia Corbett have long been rivals and continue to have an antagonistic relationship well into adulthood. Julia, married to a Quaker social worker, is a successful novelist of domestic life, and Cassandra is a bookish and introverted Oxford professor. As children, they played "the game"—a medieval mixture of battles and courtly romance. Both once in love with Simon Moffitt, they rekindle old hostilities when he returns to England from the Amazon. Julia writes a novel about Cassandra's affair with Simon. Cassandra kills herself; it is unclear in the end, however, which sister has won "the game."

The Shadow of a Sun. London: Chatto and Windus, 1964. New York: Harcourt, Brace, & World, 1964. Paperback, with Byatt's original title restored, *The Shadow of the Sun*, London: Vintage, 1991. Seventeen years old and terribly shy, troubled Anna Severell must contend with the fame of her aloof novelist father, Henry Severell, and her no-nonsense mother. She meets the literary critic Oliver Canning and his hyperfeminine wife Margaret. Oliver tutors Anna for a summer and convinces her to go on to Cambridge. There, she has an affair with Oliver, which leads to the breakup of his marriage and her pregnancy.

Short-Story Collections

Many of the stories in these collections are annotated separately under "Short Stories."

The Djinn in the Nightingale's Eye: Five Fairy Stories. London: Chatto and Windus, 1994. Includes "The Glass Coffin" (from *Possession: A Romance*),

"Gode's Story" (from *Possession: A Romance*), "The Story of the Eldest
  Princess," "Dragon's Breath," and "The Djinn in the Nightingale's Eye."
The Matisse Stories. London: Chatto and Windus, 1993. New York: Random
  House, 1993. Includes "Medusa's Ankles," "Art Work," and "The Chi-
  nese Lobster."
Sugar and Other Stories. London: Chatto and Windus, 1987. New York: Scrib-
  ner's, 1987. Paperback, Harmondsworth, Eng.: Penguin Books, 1988.
  Includes "Racine and the Tablecloth," "Rose-Coloured Teacups," "The
  July Ghost," "The Next Room," "The Dried Witch," "Loss of Face," "On
  the Day E. M. Forster Died," "The Changeling," "In the Air," "Precipice-
  Encurled," and "Sugar."

Short Stories

"A Lamia in the Cévennes." *Atlantic* (July 1995): 56–66. An English painter
  finds an unexpected guest in the pool at his house in the Cévennes: a
  lamia. However, too absorbed in his painting and in the exacting responsibilities of color, especially as manifested in the changing water in the
  pool, he resists her seductive promises of power and wealth. He wants to
  paint her, to capture her in pure color; she wants him to kiss her so that
  she will turn into a beautiful woman. In the end, they both achieve their
  desire, but not in the way the reader expects.
"The Djinn in the Nightingale's Eye." *Paris Bulletin* 36 (Winter 1994): 14–113.
  Also in *The Djinn in the Nightingale's Eye: Five Fairy Stories*, 93–277. A literary scholar goes to Turkey to present a paper and finds the proverbial
  genie in a bottle. She chooses her wishes wisely, and she and the Djinn
  become lovers. This simple plot is subordinate to Byatt's wide-ranging
  reflections on the human condition, contextualized within a learned literary tradition.
"Dragon's Breath." *Index on Censorship* (September 1994): 89–95. Also in *The
  Djinn in the Nightingale's Eye: Five Fairy Stories*, 73–92. Written for a
  radio program in aid of Sarajevo (storytellers from around the world read
  their stories simultaneously), this tale of a village and its destruction by a
  dragon mirrors the horror of the destruction in Eastern Europe in the
  1990s.
"The Story of the Eldest Princess." In *The Year's Best Fantasy and Horror: Sixth
  Annual Collection*, edited by Ellen Datlow and Terri Windling, 83–94.
  (New York: St. Martin's, 1993) Also in *The Djinn in the Nightingale's Eye:
  Five Fairy Stories*, 41–72. Also in *The Outspoken Princess and the Gentle
  Knight: A Treasury of Modern Fairy Tales*, edited by Jack Zipes, 182–207.
  (New York: Bantam, 1994) Instead of accepting her fate as a princess
  who sets out on a quest and fails, Byatt's princess abandons her quest and
  seeks her own adventure—and thus achieves her own desire.
"The Chinese Lobster." *New Yorker* (26 October 1992): 90–100. In *The Matisse
  Stories*, 91–134. A meditation on Matisse's place as a painter in a world

vastly different from the one in which he painted. While Matisse's greatness is never in doubt, how one might appreciate or appropriate his paintings is, as a story of sexual harassment reveals.

"Art Work." *New Yorker* (20 May 1991): 36–51. In *The Matisse Stories*, 29–90. The artistic Dennison family is paralyzed by their rigid conception of art while their Guyanese housekeeper, Sheba Brown, creates her more exuberant art in secret. When her work is finally made public, it shows her to be a recycler par excellence of the domestic detritus of women's lives—and of Western culture itself.

"Medusa's Ankles." *Women's Journal* (September 1990). Also in *Best English Short Stories III*, edited by Giles Gordon and David Hughes, 73–86. New York: Norton, 1991. Also in *The Matisse Stories*, 3–28. A middle-aged woman makes a routine visit to her hairdresser that becomes anything but routine. In a rage over her mishandled hair and her fading youth, she throws bottles, breaks mirrors—and achieves an uneasy catharsis.

"The Dried Witch." First published in *Sugar and Other Stories*, 85–111. An aging widow living in an imaginary and primitive village is frustrated by notions of propriety. She studies to become a witch, which ultimately brings about her destruction.

"In the Air." First published in *Sugar and Other Stories*, 161–84. A woman who walks her dog every day in the nearby park is haunted by fears of assault that become too real.

"Loss of Face." First published in *Sugar and Other Stories*, 112–28. Celia Quest lectures on Milton in an unnamed Asian country and confronts the ways in which cultures collide: how can people from different backgrounds come to a common understanding of a literary text? She misrecognizes an Asian colleague; they both "lose face" as a result.

"The Next Room." First published in *Sugar and Other Stories*, 57–84. Also in *The Literary Ghost: Great Contemporary Ghost Stories*, edited with an introduction by Larry Dark, 257–81. New York: Atlantic Monthly Press, 1991. A woman must live with her parents' legacy of meanness as she hears them constantly bickering through the wall after their death.

"Precipice-Encurled." *Encounter* 68 (April 1987): 21–31. Also in *Sugar and Other Stories*, 185–214. Robert Browning meditates on his life and art and is part of a story of unrealized love.

"Racine and the Tablecloth." First published in *Sugar and Other Stories*, 1–32. About the difficulties and loneliness of being smarter than most; young Emily Bray struggles with the unkind and insensitive headmistress of her boarding school.

"Rose-Coloured Teacups." First broadcast on BBC Radio 3. First published in *Sugar and Other Stories*, 33–38. Now married with a daughter of her own, a woman imagines her mother at a tea party in her rooms at college, and regrets choices made.

"Sugar." *New Yorker* (12 January 1987): 28ff. Also in *Sugar and Other Stories*, 215–48. The fulcrum of the story is a hospital room in Amsterdam in which the narrator's father lies dying of cancer. From this locale—spatial and mental—the narrator ranges backward in time and place as she reflects upon her family.

"The Changeling." *Encounter* 64 (May 1985): 3–7. Also in *Sugar and Other Stories*, 147–60. Josephine Piper writes about fear, partially as a way to keep her own at bay. When Henry Smee, a troubled, withdrawn young man, comes to stay with her, his resemblance to a character she created—based on herself—begins to stir up her long-repressed feelings.

"On the Day E. M. Forster Died." *Encounter* 61 (December 1983): 3–9. Also in *Sugar and Other Stories*, 129–46. Mrs. Smith, a writer who has just outlined her next book and is filled with excitement and triumph at the prospect of beginning, crosses paths with an acquaintance whose story of paranoia and conspiracy foreshadows her own death.

"The July Ghost." First broadcast on BBC Radio 3. In *Sugar and Other Stories*, 39–56. Also in *Firebird*, edited by T. J. Binding (London: Allen Lane/Penguin, 1982); *Black Water 2: More Tales of the Fantastic*, edited by Alberto Manguel, 164–79 (New York: Clarkson/Potter, 1990); and *Modern Ghost Stories by Eminent Women Writers*, edited by Richard Dalby, introduction by Sara Maitland, 1–14 (New York: Carroll and Graf, 1992). A Jamesian story of a woman too sensible to see her own son's ghost; she can only be solaced secondhand, through her lodger, who is able to see the ghost.

Poems

"Dead Boys." *Times Literary Supplement* (2 December 1994): 27. A poem of grief, loss, and memory.

"Working with Clichés." *The Timeless and the Temporal: Writings in Honour of John Chalker by Friends and Colleagues*. Edited by Elizabeth Maslen. London: Queen Mary and Westfield College, Department of English, 1993. 1–3. A poem "about" the figure of Proteus, with an epigraph by Toni Morrison on the function of clichés.

"A Dog, a Horse, a Rat." *Times Literary Supplement* (24 May 1991): 22. A lament—mourning and loss touched with anger and disbelief.

Nonfiction

Book-Length Scholarly Studies

Imagining Characters: Six Conversations about Women Writers, by A. S. Byatt and Ignes Sôdrè. Edited by Rebecca Swift. London: Chatto and Windus, 1995. Forthcoming in the United States (Vintage Press).

Iris Murdoch. Edited by Ian Scott-Kilvert. London: Longman/British Council, 1976. A short study of Murdoch's work published in the *Writers and Their Work* series, a British equivalent of the Twayne Authors Series. Based on *Degrees of Freedom: The Novels of Iris Murdoch.*

Wordsworth and Coleridge in Their Time. London: Thomas Nelson, 1970. New York: Crane Russak, 1973. London: Hogarth Press, 1989 (under the title *Unruly Times*). A collection of six essays exploring aspects of English life in the Romantic period, and Wordsworth and Coleridge in context.

Degrees of Freedom: The Novels of Iris Murdoch. London: Chatto and Windus, 1965. New York: Barnes and Noble, 1965. Examines the relationship between Murdoch's novels and her use of symbolism, fantasy, and myth. More important, it is a study of how Murdoch works out her particular philosophy in her fictional world.

Edited Works

Eliot, George. *The Mill on the Floss.* Edited and with an introduction (7–41) and notes by A. S. Byatt. London and New York: Penguin 1979; reprint, 1985.

————. *Selected Essays, Poems, and Other Writings.* Co-edited with Nicholas Warren, introduction (ix–xxxvii) by A. S. Byatt. London and New York: Penguin, 1990.

Collected Essays

Passions of the Mind: Selected Writings. London: Chatto and Windus, 1991. New York: Random House/Turtle Bay Books, 1992. A collection of scholarly essays, reviews, and prefaces written between 1969 and 1991 on Victorian writers and twentieth-century British and American authors, along with a meditation on Van Gogh's art. The collection includes the following in alphabetical order:

"Accurate Letters: Ford Madox Ford" (93–108). A combination of two previously published essays: a preface for *The Fifth Queen* and a review of the Bodley Head reissue of Ford's complete novels. Byatt says of Ford that he is "a writer much admired by writers, but comparatively neglected by scholars and the general public." The reprinting of his novels is a good time "to re-establish his reputation, not only as an author of three or four novels better than most English novels, but as a thinker about the nature of writing, and the craft of fiction." Byatt then focuses on Ford's historical novel *The Fifth Queen*: "concerned with sex, love, marriage, fear, lying, death and confusion" and the balance of power as a real force in our lives. She also discusses *The Good Soldier* and *Parade's End.*

"Barbara Pym" (241–44). A combination of two previously published reviews. Pym's *An Academic Question* is an "attempt to write something 'sharp' and 'swinging' about a provincial university." Its mixture of first- and third-person makes it "thin and unappealing." Byatt then leads into a general consideration of Pym's prominence, especially as a subject of scholarly study.

"Charles Rycroft: *The Innocence of Dreams*" (261–64). First published as "Downstream" [review of *The Innocence of Dreams* by Charles Rycroft], *New Statesman* (4 May 1979): 646. Byatt is fascinated by this psychoanalyst's reading of dreams and their connections to the imagination.

"Coleridge: An Archangel a Little Damaged" (253–60). First published as a review of *Coleridge: The Damaged Archangel* by Norman Fruman, *New Statesman* (May 1979). A review of Fruman's biography of Coleridge turns into a sympathetic assessment of Coleridge's work.

"Elizabeth Bowen: *The House in Paris*" (217–24). First published as an introduction to *The House in Paris* by Elizabeth Bowen (Harmondsworth, Eng.: Penguin, 1976). This introduction to Bowen's novel is particularly interesting as a case-study of one reader's reading: Byatt describes her experiences reading *The House in Paris*, first as a child, then as a teenager, and finally as an adult. Byatt connects the personal with larger ideas: What is "modern"? What distinguishes the "modernist" novel from the Victorian novel? What can be said about the supremacy of plot? "*The House in Paris* is a novel about sex, time and the discovery of identity."

"George Eliot: A Celebration" (63–67). First published as a special pamphlet issued with Penguin's boxed set of the novels of George Eliot (Harmondsworth, Eng.: Penguin, 1990). Byatt appreciates in Eliot's essays the "deployment of a clear mind and a lot of information" and describes her essays as "sharp, trenchant, satirical, in places wildly funny." Byatt says that "she offers us scope, not certainties."

"George Eliot's Essays" (68–90). First published (in slightly different form) as introduction to *George Eliot: Selected Essays, Poems, and Other Writings* (Harmondsworth, Eng.: Penguin, 1990). Eliot was "sceptical, unconventional," in her major essays, written between 1854 and 1857 for the *Westminister Review*. Byatt connects these essays on "religious scientific ideas" to Eliot's fiction. An analysis of these essays, Byatt argues, is a way to understand Eliot's developing ideas about fiction.

"An Honourable Escape: Georgette Heyer" (233–40). First published in *Nova* (June 1969). "Escape literature can exist to satisfy people's fantasies— sexual and social—at the expense of probability and 'truth.'" But Byatt defends another kind of escape literature, exemplified by Heyer, that can "provide simple release from strain." She praises Heyer's richness of detail in the depiction of everyday life.

"Monique Wittig: *The Lesbian Body*" (245–50). First published as "Give Me the Moonlight, Give Me the Girl" [review of *The Lesbian Body* by Monique Wittig, translated by David Le Vay], *New Review* 2 (July 1974): 65–67. More of a summary than an actual critical engagement; Byatt is disturbed by the violence that she perceives in Wittig's prose.

"'The Omnipotence of Thought': Frazer, Freud, and Post-Modernist Fiction" (110–46). First published in *Sir James Frazer and the Literary Imagination: Essays in Affinity and Influence* edited by Robert Fraser, 270–308 (London: Handmills, Basingstoke, Hampshire, 1990; New York: St. Martin's Press, 1991). Discussion of a group of novels that uses *The Golden Bough* as a "means of patterning their narratives"—books by Iris Murdoch, Anthony Powell, Saul Bellow, Muriel Spark, and Norman Mailer. Part of Byatt's discussion of Iris Murdoch is drawn from her 1965 book *Degrees of Freedom*.

"People in Paper Houses: Attitudes to 'Realism' and 'Experiment' in English Post-war Fiction" (147–68). First published in *The Contemporary English Novel*, edited by Malcolm Bradbury and David Palmer, 19–41 (London: E. Arnold; New York: Holmes & Meier, 1979). Byatt puzzles out the problem of realism in the novel, especially in the 19th-century novel and the contemporary "modernist" novel. The focus is on Doris Lessing, Iris Murdoch, C. P. Snow, and Angus Wilson, but Byatt touches on Kingsley Amis, John Fowles, James Joyce, J. R. R. Tolkien, and others. Byatt locates the conflict over realism in a prescriptivism that originated in literary criticism. She develops the idea of the "greedy reader," turned writer, who is so steeped in reading that she or he cannot help but create an allusive, multilayered text.

"Robert Browning: Fact, Fiction, Lies, Incarnation and Art" (21–62). Expanded version of introduction to *Robert Browning: Dramatic Monologues* (London: Holio Society, 1991). Browning is one of the greatest English poets, but underappreciated because he was so prolific and hard to categorize. He is also a great love poet, partially because he "sees women as complex human beings." His chief greatness is found in, of course, the dramatic monologues. Byatt discusses as a central text Browning's "Karshish," then moves on to psychology, the New Testament, George Eliot, and others. Browning "is a poet who writes men and women, all separately incarnate, all separately aware in their necessarily and splendidly limited ways, of infinite passion and the pain of finite hearts that yearn."

"A Sense of Religion: Enright's God" (177–94). First published in *Life by Other Means: Essays on D. J. Enright*, edited by Jacqueline Simms, 58–74 (Oxford: Oxford University Press, 1990). "Anger with God for being absent is one form of the Enright religion." An extended consideration of Enright's poetry and the place and function of religion. Byatt shares with Enright a sense of the "deadness of modern religion" and a questioning of humanity's relation, or nonrelation, to God.

"Still Life/Nature Morte" (3–13, with English translations of French quotations). First published in *Cross References: Modern French Theory and the Practice of Criticism*, edited by David Kelley and Isabelle Llasera, 95–102 (London: Society for French Studies, 1986). What starts out as a discussion of *The Virgin in the Garden* and *Still Life* ends up as a wide-ranging meditation on metaphor and its real presence in Byatt's intellectual and everyday life.

"Sugar/Sucre" (14–18). First published, under the title "Sugar," as an introduction to Byatt's short story of the same title for French translation (Paris: Editions des Cendres, 1989). A discursive history of the genesis of "Sugar," a history that, typically for Byatt, becomes caught up in larger questions—here, the power of art as mimetic or not.

"Sylvia Plath: *Letters Home*" (225–29). First published as a review of *Letters Home*, edited by Aurelia Schober Plath, *New Statesman* (23 April 1976): 541. Byatt is interested in Aurelia Plath and her relationship with her daughter Sylvia; she sees Plath's life as a "process of mask-making and character-building."

"The *TLS* Poetry Competition" (174–76). First published as "Writing and Feeling" *Times Literary Supplement* (18 November 1988): 1278. After reading 960 poems for a literary competition, Byatt is struck by how bad the poetry is—and also by how moved she is by it. How can people write poetry if they cannot engage with language and wordplay? There is something to be said for experimenting with verse forms, versus free verse.

"Toni Morrison: *Beloved*" (230–32). First published as a review of *Beloved* by Toni Morrison, *The Guardian* (October 1987). Byatt describes the novel as "huge, generous, and gripping."

"Van Gogh, Death and Summer" (265–302). Expanded version of "After the Myth, the Real," review of *The Van Gogh File: A Journey of Discovery* by Ken Wilkie; *Young Vincent: The Story of Van Gogh's Years in England* by Martin Bailey; *The Love of Many Things: A Life of Vincent Van Gogh* by David Sweetman; and *Vincent Van Gogh: Christianity versus Nature* by Tsukasa Kodera, *Times Literary Supplement* (29 June–5 July 1990): 683–84. What begins as a review of four books on Van Gogh ends up to be an excursus on Van Gogh and his connection to and embodiment of larger questions having to do with art, passion, and religion. Van Gogh's "obsessive trajectory" of a life has become a "hagiography," Byatt argues.

"Willa Cather" (197–216). A combination of previously published introductions to Cather's novels: *O Pioneers!* (afterword) (London: Virago Modern Classics, 1983); *Death Comes for the Archbishop* (London: Virago, 1981); and *The Professor's House* (London: Virago, 1980). Byatt writes admiringly of Cather's sentences, "which are so unexpected, so apparently fluent and artless, so precise and muscular and exact." Byatt focuses on Cather's understanding of the discovery of her own voice, her glorying in the "undifferentiated earth," in *O Pioneers! The Professor's House* contains "bright air, human muddle, stuffy rooms and the truth of the last hard bed." Byatt admires the pace of *Death Comes to the Archbishop*, Cather's defining of "America."

"William Golding: *Darkness Visible*" (169–73). First published in *Literary Review* (May 1979). Byatt admires the "fine frenzy in the way [that Golding and other like writers] force visions of light and blackness on the reader." *Darkness Visible* is a story of a boy—a visionary, both real and false—that is "spattered with clues and signs, clotted with symbols and puns."

Uncollected Essays (alphabetical)

"A. S. Byatt on *Angels and Insects*." *Architectural Digest* (April 1996): 100–08. Byatt discusses the romance of the English country house and Arbury Hall (Warwickshire) where *Angels and Insects* was filmed, along with the genesis of her novel.

"The Dislikable Gwendolen: A Conversation on George Eliot between A. S. Byatt and Ignes Sôdrè." *Times Literary Supplement* (6 October 1995): 19–20. Byatt and Sôdrè discuss Gwendolyn Harleth in Eliot's *Daniel Deronda*. Excerpt from *Imagining Characters*.

"The Hue and Cry of Love." *New York Times*, 11 February 1991, A15, A19. A tongue-in-cheek deconstructive reading of "Roses are red / violets are blue."

"Insights Ad Nauseam." *London Times Literary Supplement* (14 November 1986): 43–63.

"Love's Rhyme Knows Reason." *New York Times*, 14 February 1992, A19, A29. Byatt brings contemporary literary criticism to bear on the rhyme, "Roses are red / violets are blue," continued from "The Hue and Cry of Love," published in the *Times* the year before.

"The Lyric Structure of Tennyson's *Maud*." In *The Major Victorian Poets Reconsidered*, edited by Isobel Armstrong, 69–93 (London: Routledge & Kegan Paul, 1969; Lincoln: University of Nebraska Press).

"The Obsession with Amorphous Mankind." *Encounter* (September 1966): 63–69.

"Reading, Writing, Studying: Some Questions about Changing Conditions for Writers and Readers." *Critical Quarterly* 35, no. 4 (Winter 1993): 3–7. "I am passionately in favour of keeping alive the teaching of as much of the past that can be managed." Asks difficult questions about the makeup of the literary canon.

"Real People and Images." *Encounter* (September 1966): 71–78.

"Wallace Stevens: Criticism, Repetition, and Creativity." *Journal of American Studies* 12, no. 3 (1978): 369–75. Review of several books on Stevens.

Prefaces and Introductions (alphabetical)

Bowen, Elizabeth. *The House in Paris* [introduction]. See "Collected Essays."
Browning, Robert. *Dramatic Monologues* [introduction]. See "Collected Essays."

Byatt, A. S. Introduction to "Sugar". See "Collected Essays."

Cather, Willa. *Death Comes for the Archbishop* [introduction]. See "Collected Essays."

———. *A Lost Lady* [introduction]. London: Virago, 1980.

———. *My Antonia* [introduction]. London: Virago, 1980. Byatt's focus is on Cather's "wisdom of intuition" (Byatt quotes Cather, who quotes Bergson). Never mind the flaws of plot and climax; for Byatt, what is important in Cather is the "faithful imitation of the process of memory" and "mastery of pace."

———. *O Pioneers!* [afterword]. See "Collected Essays."

———. *The Professor's House* [introduction]. See "Collected Essays."

———. *Song of the Lark* [introduction]. London: Virago, 1989.

Eliot, George. Special pamphlet issued with Penguin's boxed set of her novels. See "Collected Essays."

Eliot, George. *Selected Essays, Poems, and Other Writings* [introduction]. See "Collected Essays."

Ford, Ford Madox, *The Fifth Queen* [preface]. See "Collected Essays."

Jane Austen's The History of England. Chapel Hill, NC: Algonquin Books, 1993. v–viii. Appreciative assessment, especially of the "gleeful self-mockery" of Austen's tone.

Paley, Grace. *Enormous Changes at the Last Minute* [introduction]. London: Virago, 1979.

———. *The Little Disturbances of Man* [introduction]. London: Virago, 1980.

Reviews (alphabetical)

"George and His Dragons." George Steiner, *No Passion Spent: Essays 1978–1996*, and *The Deep of the Sea and Other Fiction. The Observer* (7 January 1996): 14. Steiner is "many-tongued, proudly intellectual, and deeply serious." Byatt calls one Steiner short story, "The Portage to San Cristobal of A. H.," a masterpiece, and speaks admiringly of his wide-ranging essays about "the fate of the book, the nature of reading, the changes in transmission of ideas in our time."

"By Love Possessed." Gabriel Garcia Márquez, *Of Love and Other Demons. New York Times Book Review* (28 May 1995):8. Appreciative review.

Ackroyd, Peter. *Dickens* ["Dickens and His Demons"]. *Washington Post Book World* (10 February 1991): 1–2. Byatt is disappointed with Ackroyd's treatment: he "tried to write a novelist's biography, not a scholar's."

Bernier, Oliver. *Louis XIV: A Royal Life* ["All the King's Mirrors"]. *New York Times Book Review* (31 January 1988): 9. Admiring review of Bernier's biography.

Bloom, Allan. *Love and Friendship* ["The Passions of the Soul"]. *Washington Post Book World* (25 July 1993): 1, 14. Admiring review of Allan Bloom's last book. Byatt agrees that it is "most delightful, most useful—to talk about [books] in their own terms," that is, within their cultural and historical context.

Bradbury, Malcolm, ed. *The Penguin Book of Modern British Short Stories* ["Beginning in Craft and Ending in Mystery"]. *Times Literary Supplement* (13 May 1988): 527. Appreciative review of collections of short stories, noting that the English do not excel in the genre compared to writers of other countries. See "Pritchett," "Maugham, Saki, et al.," "Davin," "Dorsch," and "Sharrock."

Davin, Dan, ed. *The Killing Bottle* ["Beginning in Craft and Ending in Mystery"]. See "Bradbury."

Dorsch, T. S., ed. *Charmed Lives* ["Beginning in Craft and Ending in Mystery"]. See "Bradbury."

Ford, Ford Madox. Bodley Head reissue of the novels of Ford Madox Ford. *Times Literary Supplement* (January 1981). See "Collected Essays."

Fruman, Norman. *Coleridge: the Damaged Archangel. New Statesman* (May 1979). See "Collected Essays."

Fuller, John, ed. *The Chatto Book of Love Poetry* ["Amatory Acts"]. *Times Literary Supplement* (31 August–6 September 1990): 913. Byatt describes Fuller's collection as a "post-romantic anthology." See "McCardie."

Jacobus, Mary. *Romanticism, Writing, and Sexual Difference: Essays on the Prelude* ["The Trouble with the Interesting Reader"]. *Times Literary Supplement* (3 March 1990): 310. Review of collections of essays by the feminist theorist and Wordsworth scholar Mary Jacobus. Byatt is unhappy with "modish" readings of Wordsworth and what she describes as Jacobus's habit of "argument by wordplay." "Such glib opportunism can now excuse itself on the grounds that accuracy is impossible and uninteresting, that what a reader finds in a text is there to be found."

Lessing, Doris. *In Pursuit of the English* ["Savage Londoners," review of production by Lyric Studio, Hammersmith, London]. *Times Literary Supplement* (9 February 1990): 146. Lessing's world is well adapted to the stage.

Long, Robert Emmett. *Barbara Pym* ["Marginal Lives"]. *Times Literary Supplement* (8 August 1986): 862. See "Collected Essays" and "Pym."

Maugham, W. Somerset, Saki, et al. *The Dragon's Head* ["Beginning in Craft and Ending in Mystery"]. See "Bradbury."

McCardie, Amanda, ed. *The Collins Book of Love Poems* ["Amatory Acts"]. *Times Literary Supplement* (31 August–6 September 1990): 913. Byatt describes McCardie's collection as "quieter English statements of absolute love." See "Fuller."

Morrison, Toni. *Beloved. The Guardian* (October 1987). See "Collected Essays."

Murdoch, Iris. *The Black Prince* ["A Word Play"]. A play performed at the Aldwych Theatre, London. *Times Literary Supplement* (5 May 1989): 487. Review of the play based on the novel of the same name: a "mixture of murder story, bourgeois farce, and moral and aesthetic exploration."

Nash, Walter. *Designs in Prose* ["Working by Intuition"]. *Times Literary Supplement* (23 January 1981): 86. Review of a prose-style book.

Owen, Alex. *The Darkened Room: Women, Power, and Spiritualism in Late Victorian England* ["Chosen Vessels of a Fraud"]. *Times Literary Supplement* (2–8 June 1989): 605. Byatt has her own literary interests in 19th-century spiritualism, as *Possession* and *The Conjugial Angel* attest. Here, she reviews a feminist social history "centred on the 'power' [women] wielded in their darkened rooms." "Scholarly, intellectually scrupulous, moving and exciting."

Plath, Aurelia Schober. *Letters Home*. See "Collected Essays."

Pritchett, V. S. *The Mythmaker* ["The Greedy Reader"]. *New Statesman* (18 May 1979): 724. "Genius is a spiritual greed," writes Pritchett, and Byatt concurs: "Good writers are greedy readers." Byatt appreciates how Pritchett has resolutely avoided jargon in his wide-ranging meditation on European, Russian, and South American novelists.

———, ed. *The Oxford Book of Short Stories* ["Beginning in Craft and Ending in Mystery"]. See "Bradbury."

Pym, Barbara. *An Academic Question* ["Marginal Lives"]. *Times Literary Supplement* (8 August 1986): 862. See "Collected Essays" and "Long."

Redgrove, Peter. *The Black Goddess and the Sixth Sense, The Moon Disposes*, and *In the Hall of the Saurians* ["Control of the Life-Sources"]. *Times Literary Supplement* (12–18 August 1988): 890. Three books by the poet Peter Redgrove: the first a discourse on perception and the limits of human perception, the next two collections of poems.

Rycroft, Charles. *The Innocence of Dreams* ["Downstream"]. See "Collected Essays."

Scott, Paul. *Staying On* ["The Raj and the Great Tradition," review of the novel-turned-play broadcast on Granada TV]. *Times Literary Supplement* (9 January 1981): 33.

Sharrock, Roger, ed. *The Green Man Revisited* ["Beginning in Craft and Ending in Mystery"]. See "Bradbury."

Snow, C. P. *The Realists* ["Worldly Wise"]. *New Statesman* (3 November 1978): 586–87.

Sontag, Susan. *The Volcano Lover* ["Love and Death in the Shadow of Vesuvius"]. *Washington Post Book World* (16 August 1992): 1–2. Sontag's book is marked by "detached, energetic curiosity"; it is "slippery, intelligent, provocative and gripping."

[Van Gogh, Vincent]. "After the Myth, the Real." See "Collected Essays."

Wedgewood, C. V. *History and Hope: Essays on History and the English Civil War*. *New York Times Book Review* (8 October 1989): 25. Brief review of Wedgewood's essays on the English Civil War and the writing of history.

Wittig, Monique. *The Lesbian Body*, trans. David Le Vay ["Give Me the Moonlight, Give Me the Girl"]. See "Collected Essays."

Contributed Works (alphabetical)

Coren, Giles. "What Are You Reading at Christmas?" *London Times* (24 December 1993): 12. Coren polls a number of writers on their Christmas reading. Byatt is reading *Bees of the World* by Christopher O'Toole (the observer on the film set for *Angels and Insects*), short stories, Kipling, and Graham Greene.

"Envy: The Sin of Families and Nations." *New York Times Book Review* (18 July 1993): 3, 25–26. Also in *Deadly Sins*, Thomas Pynchon, et al. New York: Morrow, 1993. Seven authors were asked to write about one of the Seven Deadly Sins. The first letter of Byatt's essay on envy, a T, is a drawing of two intertwined snakes. "Envy grows in the deprived and in those who consider themselves deprived," argues Byatt. The opposite of envy is justice. To develop her argument, Byatt invokes children crying, "It isn't *fair*," and refers to the Bible, to allegory (*The Faerie Queene* and Ovid), and to Shakespeare, Freud, Balzac, Dickens, Browning, Coleridge—in short, she calls upon her own vast literary memory in a way that can only arouse envy in the reader.

Millet, Eva. "How Much Do the British Know about European Fiction?" *The Guardian* [European edition] (18 November 1993): 9. Millet asks this question of a number of British writers. Byatt: "The best European novels I have read over the last three years are: *The Marriage of Cadmus and Harmony, Corazon tan blanco . . . Obabakoab* and *Rituals*. All four share the quality of showing why human beings need to tell stories to each other on a very profound level."

"Obscenity and the Arts—A Symposium." *Times Literary Supplement* (12–18 February 1988): 159. The *TLS* asked writers and others to talk about definitions of obscenity. Byatt says that those with whom she is most irritated are those she would consider to be on the same side as herself: the artistic and intellectual left. She urges that the left take a good look at what it is they are defending, and she criticizes the excesses of popular culture and the obsession we have with the shock of the new.

"One Hundred Years After." *Times Literary Supplement* (2 October 1992): 8. Twelve writers reflect on Tennyson's achievement and influence. Byatt says, "I grew up on 'The Lady of Shalott' and the 'Morte d'Arthur.'. . . As a result I find the rhythms, and the images, and even whole sentences, haunting everything I write, irrelevantly and relevantly."

SECONDARY WORKS

Scholarly Studies

Ashworth, Ann. "Fairy Tales in A. S. Byatt's *Possession*." *Journal of Evolutionary Psychology* 15.1–2 (March 1994): 93–94.

Belsey, Catherine. *Desire: Love Stories in Western Culture.* Oxford, Eng. and Cambridge, Mass.: Blackwell, 1994. Belsey discusses *Possession: A Romance* in chapter 4, "Postmodern Love"; she calls it "a profoundly Lacanian novel."

Campbell, Jane. "'The Somehow May Be Thishow': Fact, Fiction, and Intertextuality in Antonia Byatt's 'Precipice-Encurled.'" *Studies in Short Fiction* 28 (Spring 1991): 115–23.

———. "The Hunger of the Imagination in A. S. Byatt's *The Game.*" *Critique: Studies in Contemporary Fiction* 29, no. 3 (Spring 1988): 147–62. The title is taken from Byatt's quotation from Johnson in *The Game.*

Cosslett, Tess. "Childbirth from the Woman's Point of View in British Women's Fiction: Enid Bagnold's *The Squire* and A. S. Byatt's *Still Life.*" *Tulsa Studies in Women's Literature* 8 (1989): 263–86.

Creighton, Joanne V. "Sisterly Symbiosis: Margaret Drabble's *The Waterfall* and A. S. Byatt's *The Game.*" *Mosaic: A Journal for the Interdisciplinary Study of Literature* 20, no. 1 (Winter 1987): 15–29.

Dusinberre, Juliet. "Forms of Reality in A. S. Byatt's *The Virgin in the Garden.*" *Critique: Studies in Contemporary Fiction* 24, no. 1 (Fall 1982): 55–62.

Fountain, J. Stephen. "Ashes to Ashes: Kristeva's *Jouissance*, Altizer's *Apocalypse*, Byatt's *Possession* and 'The Dream of the Rood.'" *Literature and Theology: An Interdisciplinary Journal of Theory and Criticism* 8.2 (June 1994): 193–208. A postmodern excursion through a number of very different texts, including Byatt's *Possession*, in order to meditate on fragments and endings.

Gilbert, Sandra M., and Susan Gubar. *No Man's Land: The Place of the Woman Writer in the Twentieth Century.* Vol. 3, *Letters from the Front.* New Haven, Conn., and London: Yale University Press, 1994. Despite their differences, Toni Morrison's *Beloved* and *Possession: A Romance* share in a project to construct "integrated maternal figures in order to examine the ways the procreative/creative mother can potentially give birth to newfound lands and legends." Enumerates a number of different kinds of possession in the novel, with a focus on "aesthetic inheritance."

Giobbi, Giuliana. "'Know the Past: Know Thyself': Literary Pursuits and the Quest for Identity in A. S. Byatt's *Possession* and in F. Duranti's *Effeti Personali*," *Journal of European Studies* 24, no. 1 (March 1994): 41–55. Focuses on the elements of the detective novel as a way to interpret how the main characters in both novels work out their identity on a literary quest.

———. "Sisters Beware of Sisters: Sisterhood as a Literary Motif in Jane Austen, A. S. Byatt, and I. Bossi Fedrigotti." *Journal of European Studies* 87 (September 1992): 241–58. Interprets *The Game* as a rewriting of Jane Austen's *Sense and Sensibility.*

Gitzen, Julian. "Byatt's Self-Mirroring Art." *Critique* 36.2 (Winter 1995): 83–96. Byatt often employs a mirror-image framework in her works.

While her characters face real-life situations, they are made larger than life through their association with myth and legend.

Hotho-Jackson, Sabine. "Literary History in Literature: An Aspect of the Contemporary Novel." *Moderna-Sprak* 86, no. 2 (1992): 113–19.

Janik, Del Ivan. "No End of History: Evidence from the Contemporary English Novel." *Twentieth Century Literature* 41.2 (1995): 160–90. Novelists who integrate history into their fiction affirm its importance in a postmodern world.

Kenyon, Olga. "A. S. Byatt: Fusing Tradition with Twentieth-Century Experimentation." In *Women Novelists Today: A Survey of English Writing in the Seventies and Eighties*, 51–84. New York: St. Martin's Press, 1988. The most comprehensive study of Byatt, her work, and her work in context through 1988. Includes remarks by Byatt on her work and on literature in general made in various talks on the radio and in person.

Shinn, Thelma J. "'What's in a Word?': Possessing A. S. Byatt's Meronymic Novel." *Papers on Language and Literature* 31.2 (Spring 1995): 164–84. A "meronym" denotes a condition which contains opposites which exist side by side. In *Possession*, this is exemplified by the binaries of past/present, romance/realism, prose/poetry.

Westlake, Michael. "The Hard Idea of Truth." *PN Review* 15:4 (1989): 33–7. A brilliant meditation on *Still Life* and Byatt's intentions: "The novel's hesitations, contradictions and formal equivocations, its failure to secure the stability it seeks, can be read productively as an index of our larger cultural crisis."

Yelin, Louise. "Cultural Cartography: A. S. Byatt's *Possession* and the Politics of Victorian Studies." *Victorian Newsletter* 81 (Spring 1992): 38–41.

REVIEWS

Novels

Angels and Insects: Two Novellas (Morpho Eugenia and The Conjugial Angel)

Adams, Phoebe-Lou. *Atlantic* (May 1993): 130. "Romantic fantasies, written with grace."

Barber, David. "Fine Grain of an Age." *Boston Globe*, 2 May 1993, B45:5. "[T]he truest measure of Byatt's passion for the 19th century may well be her conviction that thick narrative and craftly storytelling can survive."

Butler, Marilyn. "The Moth and the Medium." *Times Literary Supplement* (16 October 1992): 22. Calls Byatt a "Victorianist Iris Murdoch"; she has abandoned the pretense "that life is what she is imitating in favour of full-hearted literariness." In blending fiction and criticism, perhaps Byatt has invented a new genre: "ficticism."

Coates, Joseph. "A. S. Byatt's Victoriana." *Chicago Tribune*, 13 June 1993, 14, 3.1. A study in the "passionate eroticism and humane values of the Victorian era."

"Forecasts." *Publishers Weekly* (1 March 1993): 40.

Gale, Iain. "Drawing on the Text." *The Independent* (20 June 1992): arts sect., 32.

Gribbin, John. *New Scientist* (20 March 1993): 41–42. "The hothouse feeling [of *Morpho Eugenia*] makes for a compelling read, and the scientific flavour is nicely integrated into the story."

Hawthorne, Mary. "Winged Victoriana." *New Yorker* (21 June 1993): 98–100. Harald Alabaster's "compulsive hoarding of nature . . . suggests Byatt's appropriation of the past." "In conjuring up a time that engages her so intimately, Byatt herself becomes a kind of medium—our conduit to a lost world."

Heaney, Patricia. *Library Journal* (15 April 1993): 125.

Hughes, Kathryn. "Repossession." *New Statesman* (6 November 1992): 49–50. *Angels and Insects* is more erotic than *Possession: A Romance*.

The Independent (24 October 1993): reviews sect., 48.

Kemp, Peter. "A Near Myth." *London Sunday Times*, 18 October 1992, 13. "The Victorian age is proving a marvellous museum for A. S. Byatt's imagination." Prefers *Morpho Eugenia* to *The Conjugial Angel*.

Kendrick, Walter. *Yale Review* 81, no. 4 (October 1993): 135–37. "We can at last stop blaming the Victorians and start reading them on their own terms. Byatt has done so with sympathy and affection."

Lesser, Wendy. "Séance and Sensibility." *New York Times Book Review* (27 June 1993): 14. This "heavily laden vehicle motors along smoothly if slowly." Lesser thinks there is too much quotation and detail.

Levenson, Michael. "The Religion of Fiction." *New Republic* (2 August 1993): 41–44. Byatt's "postmodernity finds its ground in something else, something older, namely an earnest attempt to get back before the moderns and revive a Victorian project that has never been allowed to come to completion. What you have in Byatt is an odd-sounding but perfectly intelligible creature, the postmodern Victorian." More than a book review; an incisive study of Byatt's work in the context of her oeuvre.

Lewis, Tess. *Belles Lettres: A Review of Books by Women* 9, no. 1 (Fall 1993): 28.

Lezard, Nicholas. "Conscience and Kylie." *The Guardian* (2 November 1993): 11.

Masello, Robert. "A Cloud of Butterflies." *Los Angeles Times*, 13 June 1993, BR 8:1. "Sly, but serious, fun . . . a pair of tales that neatly bracket, and illuminate, an era."

Norfolk, Lawrence. "Troubled Souls: Tales of Murder, Mystery and Obsession—*Angels and Insects: Two Novellas*." *Washington Post Book World* (2 May 1993): X1. "Brief visions of a world which Byatt understands uniquely well: 19th-century England and . . . men and women."

Oldham, Gerda. *Antioch Review* 51, no. 4 (Fall 1993): 653. Summary of the novellas.

Phillips, Robert. *Hudson Review* 46, no. 4 (Winter 1994): 766. "Byatt's language is almost monstrously rich. . . . Byatt seems determined to out-Murdoch Iris Murdoch."

Rossen, Janice. *World Literature Today* 68 (Winter 1994): 141–42.

Rubin, Merle. "Seen in a Victorian Mirror." *Christian Science Monitor*, 25 May 1993, 13. Her prose has a "Pre-Raphaelite vividness of color and detail." If Byatt errs, it is in "taking the past too literally: of failing to find out more about the Victorians than the Victorians already knew about themselves."

Tate, J. O. *National Review* 45, no. 16 (23 August 1993): 60. *Angels and Insects* seems "to add up to a Hamlet without the prince, or a Masterpiece Theater without a masterpiece."

Taylor, Paul. "A Mixed Benison from Tennyson." *The Independent* (25 October 1992): reviews sect., 28. "Byatt has a high mind and a heavy hand."

Wallace-Crabbe, Chris. "A. S. Byatt: Rich Tables, Hectic Parlours." *Scripsi* 8 (1992–93): 190–94.

Washington Post Book World (24 April 1994): X12.

Possession: A Romance

Brookner, Anita. "Eminent Victorians and Others." *Spectator* (3 March 1990): 35. *Possession* "is inordinate, but not indiscriminate; it is unfashionable; it is generous, teeming with more ideas than a year's worth of ordinary novels."

Conroy, Sarah Booth. "The Magic Brew of A. S. Byatt." *Washington Post Book World* (29 November 1991): D1, 9. A "delicious fruitcake fiction." "Her books are full of things glimpsed out of the corner of the eye, dimly heard, difficult to explain." Conroy also interviews Byatt and includes quotations.

D'Evelyn, Thomas. "A Book about Books." *Christian Science Monitor*, 16 December 1990, 13. "This improbably buoyant novel combines Shakespearean romance (chaste lovers, guilty passion, children lost and found), detective novel suspense (lost correspondence, visits to scenes of the crime, a coffin disinterred on Halloween), satire on academic fashions . . . and a pastiche of styles from Browning to Emily Dickinson."

———. "A Book about Books." *Christian Science Monitor*, 16 November 1990.

Dirda, Michael. "The Incandescent Spell of *Possession*." *Washington Post*, 17 October 1990, C1, C7. "Wow!" Byatt "aims to show how some literary professionals, obsessed with textual questions, Lacanian psychology, or deconstruction, may blind themselves to the sheerly human, the actual feelings, in poems."

Evening Standard 32 (Summer 1991): 77. "In the Murdoch class."

Feinstein, Elaine. "Eloquent Victorians." *New Statesman* (16 March 1990): 38. *Possession* is "a poet's novel."

Gray, Paul. "Winner." *Time* (5 November 1990): 94. Byatt has acknowledged
the influence of Umberto Eco and John Fowles: "manifest intelligence,
subtle humor and extraordinary texturing of the past within the present
make *Possession* an original, and unforgettable, contribution."

Howe, Fanny. "Love between the Pages." *Commonweal* (25 January 1991): 69.
Possession asks, "What is a possession and what is unpossessable?" The
novel is "reactionary in its contempt for feminism . . . and in its fundamental desire to recover that lost and well-loved world [of Victorian
England]."

Hulbert, Ann. "The Great Ventriloquist." *New Republic* (7–14 January 1991):
47ff. Reprinted in *Contemporary British Women Writers: Narrative Strategies*, edited by Robert E. Hosmer, Jr. (New York: St. Martin's, 1993),
55–61. *Possession* is a "tour de force of university fiction." Hulbert is conscious of Byatt's postmodern consciousness; at the same time, she
believes that Byatt "challeng[es] the reigning theories of linguistic inde-
terminancy." The novel is an "occasion for an exhilarating, virtuoso, and
at times exhausting exploration of the many ways language has of
speaking."

Jenkyns, Richard. "Disinterring Buried Lives." *Times Literary Supplement* (2–8
March 1990): 213–14. As have other reviewers, Jenkyns makes a comparison between the poet Ash, who in *Possession* has the epithet "the
Great Ventriloquist," and Byatt; he applies to Byatt what she says
about the imaginary Ash and his "unwieldy range." He juxtaposes
Byatt's achievement with those of David Lodge, Dennis Potter, Angus
Wilson, Margaret Drabble, Alison Lurie, Evelyn Waugh, not so much
to compare admiringly but to cavil about a "lapse into a conventional
cast of mind." "Ash is too perfectly of his time to come fully alive . . .[*Possession*] "has earned the right to be judged by high standards, so it is
worth probing its weaker side . . . [it] gain[s] much of its *élan* from the
way in which it bursts out of the confines of the campus novel to revel in
the delights of a boldly romantic narrative, with a gloriously melodra-
matic climax." In the tradition of *Great Expectations* and *Felix Holt*. "One
wonders if there is not a repressed Byatt, more robustly reactionary than
she knows, longing to burst out and declare that traditional country life
is best, and the modern world is scruffy and smutty, and what a girl
needs is a strong, handsome man to look after her."

Johnson, Diane. "The Best of Times." *New York Review of Books* (28 March
1991): 35ff.

Kaiser, Mary. *World Literature Today* 5, no. 4 (Autumn 1991): 707. "Byatt's
primary allegiance is with the tradition of the serious, realistic novel,
wherein deep sympathy for individual human beings is a central value."
Kaiser continues: "Byatt is committed to uncovering the truth about
human experience." *Possession* is "without doubt a postmodernist novel . . .

a triumphant example of a new phase of postmodernism, the literature of repletion rather than the 'literature of exhaustion,' in John Barth's famous phrase."

Karlin, Danny. "Prolonging Her Absence." *London Review of Books* (8 March 1990): 17–18.

Kemp, Peter. "An Extravaganza of Victoriana." *London Sunday Times*, 4 March 1990, H6. "Wholeheartedly intelligent."

Kerley, Gary. "A. S. Byatt's Intriguing Romance Explores Roots of *Possession*." *Atlanta Journal Constitution*, 25 November 1990, N11.

Kirkus Reviews 58 (15 August 1990): 1107.

Koning, Christina. "Ladies of Letters Look in the Mirror." *The Observer* (11 March 1990): 68.

Lehman-Haupt, Christopher. "When There Was Such a Thing as Romantic Love." *New York Times*, 25 October 1990, C24. Recalls Fowles, John Palliser's *Quincunx*: "witty and sometimes even moving commentary on the cycles of history and the contrast between the pre-Darwinian age and the age of post-modernism . . . about speech, language, the pleasure of reading, the singularity of reading . . . brilliant mimicry of Victorian poetry too often reflects its tedium as well as its complexly patterned obsessiveness." Quibbles with Byatt's depictions of scenes with Ash and LaMotte that break with her realistic, multiple point-of-view narrative.

Marshall, Brenda K. "Parallel Lives." *Women's Review of Books* (May 1991): 6.

McAleer, John. "Satirizing the Academy." *Chicago Tribune*, 18 November 1990, 14, 6.3.

New York Times Book Review (2 December 1990): 81. Listed as Editors' Choice of the best books of 1990.

Oates, Joyce Carol. *Vogue* (November 1990): 274ff. "As an exploration of love in our overly verbalized and obsessively analyzed era, *Possession* manages to be both sophisticated and sentimental." It is "lushly sensuous in detail as a Pre-Raphaelite painting." "The theme of connectedness and of powerful literary influences is central to *Possession*, and one senses from Byatt's sunny equanimity of tone that such indebtedness is hardly meant to be covert."

Oldham, Gerda. *Antioch Review* (Spring 1991): 302. Byatt takes "amiable potshots at feminists, deconstructionists, and literary critics." *Possession* does not "peter out or become tiresome both for the author and the reader."

Parini, Jay. "Unearthing the Secret Lover." *New York Times Book Review* (21 October 1990): 9. Includes interview sidebar by Suzanne Cassidy: "How to Write a Novel: Start with Two Couples" (11). A "gifted observer, able to discern the exact but minor details that bring whole worlds into being." Compares Byatt to Wodehouse, Lodge, Borges. Cropper a "cross between Leon Edel and Liberace."

Prescott, Peter. "Why Byatt Possesses." *Newsweek* (21 January 1991): 61. Includes brief interview with Byatt by Jennifer Foote ("Out from Sister's Shadow"). *Possession* is about "the grip with which the past controls the present." "It's exhausting, but it's all utterly convincing."

Pritchard, William H. "Fiction Chronicle." *Hudson Review* 44 (Autumn 1991): 500. "Like the Burne-Jones on the cover, *Possession* is heavily and ornately overlaid with literariness."

Publishers Weekly (24 August 1990): 54. Byatt succeeds in projecting "diverse and distinct" voices; she is, more than Ash, "the great ventriloquist." Byatt engages in a "subtle questioning of the ways readers and writers shape, and are shaped by, literature."

Rifkind, Donna. "Victorians' Secrets." *New Criterion* (February 1991): 77–80.

Rome, Linda L. *Library Journal* (1 November 1990): 123. In full: "[*Possession*] is as sumptuous as brandy-soaked Christmas fruitcake, dense with intrigue, beguiling characters, and a double-edged romance that bridges Victorian England and modern-day academia. At once literary and highly readable, the book boasts a compelling narrative that exposes the real life behind the art of two Victorian poets . . . and contrasts their passion for life with that of . . . contemporary scholars who stumble upon romance hidden in dusty papers. This wonderfully written work is highly recommended."

Rothstein, Mervyn. "Best Seller Breaks Rule on Crossing the Atlantic." *New York Times*, 31 January 1991, C17ff. Byatt, in a telephone interview with Rothstein, says that *Possession* is "like the books people used to enjoy reading when they enjoyed reading. It has a universal plot, a classic romantic plot and a classic detective plot. . . . People can get the sort of pleasure out of it they got out of the old romantic novel." She also says that it is a human desire to read about the past, which is why we like Eco and Fowles. Byatt continues: "I think we're still living at the end of the Victorian era, at least philosophically, in the way we think and in the way we try to understand the world. We've moved on technologically, but the foundations of our ideas are still there, if you think of Freud and sexuality, or Darwin and the naturalists. It all turns around the idea of the death of Christianity, the disappearance of God, and I think morally our world doesn't quite know what has been put in its place. . . . Does the scholar possess the poet or does the poet possess the scholar?" On Tennyson's rhythm in the poetry of Ash: "I crossed [Emily Dickinson] back with Christina Rossetti to make her more ordinary and more English." Byatt adds that she is tired of being compared with her sister.

Schwartz, Gil. "What to Read on Vacation." *Fortune* (26 August 1991): 113–116. In full: "*Possession* . . . is a churning, lusty, circuitous tale of some 550 pages with a Shakespearean number of characters and enough atmosphere to make Umberto Eco sneeze. It is also without question the best buy per pound on the shelves today, and heavy enough to hold down the entire side of a picnic blanket, not to mention your imagination, for about three weeks, minimum. Now that's value."

See, Carolyn. "At a Magic Threshold." *Los Angeles Times*, 28 October 1990, BR2, 13. A "masterpiece of wordplay and adventure."

Smith, Anne. "Sifting the Ash." *Listener* 123 (1 March 1990): 29.

Stout, Mira. "What Possessed A. S. Byatt? A British Novelist's Breakthrough Surprises Everyone but the British Novelist." *New York Times Magazine* (26 May 1991): 12ff. Part profile, part review.

"Summer Reading." *Observer* 24 (June 1990): 50.

Taylor, Robert. "*Possession*: Victorian Story with Romance, Poetry." *Boston Globe*, 24 October 1990, 83.

Thurman, Judith. "A Reader's Companion." *New Yorker* (19 November 1990): 151ff. "Responsive quotation is her preferred form of foreplay." Maud "comes to embody the cerebral excesses and solipsisms of Byatt's style." "The modern politics of knowledge forces academic writers to develop strategies for placing themselves beyond criticism. The trick, apparently, is to deconstruct one's own text defensively rather than surrender any fertile passage to an invading analyst." "Byatt wants to prove that she can write anything and everything, and nearly succeeds. Now she needs to abandon her unreadability—her pedantic insistence that we savor the minutiae, the ironies, and the heroics of her struggle with all that can't be said."

Trucco, Terry. "Brit Wit's Lit Hit: Antonia's Anonymous No More." *Wall Street Journal*, 6 December 1990, A16.

Still Life

Burgess, Anthony. *The Observer* (1 December 1985): 17. "Transcend[s] mere history in its evocation of the human condition."

Christian Science Monitor, 16 October 1985, 22. "Mental paintings full of color and light."

Lewis, Roger. "Larger than Life." *New Statesman* (28 June 1985): 29.

London Review of Books (18 July 1985): 17.

Mars-Jones, Adam. "Doubts about the Moment." *Times Literary Supplement* (28 June 1985): 720.

McManus, Jeanne. "Brain Children in Britain." *Washington Post Book World* (22 November 1985): B18. "How refreshing to have braininess—not drugs, not incest—be the problem that plagues a family."

Merkin, Daphne. "Writers and Writing: The Art of Living." *New Leader* (10 February 1986): 17.

The Observer (14 December 1986): 23.

Rose, Steven. *New Statesman* (27 November 1987): 33. "Immaculate observation of place, period, class and gender."

Sage, Lorna. "How We Live Now." *The Observer* (23 June 1985): 22. "Witty, clogged with details, bookish, elaborate, chatty, didactic."

Vincent-Davis, Diana. *Library Journal* (15 November 1985): 109. For both
    characters and author, "intellectual passions are as all-encompassing as
    emotional ties . . . opaque, challenging, and rewarding."
West, Paul. "Sensations of Being Alive." *New York Times Book Review* (24
    November 1985): 15. Byatt has an "acute, supple mind not always pri-
    marily interested in the narrative mode as such. She excels at finely
    attuned brooding and in emphatic introspection. . . . A psychological
    novelist, enthralled by the sensation of being alive. . . . She does what
    Dreiser called 'chemisms' with the rippling, elated touch of a Virginia
    Woolf."

The Virgin in the Garden

Adams, P. L. *Atlantic* (April 1979): 99.
Bernikow, Louise. "The Illusion of Allusions." *Ms.* (June 1979): 36–38.
Bradbury, Malcolm. "On from Murdoch." *Encounter* 30 (July 1968): 72–74.
Choice (September 1979): 828.
Critique 24 (Fall 1982): 55.
Dinnage, Rosemary. "England in the 50s." *New York Times Book Review* (1 April
    1979): 20. "[G]rave, solid, ample as a Yorkshire tea, with deliberate
    hints of the Northern tradition of Mrs. Gaskell and Charlotte Brontë."
Irwin, Michael. "Growing up in 1953." *Times Literary Supplement* (3 November
    1978): 1277. "The stories, skilfully alternated, are linked by cunning
    echoes and symbolic commentary. The author's commitment is to her
    ideas rather than to the imaginative life. . . . Most of the main characters
    are chronically literary. . . . The oddest defect in the novel, granted the
    writer's obvious thoughtfulness and sensitivity, is the stodginess of some
    of the prose. . . . This is further evidence, perhaps, of the writer's compar-
    ative lack of interest in the routine chores of realist fiction."
King, Francis. "Grand Scale." *Spectator* (2 December 1978): 26–27.
Murdoch, Iris. "Force Fields." *New Statesman* (3 November 1978): 586. A
    "large, complex, ambitious work, humming with energy and ideas."
New York Times Book Review (15 March 1992): 28. Brief notice.
Thwait, Anthony. "The New Elizabethans." *The Observer* [London] (5 Novem-
    ber 1978): 30. Comments on Byatt's "sardonic playfulness."
Paulin, Tom. "When the Ghost Begins to Quicken." *Encounter* (May 1979):
    72–77. "It is unfortunate that Byatt will always be compared with Iris Mur-
    doch. . . . She is erudite, talented, and witty—just right for those who love a
    leisurely English novel chatting of everything under the English sun."
Pendleton, Dennis. *Library Journal* (15 February 1979): 511.
Widman, R. L. "Shades of Brit Lit." *Washington Post*, 16 March 1979, B2. "Fair-
    ly reeks with Lawrentian passion and emotion, seethes across Hardyesque
    landscapes and wallows in characters who are too frequently pale imita-
    tions of Iris Murdoch's creations."

The Game

"Child's Play." *Times Literary Supplement* (19 January 1967): 41. Generally critical.
Craig, Patricia. *Times Literary Supplement* (9 March 1984): 259.
Flannery, Joseph. *Best Sellers* (1 April 1968): 2. "To enjoy this novel one must prefer reflectiveness to action." Finds the characters less than engaging and the pace too leisurely; while not an academic novel, some knowledge of academe helpful. "To understand Cassandra, and she is much more difficult than Julia, it is well to know something of the tangled Arthurian romances. And to enjoy the book it is imperative to understand Cassandra."
Levin, Martin. "Reader's Report." *New York Times Book Review* (17 March 1968): 36. "The father's passive idealism, Simon's belief in original sin, Cassandra's view of the order and harmony of the universe, and Julia's ritualistic religion are truly part of the action."
Manning, Olivia. "The Life Hater." *Spectator* (13 January 1967): 49–50. "The novel uses literature to create literature . . . [it] is good in the way that the novels of Iris Murdoch are good."
The Observer (18 December 1983): 29.
Rhode, Eric. "School Code." *New Statesman* (13 January 1967): 54. "Byatt writes with concern about God, myths, and haughty academic women, but is inexact about television."
Ringer, A. C. *Library Journal* (1 March 1968): 1018.
Rogers, Michael. *Library Journal* (15 February 1993): 197.
Sackville-West, Sophia. "Christmas Books." *Evening Standard* (10 December 1992): 46. "[O]ne of the best evocations of sibling rivalry ever."

The Shadow of the Sun

Levin, Martin. *New York Times Book Review* (2 August 1964): 32.
"Living with a Genius." *Times Literary Supplement* (9 January 1964): 21. Critical, saying that Byatt is "a very feminine writer" in her attention to "emotional nuance."
New Yorker (26 September 1964): 206. Critical.
Spector, R. D. *Book Week* (30 August 1964): 14.

Short Stories

The Djinn in the Nightingale's Eye: Five Fairy Stories

Adil, Alev. "Obeying the Genie." *Times Literary Supplement* (6 January 1995): 20. Comments on Byatt's "rich and archaically extravagant language" and on her exploitation of narrative.
Craig, Patricia. "Fantasy with One Foot on the Ground." *Spectator* (7 January 1995): 31. "[A] cerebral extravaganza, bristling with ideas."

Dunmore, Helen. "Magic in the Palm of a Hand." *Observer* [London] (1 January 1995): 17. Appreciative review.

The Matisse Stories

Baele, Nancy. "Matisse Spirit Haunts Byatt's Stories." *Ottawa Citizen*, 6 February 1994, D6.

Bawer, Bruce. "What We Do for Art." *New York Times Book Review* (30 April 1995): 9–10. Byatt's "characters are credible, their encounters authentically complex, their environments vividly delineated."

Clark, Alex. "Artists and Models." *Times Literary Supplement* (14 January 1994): 21. Byatt turns to the "indeterminate and ambiguous nature of representation itself."

Dyer, Geoff. "Precious in the Pink." *The Guardian* (11 January 1994): G8. "We need to look at these stories in two ways—as stories and as dramatised essays on Matisse—to come up with a compound verdict that does justice to the twin impulses behind them. . . . As you would expect, there is a lot of colour in Byatt's writing, but it is ornamental rather than animate. . . . In what is almost a mirror image of Matisse's art, Byatt's prose contrives to be both exquisite *and* bland."

Glendinning, Victoria. "Pleasure Principles." *London Times*, 30 December 1993, Books, 32. "Byatt's short stories touch the heart more immediately than do her novels."

Halpern, Sheryl. "Just a Bit of Byatt; Thin but Satisfying Read." *Montreal Gazette*, 26 March 1994, I3. "Serene Matisse prints and sketches may frame these three stories, but they're about less-than-serene Matisse-lovers: middle-aged academics and artistic also-rans who see themselves and their desires in the master's nudes, interiors and still lifes."

Jeffries, Stuart. *The Guardian* (4 November 1994): T19. "Three rich, satisfying stories. Ease and fierceness mingle in them—the same qualities that one can detect in Matisse's late paintings: there is . . . ease in the storytelling and fierceness in moral and aesthetic judgments."

Kelman, Sue. "The Painted Words of A. S. Byatt." *Toronto Star*, 19 March 1994, K12. The "richest and most satisfying collection of short fiction I have ever encountered . . . contain[s] everything that makes Byatt a great writer. Each brief plot holds a breathtaking twist, but the plot is not the point. As always, the reader's intellectual curiosity is taken for granted. . . . Byatt is attempting literally to paint with words, to convey physical sensations from the taste of food to the weight of heartache."

Kemp, Peter. "Still Lives." *London Sunday Times*, 2 January 1994, Books, 1. "Hits the imagination's retina with all the vibrant splatter of an exploding paintbox. . . . Ecstatic receptivity to colour is one of Byatt's ways of blazoning the affinities these stories have to the paintings of the artist who inspired this book. . . . Letting her imagination loose in an area somewhere between cultural commentary and creativity has always been Byatt's approach to writing fiction. . . . The three slim tales . . . attractively manifest her ability to metamorphose her thinking about cultural icons into thought-provoking fiction."

Lezard, Nicholas. "Books: Round-Up." *The Guardian* (8 November 1994): T10. "These are polished, perfected works, almost suspiciously so; and the book's luxurious production values suggest an artefact that is designed, like a bogus appreciation of Matisse himself (not to suggest that Byatt is in any way fraudulent herself), to advertise a factitiously 'tasteful' sensibility."

Macdougall, Carl. "Teasing Tales from Matisse." *Glasgow Herald*, 8 January 1994, 12. The "stories wander into a failed marriage, artistic deception, a child's suicide and its effect on those who remain."

McWilliam, Candia. "Death, Decay and Hairdos." *The Independent* (9 January 1994): reviews sect., 31. "Byatt carries off her naked intellectuality by giving equal rein to her intense visual recall and a response to colour that is as powerful as her moral sense. The subject implicit in all three stories is mortality, recalled again and again by unceasing minute changes in what is alive and bound for death."

Roberts, Michele. "Matisse: All the Nudes That's Fit to Print." *The Independent* (22 January 1994): 30. "These new stories, while concerned with the modern, in terms of their subject matter still pay homage to the kind of realism perfected a hundred years ago. . . . The stories open out like a triptych, hinged together by their common inspiration: the paintings of Matisse, and, in particular, the female bodies they celebrate as vehicles for colour and forms, colour as form. . . . The beauty of the writing is so pleasurable that it's a shock to realise that the stories are about not only *luxe, calme et volupté* but also about cruelty, destruction, selfishness, dishonesty and self-annihilation."

Robson, David. "Painting in Prose." *Daily Telegraph*, 9 January 1994, 4. A "masterpiece of its kind. Each piece works perfectly in its own right and they enjoy a unity, both of theme and of style, which makes for a deeply harmonious product. Very little actually happens in the stories, and the leisurely tempo of the narrative enables Byatt to deploy her formidable skills as a word-painter to construct dense visual portraits of the characters and their physical ambience; but the things that do happen have a seismic significance. . . . Byatt's prose style is ornate and her sentences have a way of sprouting exotic tendrils but, when simplicity is called for, she does not let you down."

Sowd, David. *Library Journal* (1 April 1995): 127.

Spurling, Hilary. "The Art of the Sensual." *Daily Telegraph*, 8 January 1994, books sect., 9. "Matisse is present, so to speak, as undertext, or as a kind of marker for these heroines to aim off at an oblique angle. . . . Interesting perhaps is the way in which Matisse's paintings . . . ride high above the surface of these stories: powerful, majestic, sensuous images, imposing their own equilibrium and detachment on the casual turbulence of daily life."

"Summer Reading: Holiday Booking." *The Independent* (3 July 1994): Sunday review sect., 32. "Readers who find the fastidious intellectualism of her full-length fiction too much of a good thing may enjoy these three novellas, each using the gloriously suggestive paintings of Matisse to explore big questions of life, death and sensibility."

Sugar and Other Stories

British Book News (December 1987): 792.

Cunningham, Valerie. "Ladies of the Lakes." *The Observer* (5 April 1987): 25.

Cushman, Keith. *Studies in Short Fiction* 25 (Winter 1988): 80–81.

Duchene, Anne. "Ravening Time." *Times Literary Supplement* (10 April 1987): 395. Would prefer sequel to *Still Life*.

Durrant, Sabine. "Shavings and Splinters." *New Statesman* (15 May 1987): 30. "Images and ideas are linked by association; memory, myth and metaphor are interwoven. The least successful stories are too long and lack impetus, the best are fascinating explorations into the process of creation."

Hargreaves, T. *Hermanthena* 142 (1987): 77–78.

Lively, Penelope. *London Evening Standard* (Summer 1991): 77. A "bright sensual prose."

New Directions for Women (November 1987): 22.

Schwartz, Lynne Sharon. "At Home with the Supernatural." *New York Times Book Review* (19 July 1987): 5. Byatt "chooses the leisurely, meditative mode of Henry James, E. M. Forster, and George Eliot." She "ventures into . . . unfashionable territory—where a moral universe is presupposed and every act is laden with more, not less meaning than it can readily bear." Byatt's gift "is not so much in unraveling the complexities of the ordinary as in sensing its uncanny and nightmarish aspects."

Soete, Mary. *Library Journal* (August 1987): 139.

Spufford, Francis. "The Mantle of Jehovah." *London Review of Books* (25 June 1987): 22–23. This review of *Sugar and Other Stories* is more an extended assessment of Byatt's work through 1987 than a simple review. She classifies Byatt's work as belonging to the genre of the English social novel.

Steinberg, Sybil. *Publishers Weekly* (22 May 1987): 65. "For judicious readers, the literary overtones of a probing writer will provide considerable pleasure."

Nonfiction

Passions of the Mind

Berne, Suzanne. *New York Times Book Review* (22 March 1992): 16. *Passions* "will delight the very literary and intimidate everyone else."

Cunningham, Valentine. "The Greedy Reader: A. S. Byatt in the Post-Christian Labyrinth." *Times Literary Supplement* (16 August 1991): 6. Connects *Possession* with *Passions*. "The postmodern is very much the post-Victorian." Appreciative.

Espey, John. "A Critical Byatt Examines the 'Habits of the Mind.'" *Los Angeles Times*, 26 March 1992, E8.

Grumbach, Doris. "Affinities and Affections." *Washington Post Book World* (29 March 1992): 11.

Irvine, Ann. *Library Journal* (1 March 1992): 90. "The writing is brilliant, requiring a substantial awareness of English literature and command of the language."

Roberts, Michele. "Greed Reading." *New Statesman* (9 August 1991): 38. Begins with a consideration of *Possession* and describes *Passions* as a "display of journalistic and scholarly versatility." Several essays assert "both the sophistication of realism as a narrative practice . . . and its feasibility." Roberts is critical of Byatt's treatment of Wittig.

Rubin, Merle. "A Writer Reviews Other Writers." *Christian Science Monitor*, 31 March 1992, 13.

Showalter, Elaine. "Slick Chick." *London Review of Books* (11 July 1991): 6.

Swanson, Stevenson. "A. S. Byatt on the Perils and Pleasures of Realism." *Chicago Tribune*, 15 March 1992, 14, 7:2.

Taylor, Robert. "A. S. Byatt's Essays Explore Her Passion for Literature." *Boston Globe*, 11 March 1992, 66. "Provocative gathering of critical writings . . . academic in an old-fashioned, thoroughly refreshing way . . . [Byatt's] purpose [is] to investigate the realm of truth bordering and sometimes overlapping the territory of fiction."

Wordsworth and Coleridge in Their Time (Unruly Times)

Bach, Bert C. *Library Journal* (1 February 1973): 421.

Books and Bookmen (November 1965): 28.

Degrees of Freedom

Bradbury, Malcolm. "The Romantic Miss Murdoch." *Spectator* (3 September 1965): 293.

Choice (March 1966): 32.

Hicks, Granville. "Easter Monday Nights." *Saturday Review* (30 October 1965): 41–42. "[Byatt] is particularly enlightening on . . . Murdoch's various attempts to combine symbolism and realism. . . . she is appreciative of virtues."

"Murdoch's Net." *Times Literary Supplement* (29 July 1965): 630. "Byatt is as well qualified as any other critic to disdain the ups and downs of literary fashion. . . . But more important . . . is that this is an attempt by an ordinary reader—that is to say, someone who reads for pleasure—

to get to grips with the philosophical ideas of a professional philosopher."

Interviews

Dusinberre, Juliet A. In *Women Writers Talking* edited by Janet Todd, 181–95. New York and London: Holmes & Meier, 1983.

Grove, Valerie. "Academic Reflections in a Victorian Climate." *London Sunday Times*, 21 October 1990, 3.3.

Kellaway, Kate. "Self-portrait of a Victorian Polymath." *London Observer* (16 September 1990): 45.

Picardie, Justine. "Women's Writing Is More than That." *London Sunday Times* 5 April 1987, 55. Also see, under reviews of *Possession: A Romance*: Sarah Booth Conroy, "The Magic Brew of A. S. Byatt"; Jay Parini/Suzanne Cassidy, "Unearthing the Secret Lover"; Peter Prescott/Jennifer Foote, "Why Byatt Possesses"; Mervyn Rothstein, "Best Seller Breaks Rule on Crossing the Atlantic."

Biographical and Bibliographical Sources

Contemporary Authors, new revised series 13, 91–92. Detroit, MI: Gale Publishing, 1991.

Contemporary Authors, new revised series 33, 70–71. Detroit, MI: Gale Publishing, 1991.

Current Biography Yearbook, 99–103. New York: Wilson, 1991.

Hosmer, Robert E., Jr. Bibliography. In *Contemporary British Women Writers: Narrative Strategies*, edited by Robert E. Hosmer, Jr., 61–65. New York: St. Martin's, 1993.

Musil, Caryn McTighe. "A. S. Byatt." In *Dictionary of Literary Biography* 14, no. 1, 194–205. Detroit, MI: Gale Publishing, 1983.

Index

The Author

Kathleen Coyne Kelly received her Ph.D. from the University of North Carolina at Chapel Hill and now teaches medieval literature and composition theory at Northeastern University in Boston, where she is an associate professor and director of the Basic Writing Program. Kelly is also interested in medievalism in nineteenth- and twentieth-century literature. Her research on medieval themes and motifs in modern literature grows out of her longtime fascination with the ways in which the Middle Ages have been perceived and constructed by postmedieval societies, including contemporary culture. Kelly's scholarly interest in A. S. Byatt was sparked in part by Byatt's use of medieval literature and medievalism in *Possession: A Romance*.